Manifesting Prosperity

From the Inside Out

By

Tammi Baliszewski, Ph.D.

Manifesting Prosperity
From the Inside Out

Tammi Baliszewski, Ph.D.

The purpose of this book is to educate and entertain. The author and/or publisher do not guarantee that anyone using these techniques, suggestions, tips, ideas or strategies will meet with success. The author and/or publisher shall have neither liability nor responsibility to anyone with respect to any loss or damage caused, or alleged to be caused, directly or indirectly by the information contained in this book.

Expanding Heart Publishing
142 Palmetto, #551
Eagle, Idaho
ISBN-13: 978-0-9831282-2-9
ISBN-10: 0983128227
Printed in the United States of America

This book is dedicated to Spirit,

my husband Steve,

and all the souls ready to say

YES to Prosperity!

Praise for

Manifesting Prosperity

"This book isn't just about getting rich, it is about enriching your life on every level. Tammi's style is clear, direct, comprehensive and to the point. I have enjoyed her wisdom and applied it in my own life. I truly believe if you apply yourself, you too will experience more love, greater prosperity and deeper fulfillment."

~ **Vanna White,** Television personality, film actress and hostess of Wheel of Fortune

"I had everything I could want — except CASH. *Manifesting Prosperity* helped me clear my vision of myself, perceive my value, re-frame my limiting beliefs, and heal my issues around money. Immediately - I mean within three weeks! - my income more than tripled. After two years my financial abundance continues to blossom, and shows no sign of abating - for which I credit the information, anecdotes and exercises in this unique and comprehensive guide to prosperity."

~ **Penny Orloff**, singer, actor, frequent contributor to *Chicken Soup for the Soul*, and author of *Jewish Thighs on Broadway*

"If you are ready for prosperity, you have the perfect guide for it in your hands! This is one of those magical books that hits home no matter where you open it or what you read. Enjoy it in tidbits and get what you need, or go slow, do the exercises, and experience epiphanies, deep healing and true transformation. Tammi's material is what I believe in, teach and apply in my own life to manifest abundance, success and fulfillment."

~ **Dee Wallace**, author of *Conscious Creation, The Big E, Bright Light*, healer, channel and actress.

"If you sincerely want to increase your prosperity and enrich your life with more money, love, purpose or joy, these pages provide the insights and tools to do just that. *Manifesting Prosperity from the Inside Out* is a brilliant mix of heart, spirit and practical action. Reading it can change your life on every level."

~ **Martia Nelson**, author of *Coming Home: The Return to True Self* and coach to women of affluence, influence and leadership.

"I have read many books about prosperity but Tammi's is different. It gives you the tools to reprogram yourself in your inner world, so you will no longer struggle with money in your outer world. I am confident this book can help *anyone* who is really ready to claim greater prosperity!"

~ **Bob Burnham**, Author of the # 1 Amazon Best Seller: *101 Reasons Why You Must Write A Book: How To Make A Six Figure Income By Writing & Publishing Your Own Book.*

Acknowledgements

With a warm heart and immense love, I want to acknowledge and extend gratitude to all who have been a part of this prosperity adventure. It has been a wonderful journey and a profound learning experience.

Thank you to my "Prosperity Support Group," Niki Fretwell, Jennifer Cochran, Doug Armentrout, Rollene Billings, Anna Ross, Debra King, Annie Lyon, Paige Daniel and Tarah Gibson—you were PRICELESS in this process. You helped me refine the exercises, hone the material and were powerful teachers. I love all of you whole heartedly.

I am grateful to Rosemary Sneeringer and Penny Orloff! You both put your heart into this book and brought it to the next level. You are a couple of the best friends, spiritual path mates and editors a girl could ask for! I love you both unconditionally and completely!

Thank you to my family of the heart: Jody Ermold, Peter Bellon, Stephen Michas, Gina Deeming, Michele de Reus, Denise Drazkowski, Marla Steenson, Wendy Baker, Morrighan Lynn, Frankie Peschl, Larry Hickey, Tamu Ngina, Trevor Laing, George Frisbie, DK Brainard, Vicki Russell, Owen Jones, Samantha Fewox, and and Jack Schwartz, you are always there when I need you and I hope you know I am here for you too.

Thank you to my CA family, Vanna White, John Donaldson, Christopher Rodgerson, Sabrina Faith, Treesa Robinson, Kathy Ziegler, Paul Heussenstamm, Cynthia Kelvin, Martin Genis, Pam Stanley, Dedra Whitt, Phyllis Coblentz, Shawn Pelofsky, and Davis Ehler. I know you recognize your success stories woven through this book. Thank you for being part of the story of my life, I appreciate you deeply.

Thank you to Bob Burnham, you have been a wealth of information, an amazing source of support and a wise teacher. It is an honor to create, play and prosper with you! Thank you Kathryn Bartman for your patience and for holding my hand through this publishing process. Thank you Cindy Simpson, for your very prompt and inspirational messages, you make me smile! And deep appreciation for you Susan Veach for your diligence, professionalism and creativity with my interior design and cover art. You are an amazing team and I am so fortunate to have you on my side!

Thank you to my teachers and living examples of prosperity consciousness, Martia Nelson, Emily Bouchard, Fred Choate, Greg and Terry Burkhart, Robert Costero, Dee Wallace, Drs. Ron and Mary Hulnick, Dr. Paul Leon Masters, Gavin Frye, and all of the masters and examples of prosperity I quote throughout this book. I love listening, watching and learning from you.

Thank you Brent Carey for the forum called Empower Radio, You are a rock star and a touchstone of kindness and faith. Thank you for believing in my abilities as a radio host before I did. I am so proud of you and proud to know you!

Thank you also to my incredible producers and all of my wonderfully brilliant guests. I LOVE having conscious conversation!

I love my Facebook and Twitter friends (you know who you are!). Thank you for your friendship, connection and support. It is my honor to connect with you and support you as well. You make me smile and inspire me everyday!

Thank you to my family, Judy Butler, Tonda, Ron and Kennedy Mason, Donald and Jorun Baliszewski, Malia and Maja, Allen, Conner and Mindy Maguire, Sam, Rick, Bob, Chet and Cindy Jewett, and my adorable Jerry Frank. A loving shout out to Terry and Barbara Peel, and Sharon and Rick Cope. I love learning, teaching, laughing, playing and celebrating with you!

Thank you to Logan and Carter Peel, you are a great source of amusement and joy. It is an honor to be your step-monster.

Immense appreciation and love to my husband, Steve Peel. You are my best friend, cheerleader, advocate, voice of reason, soul mate, playmate, creative ally, source of great joy and so much more. God sure knew what He was doing when He brought me you!

And finally, a HUGE THANK YOU and acknowledgment to my readers. May this information light the way for you to attract, claim and receive all that you desire and deserve in the world. I am holding you in my heart as you journey through this material and as you venture forward on your prosperity path. Please be in touch with me if I can support you in any way.

May you be blessed with grace, ease, joy, success, fulfillment, great love and profound prosperity,

Tammi Baliszewski, Ph.D.
www.tammibphd.com

Contents

Introduction

*Within you is the divine capacity to manifest and attract
all that you need or desire.*

~ Wayne Dyer

Welcome to *Manifesting Prosperity From the Inside Out*. If
you are tired of struggling financially or doing things you
do not want to for money, this material was created for you. If you
are ready to claim greater prosperity on all levels, this information
and these exercises can help you cultivate the mental, emotional,
psychological and spiritual environment you need to manifest what
you deserve and desire in the world.

The foundation of my beliefs and these teachings are a blend
of psychological and spiritual principles; one without the other is
incomplete. It is important to heal limiting beliefs and subconscious conditions from our childhood. It is also important to line
up with our Higher Selves and cultivate a relationship with that
"Something Greater" which can be referred to as God, Spirit, Om,
The Universe, Source, Creator and/or Creative Intelligence. You
may have your own word or words to describe the energy that
moves the planets around the sun, is responsible for the grass being

1

green and the beating of your heart. It is much more effective to partner and co-create with this energy rather than rely solely on our own understanding.

When we do the work to heal the limiting content in the subconscious mind, acknowledge our worthiness, take responsibility for our thoughts, feelings and actions, cultivate our creativity and invite Spirit to co-create with us, miracles happen, grace is guaranteed and the sky is the limit!

While it is true some people manifest prosperity more easily than others and we all have unique soul lessons, karma, contracts and curriculum, at the core level we are all abundant and directly connected to Source Energy. Every single one of us has the ability to tap into the Divine within, access principles of prosperity and claim abundance for ourselves in the physical world. Most of us were just not taught how to do it. My intention is to support you in clearing out anything that is not serving you, assist you in implementing these principles and help you in attracting your divine inheritance.

The "Inside Out" method is not a quick fix, but rather a healing journey. At times you may find yourself feeling overwhelmed or emotional. Relax, pace yourself and set the intention to enjoy the journey. With the prosperity process, it is better to take solid, steady steps and be the tortoise rather than the hare. This material is designed to meet you where you are and take you as far as you intend to go. What you put into it is what you will get out of it. Some of the information may seem strange and new, or you may be familiar with all of the concepts. Some of the exercises may seem unusual and/or repetitive, but here's the deal: THEY WORK! I invite you to open your mind and have fun with the manifesting prosperity experience.

I am presenting you with a roadmap, guide and an enormous buffet of opportunities to manifest greater health, love, fulfillment, creativity and abundance. You will find I approach prosperity from many different directions, altitudes and angles, including: energetically, psychologically, scripturally, intellectually, historically, scientifically, creatively, subconsciously and spiritually. If you don't like what you are reading, keep going—it will change. Feel free to cherry pick; take what works for you and leave the rest. With that being said, I am *absolutely confident* if you are sincere in your intentions to manifest greater prosperity, and you participate in the exercises wholeheartedly, your life will improve in remarkable, unforeseen and miraculous ways.

To further energize your prosperity journey, connect with a friend or a group of like-minded people, and go through the book together. Gather together on a weekly basis and share your lessons, revelations and wins. See the best in each other, give each other feedback and cheerlead for one another. When two or more come together for the sake of up-leveling in consciousness, expansion and creation, it is promised that Spirit will be there supporting you in the process.

May you be blessed with grace, ease, enlightening surprises, miracles and joy on your prosperity adventure. If you have questions or would like additional support, please visit my website at www.tammibphd.com or write to me at tammibphd@gmail.com. I look forward to connecting with you and hearing your stories of success!

PART ONE

The Elements of Prosperity

Chapter 1

Prosperity – Who Is It For?

*It's God's will for you to live in prosperity
instead of poverty.*

~ Joel Osteen

Prosperity. It seems elusive. Is it because a comfortable, joyful and abundant life is meant for only a select few—the "lucky people" who are born into wealth, marry into it, or just innately know how to navigate this Earthly reality? A significant number of people struggle financially and live in fear. And on some level this makes sense; if you look around, the world clearly appears to be an unsafe, crazy and scary place! There are issues of global warming, natural disasters, the depletion of Earth's resources, the devastation of war, terrorism, violence, chaos, greed and the unpredictable state of the economy. In fact, the majority of people on this planet are living in a state of stress and lack.

Much of what we observe in the media is fear-based and focused on the negative. It seems many in positions of power are willing to lie and cheat for personal gain, politicians appear to lack moral values and the Earth is frequently ravaged for profit. There is also constant focus on the negative state of the economy. It seems we cannot watch the news without hearing about the volatility of the stock market, the national debt, the lack of jobs and the struggles within the housing market. The facts are a significant percentage of people lost value in their homes, lost their homes altogether and are struggling to regain a solid financial footing in the world. In other words, adherence to fear and faith in lack is running rampant.

Problems are inevitable if we look to the world for our sense of security. If we spend a significant amount of time watching the news or reading newspapers looking for a glimmer of hope, hope may never come. When we look to something outside of ourselves for a sense of safety we give away our power because we are relying on false idols, fallible human beings and worldly circumstances to change so we might relax, feel soothed, comforted and reassured. In truth, there is no real safety and security "out there." Safety is a state of being and can only be achieved by relaxing into the space of love and peace within.

> *True safety and a strong sense of*
> *security can only come from our*
> *connection to that "Something Greater"*
> *and from deep within ourselves.*

The "facts" are things are tough on planet Earth. The "truth" is we are each an aspect of a powerful, infinite, loving Creator. As human beings we have the great honor, privilege and double-edged sword of free will and choice. We have the awesome opportunity (and challenge) to be the demigods of our reality. However, most of us were not taught this. Most were taught to believe what we were told by parents, teachers and society. Most look to people, places and things outside of themselves in a position of neediness, hoping and praying for salvation. However, salvation and authentic power can only come from our connection to Source, remembering the truth about ourselves and accessing the immense power that resides within our own hearts and souls. So, ultimately, the problem of poverty and lack is not a problem of the economy, but rather a problem in our own consciousness.

Much has been written on manifesting prosperity and the subject has been brought to the forefront due to the best-selling books of Abraham-Hicks and the Law of Attraction. There is also the notoriety and success of *The Secret*, the creative endeavor of Rhonda Byrne. Her DVD and book include teachings from Jack Canfield, Michael Beckwith, Bob Proctor, John Gray, Neale Donald Walsch and many other wonderful teachers. But the genre has a long heritage going back hundreds, even thousands of years. Both Jesus and Buddha spoke of prosperity principles. Other respected teachers of prosperity include P.T. Barnum in his book *The Art of Money Getting* (1880), Florence Scovel Shinn with her books *The Game of Life* (1925), *The Power of the Spoken Word* (1928), *Your Word is your Wand* (1940) and *The Secret of Success* (1945). James Allen wrote *The Path of Prosperity* in 1905, Charles Fillmore wrote

Prosperity in 1936, Napoleon Hill wrote *Think and Grow Rich* in 1960 and *The Master Key to Riches* in 1965.

The principles addressed in these classics have much in common with more recent works and can be a source of support and guidance for those wanting to claim and experience a life of greater success. What all of these teachers seem to agree on is that prosperity an *energy, a mindset* and a *state of being.*

True prosperity occurs when a person understands their immense innate value, is confident in their power, has faith in the positive and is aligned with Spirit/Source/God/the Universe.

My intention with this material is to thoroughly explore prosperity consciousness and give you the steps to tap into it, claim it and put it into action for yourself. I will share stories from people who have made the journey from financial woes to great wealth and powerful advice from some of the most prosperous people on the planet. I will also share wisdom from respected spiritual teachers, prosperity lessons from clients and students, as well as my own understandings on the path from surviving to thriving. All of this material is designed to support and inspire *YOU* in saying *YES* to your personal power, *YES* to the energy of abundance and *YES* to manifesting greater prosperity—*if* you are ready and *if* you really want to!

No person who ever lived up to their potential or manifested great prosperity did so without first committing to themselves and their purpose. Prosperity does not happen if you have one foot in and one foot out of the process, nor does it happen by accident. So, if you are ready to put both feet in, and commit to your prosperity journey, get a journal and let's go! This work WORKS—not because I say so, but because it is spiritual law.

Exercise #1 – Commitment and Intention

I invite you to get a notebook or journal devoted to your "Prosperity Adventure." Set your prosperity intentions and *write them down.* Intention setting is a powerful way of claiming and anchoring what you want in the physical world. In order for the branches to go high, and manifest the fruits of prosperity, the roots need to go deep. Open your mind and heart to fully committing to this human adventure. You do not need to know the details of how things are going to unfold, or when things are going show up, just consider and claim your priorities, desires, hopes and dreams and *write them down.*

The Universe is creative, generous, lavish and abundant and by committing to yourself, and setting your intentions, it is like programming your desired destination on a vehicle navigation system. This is a very powerful first step in co-creating and aligning with the Universe and claiming your prosperity. Now, open your mind to this truth: *"Anything is possible!"*

Exercise #2 – Invite the Power of the Universe to Partner With You

The same energy that holds the stars in place, moves the planets around the sun, and turns summer into fall, fall into winter and winter into spring can also support you in miraculous and astonishing ways . . .but not without your invitation. Are you ready? If so, invite God, Spirit, Creative Intelligence, Your Soul, Higher Self, or the Organizing Force of the Universe to partner with you on this journey.

You may use the following prayer or one you create yourself. Speaking it out loud creates even more power. Remember this clear and simple statement from the Bible: "In the beginning was the Word, and the Word was with God, and the Word was God." Use your words to align with Source, empower yourself and energize your prosperity adventure.

Invitation Prayer:

Spirit, Father/Mother God, Lord of All Creation:

Just now I invite you in to join me and to please light my path to prosperity. As I breathe in I invite you in, and as I exhale I am gracefully and easily releasing anything that is no longer serving me.

Just now I acknowledge and accept that I am a unique expression of The Divine, that I have valuable gifts and talents, and that I am magnificent, wonderful and worthy. I open my mind, heart and life to receive graciously all that You have for me, all that is for my highest good and the highest good of all concerned.

My intention is to step fully into my purpose, prosperity and partnership with You. I am so grateful for all the blessings in my life and all that are on their way to me now. Thank you, thank you, thank you! And So It Is!

Exercise #3 – Feel Your Prosperity NOW!

1. Prosperity is an *energy* and must be an inner experience before it can be an outer reality. Consider what it is that you want and what would make you really *feel* prosperous. Is it the career of your dreams? Is it making a certain amount of money per week? Or having a particular amount of money in your bank account or wallet? Is it the ability to write a check out for a certain amount to a family member or to your favorite charity? Is it vibrant health? Enjoying a fulfilling, healthy partnership? Receiving abundant unconditional love? Or is it the experience of freedom, respect and peace? Really consider the details of your particular definition of prosperity. Write down everything that comes forward in your journal.

2. After you have identified what exactly would make you feel prosperous, imagine what it would feel like to have, do and be all those things *right here* and *right now*. Prosperity is no longer

in your future, it is your present moment reality. Feel the details of prosperity in your mind, viscerally in your body and energetically with your emotions.

3. Utter your invitation prayer and imagine lining up with the Source of all prosperity. Know the energy of prosperity is in you, above you, around you and breathing you. Allow yourself to sit quietly in this grateful, relaxed feeling state of having your prosperity *here* and *now* for five minutes.

4. After five minutes of residing in the feeling state of your present prosperity, write down any thoughts, revelations and information that comes forward in your Prosperity Journal.

If it resonates for you, get a calendar and put an X or a heart on each day you do this mediation. Know that If you do these three exercises for 30 consecutive days, this in and of itself will *absolutely* change your life in unforeseen and miraculous ways. These are solid foundational steps that will support you in accessing and receiving great abundance, and build momentum in the direction of your positive and prosperous future.

Chapter 2

Prosperity Defined

Prosperity is a way of living and thinking, and not just money or things.

~ Eric Butterworth

One day, when I was feeling particularly sorry for myself and the tragic state of my finances, I thought to myself: "I am *worthless!*" What dropped into my awareness is: "You are *priceless!*" It was not up to anyone but *me* to assess my innate value, and it was not necessary to base it on the amount of money I earned. That thought opened my mind and supported me in setting the intention to claim my worthiness and to manifest greater prosperity.

The bottom line is we all manifest

EXACTLY what we believe we deserve.

In order to attract, create, manifest and maintain greater prosperity, we need to open our minds to the possibility that we deserve it. Not on an entitled, shallow level, "I want lots of money and deserve it because I am better than others," but rather on a very deep level: "I want and deserve success and prosperity, because I am a child of God, as we all are."

Let's explore exactly what prosperity is. According to the *Merriam Webster Dictionary* prosperity is defined as: "The condition of being successful or thriving; especially economic well-being." Wealth is the possession of money or assets. However, prosperity encompasses something much greater. I define prosperity as fulfillment in every area of our lives. This includes our relationships, our health, our finances, our purpose, our creativity, peace on the mental realm, happiness on the emotional realm and alignment with the spiritual realm. Prosperity is a sense of freedom, joy, appreciation and value on all levels. In fact prosperity can mean whatever *you* want it to mean.

Here is a wonderful definition of prosperity shared by Edwene Gaines, best-selling author and metaphysical teacher (*The Four Spiritual Laws of Prosperity*, 2005). Ms. Gaines tells us true prosperity consists of:

- A vitally alive physical body to provide a comfortable worldly home for the spiritual beings that we are.
- Relationships that are satisfying, nurturing, honest and work all the time.
- Work that we love so much that it is play.
- All the money we can spend.

Prosperity is partially about creating wealth, but it is also about celebrating this human experience, co-creating with the Universe and sharing our good fortune with others. The creation of "healthy wealth" should be about using one's imagination, maximizing creative potential and bringing valuable things into being. Our endeavors should bring us joy, and also be used to uplift and empower others. True prosperity is the energetic flow of receiving graciously and giving generously.

Prosperity is best appreciated as a circle

in which money is first manifested,

then managed well and shared to good effect.

Prosperity consciousness suggests we are responsible stewards of our reality and our wealth. Authentic abundance is an energetic exchange created from existing resources, then eventually given back in some form.

Is Poverty a Virtue?

For many people there is a stigma attached to having money and they adhere to the belief that poverty is a virtue. I love this quote from Marianne Williamson: "There is nothing noble about being poor. Poor people don't need your sympathy, they need your cash." A very powerful statement indeed! Money is like love, the more you have, the more you have to give.

In truth, money should be a means to an end and not the ultimate goal. Money is a piece of the puzzle, not the whole puzzle. The goal of moneymaking should not be to gather and hoard or to be selfish and greedy. Greed is when one is energetically saying: "I want this and I don't want you to have it." However, it is *NOT* greedy to say "I want this and I want you to have it too!"

Yes, prosperity is more than money, but money *IS* an important aspect of prosperity. Money is energy and a medium of exchange that facilitates trade. Money can give you freedom and control over your time. It can also support you in being of greater service in the world. The true goal of prosperity is to use money as a tool, allow it to guide you where you heart leads you and help you fulfill your divine purpose.

Who Do You Serve?

I love this quote from Calvin Coolidge: "Prosperity is only an instrument to be used, not a deity to be worshipped." This is confirmed in sacred text. In the New International Version of the Bible, Luke 16:13 shares: "No servant can serve two masters. Either he will hate the one and love the other, or he will be devoted to the one and despise the other. You cannot serve both God and money." So the *TRUE GOAL* is God, as stated in Matthew 6:33, "But seek first his kingdom and his righteousness, and all things will be given to unto thee." In other words, if you go for God, the gifts of the world will also be shared with you.

I am certain you have heard the quote: "Ask and it is given." It is God's pleasure to share his kingdom and riches with his children.

God is not glorified by poverty, illness and suffering, nor is God glorified by victim consciousness. God is glorified when we stand up and acknowledge the Truth of who we are as Royal Heirs to the Universe and graciously receive our Divine Inheritance.

We all have so much more power than we think. We are all aspects of Spirit, The Infinite, Our Creator, Universal Intelligence, Original Light, Brilliance, Wisdom and Love. If we come from ego (sometimes used as an acronym for "Edging God Out") and assume the posture of separation, competition and fear, it will be impossible to attract and receive divine prosperity. The goal is to relax and align *with* the energy that moves the planets around the sun, and work *with* the forces of the Universe, rather than against them.

We ALL have the potential and capacity to live

miracle-filled, co-creative, prosperous lives.

We just need to invite the energy in, claim it, surrender to it,

then relax and receive it!

You are a Unique Aspect of God!

Genevieve Behrend (*Your Invisible Power,* 1921) has stated: "Human beings exist so that the Universal Mind can be differentiated and expressed in an endless variety of personalities. Therefore, by visualizing and then bringing something into form, you are fulfilling God's will for you to be unique and powerful. You fulfill your personality by creating something out of nothing." If one ever feels ashamed about asking for what they want, they may do well to remember Behrend's idea that we are each simply a smaller version of the Universal Mind or God. It is our nature to constantly desire and bring new things into being. Behrend has also stated: "Do not fear to be your true self, for everything you want, wants you."

How exciting is that last sentence? Think about it for a moment: "Everything you want, wants you!" If you open your mind to this possibility, sit with it, contemplate it and really embrace it, your life can start moving in a more positive and powerful direction—effective immediately!

Like Attracts Like

Buddha has said: "All that we are is the result of what we have thought." Our lives and our finances are the result of our thinking. Each of us is a powerful force attracting the equivalent of what we strongly think and feel. This was the Buddha's wisdom and understanding of the "Law of Attraction."

The Law of Attraction dictates: Whatever you put your attention on through thoughts and desires becomes your reality. If you are focused on the negative and "not having" something, it will be impossible to attract it. When you are focused on the positive, residing in a place of faith and confidence, it creates a vibration where your desires can naturally be attracted and manifested.

Consider the following questions for a moment: Do you spend more time thinking about the fear of failure, or the joy of success? Are you afraid of your debt and your problems, or are you optimistic about opportunities and solutions? Every thought you think draws to you situations, people, relationships and experiences. Whether you attract positive or negative experiences will be determined by whether your thoughts are weighted more towards the positive or negative.

Your feelings and your thoughts are like powerful magnets.

Everything you manifest is first initiated by your inner reality.

If you are not spending time consciously working with these principles, you will inevitably create your life by default—through random, undirected thoughts and beliefs rolling around in your mind and heart, then manifesting in your life in chaotic and often sloppy ways. Living by default is NOT the most fun or effective way to create a prosperous and fulfilling life.

What Do You Want?

One evening after dinner, my stepson, my husband and I decided to go out for a donut. As we waited our turn in line, we stood behind a woman and overheard her request: "I will take a glazed donut, a maple bar and a raspberry-filled donut." The young man working there had a box in hand and immediately started to fill her order. The woman said: "No . . . wait. I think I will have a chocolate cake donut, a bear claw and a lemon-filled donut." In mid-maple bar manifestation, the young man stopped and put the bar back and searched around for a bear claw. The woman continued to hem and haw, then changed her mind for a third time. He put all the donuts back and stared at her, patiently waiting for her to make up her mind.

I had an epiphany; I think the Universe is the same way with us! We say we want something, then before it manifests we change our mind and decide we want something else. If we are not clear and consistent with our desires and intentions, it will make it challenging or impossible to manifest them. It would be like driving somewhere with our foot on the accelerator, then the brakes, the accelerator, then the brakes, OR with our feet on both pedals at the same time—NOT the most efficient way to arrive at our destination.

In the beginning of Rhonda Byrne's film *The Secret,* God or the Universe presents Himself as a genie. He says: "Your wish is my command." When we identify and claim something we desire, energetically it is on its way. Then, if we think: "Oh, but I probably don't deserve it," what we desire recedes before it can manifest. I have seen this happen with clients who tell me about something they want in one breath, but in the next breath they tell me why they do not want it, or cannot have it.

An "accelerator/brakes" example occurred with my client Joan. "I would love to make money with my jewelry, but people really don't have much disposable income these days. It would be awesome to make money doing what I love, but I probably should just go look for a part time job." In those two sentences, I heard Joan change her mind four times. I told Joan I heard her being incongruent, battling herself to a standstill and arguing for her limitations. She said she did not understand. I repeated back to her what she just said to me and how in those thirty seconds she was inviting then repelling what she wanted multiple times. She began to understand. I invited her to get clear about what she really wanted, and then get consistent with her thoughts and words. If you spend too much time talking about why you cannot have what you want and arguing for your limitations, that is exactly what you will manifest in your life: lack and limitation.

It boils down to this, if you want prosperity, give your attention to what you *do want,* not what you *do not want.* Be conscious, consistent, mindful and diligent with what you think and what you say. This will support you in getting solid, clear and congruent. It will also naturally strengthen your manifestation muscle and your ability to attract what you desire.

What Are Your Gifts?

You have unique, important and special gifts. Every human being does. However, in order for the world to reflect back to you the value of your gifts, you need to understand and claim them for yourself. My intention and desire was to support Joan in doing this. Now I want to support you. But, before I could teach anyone else to claim their own value, I had to do it for myself.

Years ago, when I realized I was tired of doing what I did not want to do to make money, I considered what I was really good at and what I truly enjoyed. I decided to create a "Gift Wheel." My Gift Wheel simply consisted of putting my name down in the center of a piece of paper, and then drew a circle around my name. On that circle I wrote down what my talents and gifts were and what I enjoyed. I also included my desires and intentions. Here are some of the qualities and desires I claimed on my Gift Wheel:

- I am intelligent
- I am compassionate
- I am sensitive
- I am intuitive
- I want to be of service
- I love having conscious, uplifting conversations
- I love reading self-help books
- I like to think, contemplate, meditate and write
- I love to paint and create
- I love beauty
- I love to see the best in others
- I want to alleviate suffering
- I have a desire to live an empowered, prosperous, fulfilling life and help others do the same

As I created my Gift Wheel, I was not certain there was a career there, or how I could make money being me. But now as I reflect on my Gift Wheel years later, I can see where this simple process put my future into motion and it all makes perfect sense! Rather than working hard doing what I did not love (being a massage therapist and waiting tables) I now get paid to play. I host a conscious radio program, I am an artist who is well-compensated for my paintings, a counselor, the founder of a non-profit, and the author of self-help books. However, before I could manifest this life for myself and make money for being the best of me, I had to acknowledge and claim my gifts. I also had to accept I had value, I was worthy and that I could be prosperous without having to prove myself to anyone.

I AM WORTHY!

T. Harv Eker, author of the book *Secrets of the Millionaire Mind* and teacher of prosperity principles has said: "Rich people are solution oriented, where people who are poor are beaten by their problems." Prosperous thinking is creative thinking. Prosperity is about adopting the belief *"I AM WORTHY!"* Eker has said: "You must acquire the mindset that you can be wealthy without having to prove anything. There is so much money swishing around the world, yet poor people believe there is a limited amount to go around and that you have to struggle to get your piece of the pie. Rich people, in contrast, believe that new wealth is continually created and that there is a limitless supply of money."

Become a great receiver,

a "money magnet" and celebrate

any money that comes to you,

no matter how small, and

the Universe will give you more.

In the past, I believed and experienced the need to struggle and share the pie Mr. Eker talked about. On a subconscious level I believed if I had something, it meant someone else would have to go without. Since there was only so much pie to go around, I chose to do without so no one else would be deprived. I thought if I played small and was humble it would somehow help other people. But what I learned is being a martyr serves no one. We are all wonderfully worthy and there is *more* than enough to go around. When we start to comprehend the prosperity principles, we understand that rather than a lot of people splitting up one pie, we can all have our own pie. And beyond that, we don't even have to settle for apple pie, when what we really want is coconut cream pie!

I CAN DO IT!

Sir Richard Branson is someone who understands there is more than enough to go around and has great time being an example of true prosperity consciousness. Branson is the founder and CEO of the mega-corporation, The Virgin Group, currently worth about 4 billion dollars. Although he did not come from a family of great wealth, what they did give him was something even more valuable: confidence and self-reliance. Branson marched to the beat of his own drum from early on and has said being different is not an obstacle, but almost a requirement in achieving prosperity. From an early age, Branson refused to contort and conform to the shape others preferred, but instead found his authentic shape. When we do this, we easily attract the pieces of the puzzle that naturally fit around us, the road rises to meet our feet and the physical world becomes our great friend and ally.

Branson is a big thinker—intuitive, passionate, confident—and has an enormous appetite for expansion and joy. He has said that his main criterion for entering a new market or industry is that it be fun and exciting. He attributes his success to this simple belief: "I CAN DO IT!" He believes success is a natural byproduct when one creates something they are proud of and it serves a useful purpose. Branson has said: "I can honestly say that I have never gone into business to make money. I may be a businessman in that I set up and run companies for profit, but when I try to plan ahead and dream up new products and new companies, I am an idealist." *(Losing my Virginity,* 2005).

Faith

A positive attitude, faith, confidence and affirmative thoughts draw to us unforeseen opportunities, synchronicity and support from the Universe. We all have access to this Divine Energy and co-creative process. Charles Fillmore (*Prosperity,* 1936) the founder of Unity Church, has been referred to as a way-shower and an American mystic. Fillmore has said prosperity exists in every sphere of life. "Love, money and vibrant health are the result of tuning into God, the heavens, or the essence of nature." Fillmore believed the nature of God, or the "nonphysical substance," is to give and *everything* comes from it. He has stated: "Pour your faith into its reality and it will bring forth everything you need to prosper. This substance is the source of your supply, not conditions or people." To cultivate this faith, Fillmore said we must forget any prior limiting notions about what is possible.

The more we understand matter, money and possessions

as emerging from the universal spiritual flow,

the less need there is to grasp after things and treat them

solely as our own.

When we begin to truly understand and implement the principles of prosperity, the need for competition diminishes and cooperation naturally begins to weave into our reality. When we relax into the prosperous state within, generosity, rather than stinginess, becomes our predominant energy and intention.

Most of us would agree that God or Spirit can manipulate matter and manifest at will—essentially directing physical form to come into being as the result of what is intended. The Universe is not some sort of blind mechanical force, but is persuaded and directed by consciousness and intention. Since we are an aspect of Spirit, it stands to reason that when we align our consciousness, intention and creativity with this same Universal Intelligence, "synchronicities" shall ensue, prosperity will present itself, and miracles will manifest.

Exercise #1: What is Great About You?

1. Consider what you like about yourself. What are all the qualities that make you unique, wonderful, different and special?

Think about and claim what is great about you on all levels: physically, mentally, emotionally and spiritually.

2. Write down all of the things you have identified in your Prosperity Journal. As you reflect on, acknowledge and more consciously appreciate these talents, qualities, gifts and/or characteristics, you may just find the world immediately reflecting your value back to you.

3. Consider and write down what makes you feel really vibrant, vital and alive. What brings you joy? If nothing immediately comes forward, think back to your childhood, what was *really fun* for you?

True prosperity is about finding your purpose and doing what you love, not contorting yourself for the sake of others or to make massive amounts of money. Joseph Campbell has said: "Follow your bliss." And you've probably heard the saying: "Do what you love and the money will follow." You do not have to know in this present moment how this information is going to come together. Trust the prosperity process as an unfolding experience and evolving adventure. Open your mind to the fact that you are incredibly unique, immensely valuable and wonderfully worthy. And open your heart to receive blessings of Divine support, worldly assistance, positive feedback and unexpected synchronicity!

Exercise #2: Create your "Gift Wheel"

1. In your journal or on a piece of paper, write down your full name in the center of a blank page.

2. Now draw a circle around your name. Around this circle write down all of your gifts, your talents, the things you enjoy, your greatest intentions and your deepest desires.

3. When you are complete, look at this information as a whole and complete picture of who you are at the deepest level.

4. Now imagine all of your talents, gifts, qualities and joy coming together as a career. Even if you cannot imagine the details, allow yourself to explore and enjoy expressing this wonderful expansive version of yourself in the world!

5. Next get into the feeling state of being well compensated for having fun and being your very best you.

6. Consider what it feels like to make double the amount of money you are currently making. How does it feel to make triple? Quadruple? Keep imagining, stretching, breathing, relaxing and receiving!

The Gift Wheel process can support you in seeing who you are with greater insight and clarity. It can also help you understand and claim what it is your soul wants to create and experience on your human adventure. The Gift Wheel process and feeling your prosperity can set the wheels of manifesting into motion. It can start to shift your energy, which in turn will shift your life.

Exercise #3: Create a Prosperity and Life Purpose Collage

Get some magazines and quickly go through them, tear out the pictures and words that make you feel joyful, prosperous and happy. Look for things that make your heart smile. Do not try to use your intellect or your mind to choose the images. Allow this to be more of an intuitive, feeling, heart-centered process. Once you have 20-30 images, cut them out neatly and arrange them on a poster board with a glue stick. Once you have all your images, messages and words on the board, step back look at your collage as a complete work of art. Your collage can act as a mirror to a deeper part of yourself. You can learn a great deal about who you are, what is important to you and your life's purpose. This is also very powerful and a lot of fun to do with a group of friends. When everyone is complete, take some time reviewing each person's collage and share feedback about what each person sees, feels and experiences while exploring and experiencing one another's creation.

Chapter 3

Making Friends with Your Subconscious Mind

Until you make the unconscious conscious, it will direct your life and you will call it fate.

~ Carl Jung

If the Universe is abundant and generous (which it is), and if you consciously know you want to manifest greater prosperity (which most people do), what is the problem? Why are you not easily manifesting more money, a great life, wonderful experiences and all of your hearts desires? The problem lies in the pinch in the middle of the hourglass, in the recesses of your subconscious mind. There is a significant, hidden and powerful part of you that is operating on auto-pilot and dictating your conscious waking reality. By choosing to befriend this aspect of yourself, you can more easily step into your authentic power, purpose and prosperity in the world.

If you are having financial difficulties
it means you have not convinced your subconscious mind
you will always have enough and more.

It is psychological law, whatever we desire to accomplish, we must first impress upon the subjective or subconscious mind. Prosperity in the world is simply an outer manifestation of a subconscious conviction on the part of the individual. If someone wants to grow into prosperity consciousness, they first need to grow into an IDEA and ACCEPTANCE of wealth, value and abundance.

It has been estimated the average person uses no more than 10 percent of his or her mental power. The remaining 90 percent of mental activities take place subconsciously. An analogy would be like looking at an iceberg: when you observe an iceberg only a small portion is seen above the surface of the ocean. The vast majority of the iceberg's mass is hidden below the surface. Our minds are similar—our conscious mind is the tip of the iceberg, and our unconscious mind is "beneath the surface." This is a reference to the fact that our conscious mind only does a small amount of work in terms of processing and storing the information we receive—the majority is done by our subconscious mind. So if we want to manifest greater prosperity, of course it is important to have the consent of the conscious mind. However, if we want real and lasting change, working with the subconscious mind is imperative.

Another analogy that can be used to understand the relationship between the conscious and subconscious mind is the conscious mind as the captain of the ship and the subconscious being the crew. The conscious mind, and the captain, is the aspect at the helm and giving the orders. The subconscious mind is like the crew who takes orders from the conscious mind and implements them. The conscious mind uses the five senses to gain knowledge and learns through listening, observation, experience and education. The subconscious mind perceives by intuition and images. It is the seat of emotion and the storehouse of memories. The content of the conscious mind also filters down, plants seeds, takes root and affects the subconscious mind—even after the experiences have been forgotten. When the conscious and subconscious minds are not working together, there can be confusion, discord, discomfort, chaos, frustration and struggle. When they are working together, peace, synchronicity, prosperity and happiness inevitably ensue.

Think of the subconscious mind as the storage house for all information you have ever been exposed to: all of your previous life experiences, your beliefs and your memories. Everything you have ever done, heard and seen, as well as everything you have ever felt and/or perceived, is residing in the recesses of your subconscious. The subconscious mind does not reason, understand sarcasm, or have a sense of humor. The subconscious mind will accept false information, and information meant to be a joke, as factual, literal and true.

Unfortunately, from infancy onward most of us have been exposed to negative messages, suggestions, images and experiences. As young people we all unconsciously, unknowingly and unwittingly accept information as truth when it comes from those we perceive as superior. This information, even if it was inaccurate, sarcastic or false, weaves into the fabric and foundation of our subconscious mind, our psyche, and therefore begins to set the course for our human experience.

As children we do not yet have the capacity for logic and reasoning, so this content firmly embeds itself in the subconscious storehouse. These messages and tidbits of information put down roots, and then are often forgotten. However, the subconscious mind does not forget anything. The limiting content and negative information will continue to exist, and therefore dictate and control our lives from behind the scenes.

Understanding Your Brainwaves

I personally found it very helpful to understand the physiological function of our brains. There are significant and tangible differences in the brainwaves of conscious activity vs. subconscious activity. Armed with this information, I could more effectively take responsibility to reprogram my outdated limiting beliefs. I could also accept and implement new updated positive beliefs.

Our brains have five primary frequencies: Beta, Alpha, Theta, Delta and the lesser- known Gamma waves:

Beta: Beta brain waves are associated with normal waking consciousness and a heightened state of alertness, logic and critical reasoning. Beta waves are optimal when directed attention and high levels of concentration are needed. When you are mentally focused and engaged with the external, material world, your brain is functioning at the Beta level. Although important for effectively functioning in everyday life, the higher Beta levels can also translate into stress, anxiety, panic and restlessness. The voice of Beta is the little nagging chatterbox of your inner critic, and the "Monkey Mind," which becomes louder and more relentless the higher you go in the range. It is interesting to note most adults live primarily in the Beta Wave state.

Alpha: Alpha brain waves are slower and are the gateway to relaxation and creativity. In the Alpha state you experience a sense of peace and well-being. In Alpha, the logical left brain drops its guard and allows the more intuitive, creative aspects of the mind to become accessible and influential. Alpha is optimal for programming your mind for success. Relaxing into the Alpha state heightens your imagination and intuition as well as your ability to visualize, daydream and heal. Alpha lies at the base of your conscious awareness and is the gateway to your subconscious mind.

Theta: Theta represents the realm of the subconscious and is the most elusive and extraordinary realm of consciousness. It has been said to be the realm of "creative genius." Theta waves occur during light sleep, meditation and during peak experiences. In Theta we open our third eye and can tap into suppressed aspects of our psyche, experience deep peace and our connection to the Universe. In Theta we have access to great inspiration, extrasensory perception, profound creativity and exceptional insight. Not only is being in the Theta state tranquil, pleasurable and rejuvenating, it is also very healing physically, mentally, emotionally and spiritually.

Delta: Delta frequency is the slowest and is present in deep, dreamless sleep, and in very deep, transcendental meditation. Delta is the gateway to the Universal mind, and the collective unconscious. The information received at this level is unavailable at the conscious level. Delta is associated with deep healing and regeneration, highlighting the importance of deep sleep to the healing process. (We will explore how to access these deeper states of awareness in my next chapter, "Making friends with your Higher Self.")

Gamma: Gamma brain waves denote intense focus, and are usually weak and transient in normal brain activity. Although little is known about this state of mind, initial research shows Gamma waves are associated with bursts of insight, and high-level information processing. Gamma waves are prevalent in experienced meditation practitioners, especially high in the left prefrontal cortex of the brain. This area is often associated with decreased anxiety and fear, and the increased positive emotions such as happiness, joy and bliss.

Longtime practitioners of meditation experience reduced Beta activity and have more Theta, Alpha, Delta and Gamma brainwaves. Children up to the age of seven or eight are primarily in Theta and Alpha. This means children are in an altered state of consciousness and everything that occurs is programming their subconscious mind. So again this confirms what we see and hear as a young child (even if we do not remember it) is creating the foundation of our beliefs for the rest of our lives.

Your Money Blueprint

None of us arrive on planet Earth with any thoughts or feelings about money, we are all taught what to think about it. Because children's minds are constantly in the Alpha/Theta states, they automatically absorb their parent's messages and beliefs into their subconscious minds without choice, doubt, question or discernment.

T. Harv Ekar, coined the term "Money Blueprint." Like a blueprint for a house, which is a preset design for a home, your Money Blueprint is your preset relationship with money. Your Money Blueprint is like a button that either allows money to flow to you or stops it. In other words, your Money Blueprint determines your financial life.

The vision that comes to mind is like playing pin the tail on the donkey. As children we are blindfolded, spun around and pushed off in a particular direction by our parents or primary caretakers. We don't consciously consider it, we just go in the direction we are prompted, and take what is handed to us. Many of us were raised and "programmed" by people who either didn't have a lot of money, or had a lot of negative beliefs, habits and emotional issues around it. For the most part, our parents' way of thinking and feeling about money was imprinted on us and became our way of thinking and feeling about money—until we hit a wall, we are brought to our knees, or we decide to wake up, take off the blindfold and learn to do things differently.

Another analogy would be comparing a child to an iPod. When you get a new iPod, it is empty with no recordings. Once you download songs to the memory, those songs can be played, but only those songs. There are a lot of other songs and plenty of other music in the world, but none of those options can be played on that iPod until they are downloaded onto it. Similarly whatever has been downloaded into a child's subconscious memory are the only choices available. Other choices are not an option until new material is introduced into the subconscious storehouse. Therefore we automatically act out our parent's beliefs until we are exposed to other experiences or intentionally download new ones. (This is why I have created a series of guided meditations, to assist others in downloading new positive, prosperous messages. These are for anyone ready to claim greater prosperity.)

My Money Blueprint

Like most people, the Money Blueprint handed down to me was primarily of scarcity, lack and "not enough." As a child, I often witnessed my parents fighting about money, and frequently heard the statement: "We cannot afford it." I remember feeling ashamed for being expensive and a burden on my parents. My subconscious mind was saturated with messages, information and beliefs about the elusive nature of money. I felt guilty for existing and uncertain how I could fix the problems, other than to become invisible. On some level I believed if I disappeared, so would their financial troubles.

My parents divorced when I was eight, but I would still hear them fighting about money over the phone, and about my father paying child support. Again, I experienced significant fear and guilt. I was very worried about the lack of money, as well as the lack of support and love. I remember hearing my mother say we were poor. I was worried we would not have enough to eat: I wondered if I would soon look like the poverty-stricken children in commercials with their distended bellies, with flies buzzing around their heads. Seeds of fear about the lack of money were planted deep, and then took up residence in my body, my heart and in my subconscious mind.

Further beliefs were cultivated when my mother remarried. It seemed things improved for a while, but there was still the same theme around money. When I got a little older, I learned many of my friends received an allowance. I liked the idea of being able to make my own money and asked my mother if there was something I could do to earn an allowance. She told me to ask my stepfather. This continued to contribute to my belief that men have the power and the money and are in control of it. So, I asked my stepfather if I could earn an allowance. He told me my allowance was the roof over my head and the meals I was fed. He made it clear he still expected me to work hard and do everything I was asked to do with pride and integrity, but no financial reward.

My stepfather worked three jobs and was a carpenter. I would frequently join him and help him build fences, shingle roofs, paint houses and erect sheds. I was often told to mow the lawn, clean up the yard, fold the laundry, make dinner, clean the kitchen and other household chores. Thanks to my parents, a fantastic work ethic was instilled, for which I am immensely grateful. However, I also subconsciously "took on" the belief that even though I worked hard and did good work, all I was to expect in return was a roof over my head and enough to eat . . . which ended up being the case for much of my adult life.

Perhaps as a child you have heard some of these statements: Money doesn't grow on trees; we are not made of money; we can't afford it, or: If wishes were horses beggars would ride. Many have also heard things like: Children are to be seen and not heard; don't get your hopes up; you can't do that; or don't be stupid. Perhaps somewhere along the line you heard your parents fighting about money, or maybe you took on beliefs that you were not very important or valuable. When the subconscious mind is saturated with this kind of programming, it can be next to impossible to manifest great prosperity and success as an adult. However, we all have the ability to make friends with our subconscious mind, download new material, and reprogram it if we choose.

You *can* change your Money Blueprint. One important step in the right direction is being the kind of person who is open to opportunities and what is good, rather than focused on negativity and what is bad. You either attract or repel with your thoughts and beliefs. You can choose to be optimistic or pessimistic. You are either a victim or you are empowered. You will not be able to attract a great deal of money if you are angry at the one percent, constantly complain about the economy, or carry on about how all rich people are greedy.

You begin to claim your prosperity, alter your Money Blueprint and expand the pinch in your "money funnel" when your subconscious mind accepts that you have the ability to attract and create your heart's desires. You cannot manifest prosperity and a fulfilling, joyful life without the support, partnership and agreement of the conscious and subconscious minds.

Connecting With Your Inner Child

A powerful and simple exercise that can support, shift and heal you on a very deep level is to imagine inviting your inner child to sit with you and tell them of their immense value. When I realized many of my adult challenges with money had to do with what I decided about my value as a child, I knew what I needed to do. I lit a candle and I inwardly invited my inner child to come be with me. At first she did not clearly come into focus, I found I really needed to let her know I had a sincere desire and intention to connect with her. Finally, I got a sense of her in my mind's eye; a cartoon little ragamuffin, with uneven bangs, uncombed hair, a plaid dress and scuffed shoes.

Once she came into focus, I asked her how she was. She told me she was sad. I asked her why. She said she did not feel very important or valuable and that life was hard and confusing. So, I had a heart-to-heart conversation with that younger part of myself; I told "Little Tammi" she was very important, that she was valuable, and deserved to be here and to be happy. I also told her she had magical gifts and she could help heal the world. I told her that her mother and father had their own challenges with money, but it had nothing to do with her. I told her I believed in her and wanted her to be a bigger part of my life. As I continued to communicate with my inner child, she started to transform; she was smiling and there was a twinkle in her eye. I asked her what made her happy and she said drawing pictures outside in nature. So I told her that is exactly what we would do, and the next day we did.

Connecting with my inner child is what activated the artist in me. I started drawing and painting. I made a little line of greeting cards with animals, angels and glitter that people loved. At one point my inner child mentioned she had concerns about being "a starving artist." I told her it did not have to be that way. I told her God was an artist and *very* prosperous! I consistently worked with my inner child, and inwardly affirmed and acknowledged her worth and worthiness. I even started to give her an allowance! As I did this my art started to become more valued and validated in the world. I got my line of greeting cards into several boutiques and friends started offering to pay me to create images for them. Things continued to evolve and expand and today I sell my paintings for thousands of dollars. I know none of this success could have occurred if I had not taken the initiative to work with my inner child, listen to her, comfort her and tell her what she longed to hear about her importance and power.

You step onto the path of an authentically empowered and prosperous life when you love your inner child and acknowledge his or her immense value.

When we acknowledge the inner child, and remind them of their importance and worthiness, it is amazing how our lives can begin to transform. This is an exercise anyone can do in the present moment to alter an outdated Money Blueprint, clear negative content in the subconscious mind and claim greater prosperity. I continue to connect with my inner child and constantly affirm her magic and magnificence. I would not have evolved into the artist, writer and teacher I am today without her. My inner child, as well as yours, is a vital piece of the prosperity puzzle.

The Subconscious Mind and Symbols

If you are like most people you probably don't have direct and open relationship with your subconscious mind; it is likely on automatic pilot, just doing what it does. As you open your mind to a friendship with it, start to pay more conscious attention to it, and begin to communicate with clear intentions, you open to a whole new world of potential, power and possibilities.

The good news about the subconscious mind is that it is always available to you. Its intention is to serve and to protect you. It is also receptive, suggestible and open to partnering with you. Carl Jung has said: "Attention to the unconscious pays it a compliment that guarantees its cooperation." By opening your mind to this relationship, you can access its information, and be guided by its wisdom. The subconscious mind can speak to us in the language of intuition, colors, images and symbols. Images can make the invisible visible, which can then be translated into thoughts, ideas and words. Images are the universal language, the language of the soul, and are seen in myths, fairy tales and parables.

By consciously accessing and communicating

with your subconscious mind, you can delve deep

within yourself to get the answers to your questions,

harness incredible power and tap into

profound states of inner wisdom.

A suggestion to begin cultivating a friendship with the subconscious was given to us from the tradition of Huna. Huna is a Hawaiian word adopted by Max Freedom Long (1890–1971) in 1936 to describe his theory of metaphysics, which he linked to ancient Hawaiian Kahunas or experts. Huna emphasizes practical living and harmony with three levels of consciousness or "the three selves," the conscious, subconscious and super conscious minds. (The superconscious is another term for God, higher consciousness, Christ consciousness or the collective consciousness.)

In Huna, we are invited to turn inward and ask the subconscious mind what it wants to be called. We may ask: What is your name? Who are you? What do you look like? This invitation is enough to evoke a more conscious relationship with this deeper, vital and mysterious aspect of ourselves. From this place you can begin to communicate, you can ask questions, share your thoughts and feelings, listen and learn. Partnering with this vital aspect of yourself will support you to become more aligned and congruent, help you participate more fully in life and assist you in showing up more powerfully in the world.

The subconscious mind is your friend

and when you explore it with the intention

to listen, learn, understand

and partner with it, life can become

an amazing, joy-filled, abundant adventure!

Removing Inner Blocks to Prosperity

William James was trained as a medical doctor and became a respected pioneering American psychologist and philosopher. He wrote many influential books on the science of psychology, educational psychology, psychology of religious experience and mysticism. James said the power to move the world is in your subconscious mind. "Your subconscious mind is one with infinite intelligence and boundless wisdom. Whatever you impress upon your subconscious mind will inevitably come to pass." *(Psychology: The Briefer Course, 1985).*

While it is true there may be "negative" content in the subconscious, the good news is everything there is because we put it there . . . and we have the power to change it. We can become good friends with our subconscious mind, update the software in our system and download new material. A seemingly small inner shift in the subconscious realm can create big shifts in our conscious waking lives.

An example of a small inner shift creating a big outer difference was during a session with my client "Paula." Paula was tired of struggling financially, of not being able to buy lunch for a friend or go shopping when she wanted. One day her mechanic said she needed new tires and this was the last straw. Paula finally got angry about her financial plight. She called me later that afternoon and said, "Will you please help me with this money thing?" I was happy to receive her request for support. I have found it is impossible to assist people or give them answers until they ask for help. I joyfully made an appointment for her the next day.

When Paula came to my office, I explained to her that her subconscious mind had not accepted being prosperous. However, we could easily access her subconscious through a guided meditation and find out what the block or barrier was. Then, if she wanted, I could help her release the limiting belief and reprogram her subconscious mind. Paula was ready to rock and roll! I told Paula we would do my "Divine Prosperity Guided Meditation." I explained to her the subconscious mind tends to reveal things first as symbols or images, which can then be translated into words, messages and stories. I also explained that all guided meditation and hypnosis is self-hypnosis. This process is just a way of accessing the imagination and inner knowing.

Paula was excited to get started. I invited her to get comfortable on her chair and then facilitated a brief "relaxation induction," counting backwards from 10 to 1. I had her imagine going into a healing inner sanctuary I asked her to describe the sights, smell, temperature and sounds that came forward. After she described her sanctuary to me in Technicolor detail, I invited her subconscious mind to reveal her "Divine Prosperity Treasure Chest." Paula told me she could see her Treasure Chest clearly in the distance, it was made of rich, dark wood and was glowing with gold accents. Then

I invited her subconscious mind to reveal the image of the block or barrier to her Treasure Chest. A moment later Paula described the brick wall that dropped into her awareness, it was dark red, solid, hard and cold.

Paula was confused. Why was this brick wall there and why was it preventing her from claiming her treasures? As the conversation with the brick wall ensued, we found it was not an enemy, but rather a friend. When we asked the wall to share its intention it said: "I am here to protect you and keep you safe." I asked the brick wall what it was protecting her from. It responded by sharing: "I am keeping you from being hurt, from being taken advantage of and being disillusioned. In truth, this was a very noble intention and an important job.

When I asked the brick wall what it needed to relax and transform into something more supportive so Paula could manifest her prosperity and heart's desires, it said "clear boundaries." The brick wall then gracefully transformed into a beautiful iridescent bubble, a wonderful new symbol of clear, flexible boundaries. I had Paula imagine the bubble surrounding her and it agreed it would keep her safe. I asked the bubble if it had any further wisdom or a message to share, it said: "Yes, speak your truth, soften up, lighten up and say 'thank you' more frequently." Paula happily took the advice that "bubbled up" from her subconscious mind and this guided meditation and committed to telling her truth and saying "thank you" more often. "Miraculously" Paula manifested two more clients that week and received a phone call out of the blue about doing a paid speaking engagement.

Recently when I spoke with Paula, she told me she has continually made more and more money every month, and now feels truly prosperous. She attributes a great deal of her success to her small yet profound inner shift. Paula seems very different than she did before we started the prosperity work. She has softened, lightened up, easily tells her truth in a loving way and has become very gracious. Paula continues the inner work and the "Divine Prosperity Guided Meditation." Paula joyfully shares her wonderful wins and amazing stories, and continues to manifest more money, greater prosperity and amazing opportunities.

You Are Valuable, Creative and Adored!

The truth is you are directly connected to the Source of All. You are created in the likeness of God and you are the child in whom He is well pleased. The truth is you live in a lavish, generous and abundant Universe in which everything you could ever want or need can be easily provided. You just need to open your mind to the possibility that you are deeply, truly and immensely valuable. Next surrender any unconscious constrictions, issues of unworthiness, and any limiting beliefs that prevent you from relaxing and receiving all the Universe has for you. Then say yes to your imagination and creativity, and make friends with your subconscious mind.

When your conscious and subconscious

minds are congruent and aligned, life works,

prosperity is natural and miracles happen!

Exercise #1: Releasing Outdated Beliefs

1. Take a moment and consider what you were taught about money and prosperity as a young person. Perhaps some limiting beliefs were handed down to you from your parents, other family members, teachers or friends. Consciously think, write and tell "your story" about your early experiences with money and your value.

2. After you have written your story, set the intention to clear, heal and transform any limiting beliefs. If it resonates for you do a "burning ceremony" or tear up this paper into little pieces and throw it away. The subconscious mind loves ritual ceremony and it is a powerful way of claiming completion in any area of life you would like to surrender, release and clear.

3. Now, set your intentions and write down the kind of relationship you would like to have with money from now on. Acknowledge your value and explore what prosperity feels like. Consider a new, improved, refreshed and revised relationship with money. How are things different? What does this all feel like? Really "try on" and explore this new relationship and your new reality. Allow yourself to relax into this "feeling state" of prosperity. Know the more time you spend visualizing, exploring and inwardly *feeling* prosperous the more you will be supported in manifesting this in your outer reality.

4. Do things that make you feel prosperous! What can you do that will support you in owning, embracing and accepting the experience of prosperity? Be kind and generous to yourself—

get a massage, buy yourself flowers. Is there an amazing meal you can make to celebrate yourself? Treat yourself with value, appreciation and respect and soon you will find you are being treated with greater value, appreciation and respect in the world.

Exercise #2: Connect With Your Inner Child

1. Turn off the phone so you won't be disturbed and create a sacred space for yourself. You may want to find a picture of yourself as a child. You may choose to light a candle and/or play some soft soothing music. You may also want your journal with you to take notes about what comes forward.

2. Take a few deep, healing, cleansing breaths and inwardly invite your inner child to join you. Be patient and let them know you have a sincere desire to connect with them. Imagine them in your mind's eye. They may show up as light or energy, as a cartoon, or as you actually looked as a young person. Try not to force anything or have any attachments to how things are "supposed to look."

3. Once he or she arrives, ask how they are doing, how they are feeling, and what name they would like to be called. Listen and allow this part of you to respond and say all they want to say. You may find they are happy or sad. They may have tears to shed, anger to express and/or stories to tell. Really connect with this part of you, be very present and listen deeply.

4. Now ask your inner child what they need from you to feel better now and to be a bigger part of your life. Perhaps you want to take some notes about what they want to do, where they want to go, what they think and feel. You may also ask them to share their thoughts and/or ideas.

5. Let your inner child know how important, worthy and valuable they are. No matter what has happened in the past, they are priceless and magical. Tell them all the things they long to hear and about some of great things that are in their future. If tears start to come up, allow them to flow.

6. Thank your inner child for spending time with you. Express your heartfelt appreciation in whatever way is sincere for you. Gratitude will support you in deepening the relationship and help you keep the lines of communication with your inner child open.

7. Connect with your inner child often. This is the part of you that is intuitive, creative, and powerful. You can imagine them with you in the car, or while shopping, with you at a concert, or the theater, with family or friends. When you cultivate a friendship with your inner child, you start to create a more solid foundation within yourself, and other people's opinions become less relevant. In fact, this can be one of the most positive, important and vital relationships in your life.

Any time you are hurting, there is a line of energy that goes back to an earlier time in your life. If you cultivate a conscious, kind, consistent relationship with the inner child, and integrate them into your life HERE and NOW, you heal from the inside out and relax into greater comfort within. As a bonus your life WILL change in positive and miraculous ways. I believe we become spiritual adults when we take responsibility for this vital relationship and treat our inner child the way they wish they had been treated by others. This important and powerful relationship will put you on solid ground in all of your other relationships, with your finances and in every other area of your life.

Exercise #3: Removing Inner Obstacles

In the session with Paula, a brick wall came forward as a symbol from her subconscious mind. Paula had experienced significant pain and betrayal in her life and her unconscious mind erected this wall designed to protect her. Although it had the best of intentions, it also kept her prosperity out. Once Paula made friends with the brick wall, she learned to listen to it and understand its purpose. From there, she could dialogue with it, reason with it, bless it, thank it and release it. Once this occurred, the brick wall easily transformed into a more supportive symbol: a beautiful iridescent bubble, an updated symbol of boundaries and protection.

Our outer reality is a reflection of our inner reality. As we understand and take responsibility for our inner reality, (the content of our subconscious mind), our outer reality naturally shifts and transforms. You may listen to guided meditations to support you in removing your inner obstacles. Additionally, here are a couple of more exercises that can support you in doing this deep inner healing work.

Step One: Allow yourself to take a few easy breaths and relax. Once you are in a state of inner peace you are open to receiving the messages of your Higher Self, Soul or Super Conscious mind. If you find it challenging to still your mind, consider a person or an animal for whom you have unconditional love, or you may choose to bring to mind a place in nature that brings you peace and centers you in your heart. Once you settle into your heart space, allow yourself to simply breathe and relax. Give yourself permission to drop into the realm of serenity, inner calm, "open flow" and deep peace.

Step Two: Consider an area in your life where you are challenged or are dealing with an obstacle. Ask this situation or issue to come forward as an image or a symbol. It can show up in an infinite variety of forms, some examples might include: a color, a shape, a nebulous cloud of energy, something from nature, a brick, a dagger, an animal or a ball. Have no preconceived notions about what may show up. Set the intention to trust the process and the power of your inner reality and graciously receive whatever comes forward for you. Once the image comes into focus, ask the following questions and patiently wait for the answers to reveal themselves:

1. What is your purpose or intention in my life?

2. What belief caused you to come into my reality?

3. What are you teaching me?

4. What is my soul trying to learn from this?

5. What do I need to know or do to release you? Or are you open to receiving a promotion?

6. Now ask this symbol to transform into a more effective tool or the perfect healing image for you now; something that can support you in moving forward in your life and stepping more fully into your power, prosperity and purpose.

7. Imagine this updated symbol as a friend, teacher, partner or ally. You can visualize journeying forward together on the path to manifesting and experiencing a more prosperous future. You can allow your imagination to wander and the inner vision unfold almost like a waking dream. Enjoy the feeling state and stay open to any revelations from this inwardly prosperous experience.

8. In closing, express gratitude for the situation, symbol and your subconscious mind. Keep your mind and heart open to meaningful coincidence, winks from the universe and a shift in your outer reality. And when synchronicity happens (and it will) utter a heartfelt "THANK YOU"!

You CAN reprogram the old software in your system. You CAN upload new song choices and new material. Participating in these exercises will help you cultivate a friendship with your subconscious mind and improve both your inner and outer realties. This in turn will naturally begin to transform your life and your finances. Even if it does not feel like much is happening I guarantee you it is! Simple awareness and revelation can gracefully support you in expanding the pinch in the middle of the hourglass, help you clear out the clutter in your subconscious mind, and dissolve any outdated beliefs and dueling intentions. These exercises can easily support you in releasing old outdated material and replace it with new, updated, positive information about prosperity. They can also help you understand, claim, receive, accept and manifest your immense value in the world.

Chapter 4

Aligning with Your Higher Self

Align your personality with your soul, Until that happens you won't be able to give the gifts you were meant to give.

~ Gary Zukav

Believing in prosperity can be challenging in our conscious waking life. It seems the world is intent on bombarding us with messages of scarcity and fear. Our logical, thinking mind would have us believe all that we see in the outer world, and therefore it's easy to buy into this limiting reality. If you think your power is "out there," you are in victim mode and disconnected from your soul and true source of power. If you attempt to control, convince or "get" anything from anyone, you are playing small, dancing for the mirror and living from the outside in. However, everyone, including you, has the choice, opportunity and ability to experience a more "Truth-based," expansive and empowered reality. This begins to happen when you decide to live your life from the inside out.

The great spiritual traditions of India tell us the outer world is considered to be an illusion, also referred to as "Maya." While in a conscious, alert state, and focused on the outer world, our rapid Beta brainwaves will not let us get a positive message in edgewise. In other words, we are entrenched and tangled up in Maya. To accept abundance as our birthright and experience a "Truer Truth" we need to drop into a calmer, deeper state of awareness. This occurs by virtue of slowing the brainwaves down to the powerful and peaceful territory of Alpha, Theta and Delta.

As we allow ourselves to sink into a more relaxed state of being, the veil between our conscious, subconscious and super conscious mind thins and/or dissolves. This is when we can be in direct communion with the deeper and/or higher aspects of ourselves. This is the place where we can access the wisdom of our authentic self, our Higher Self and Source. The Higher Self is the purest God-self you can access while still in human form, devoid of the heavier emotions of fear, hatred, guilt or shame. Higher Self states are blissful, filled with joy, empowerment, freedom and love.

It is exciting when we understand we have everything we need inside of ourselves to change our lives dramatically and access the most important source of power in the Universe.

Every one of us is connected to Spirit and to each other. The problems occur when we do not understand and live from this place. A vision that comes to mind for me is a wheel with a hub in the center and millions of spokes coming out from it. Each one of us represents a spoke emanating from that hub. If you go deep enough into me, and deep enough into you, we get to that hub, which can also be referred to as Source or Spirit or God. When I refer to Higher Self, Inner Being, Soul or Soul Self, I am referring to the line of energy that emanates from us, and attaches us to that central hub which is God or Source.

In truth, we can never be disconnected from God, not even for a second, it is an absolute impossibility. However, while we are in ego, pain or suffering it can *feel that way*. Often in an attempt to avoid, ignore or outrun pain, we have the enticing opportunity to distract ourselves with Maya, and chase any number of worldly experiences. Some of those options might include: shopping, eating, consuming alcohol, working out, cosmetic surgery, drugs, sex, pornography, relationships, television, movies, video games, talking on the phone, social media, sports and/or work, to name a few. However, these distractions will never bring lasting happiness. They will more than likely usher us further away from our soul and distance us from true fulfillment, freedom and authentic power. The experience of true and lasting happiness cannot be acquired from anything outside of ourselves, it is a state of being that resides deep within ourselves, and occurs by virtue of aligning with our souls.

Many people think they will finally be fulfilled when they get their body to look the way they want, achieve fame, hit the lottery, attain wealth, get approval from others or find that "special relationship." However, the experience of lasting happiness and fulfillment do not occur when something outside of oneself happens. Happiness is an inside job and occurs when one is acting in accordance with their higher nature, and aligned with his or her Higher Self.

True happiness occurs when you are in partnership

with your Higher Self.

Your ideal, prosperous life is not something you attain when you manifest all the money you want or attain any outward oriented goal. Your ideal life is activated the moment you step onto your true path, where you are expressing yourself fully in the moment and living your soul's purpose. When people talk about "finding themselves" or "being true to themselves" it comes from the deep desire to be aligned with their Higher Self. There is a profound satisfaction and peace that comes from being aligned with our soul self—this is also the state of being where prosperity naturally flows.

Creating From EGO versus IGO

I was once told from a wise and wonderful teacher that all of our pain comes from our perceived disconnection from Source. I was not certain I agreed. However, from that moment on, I checked in with myself whenever I was in pain. I had to admit, while in the throes of my suffering, I really *did not* feel connected.

I have come to understand we have two ways to create our lives, either from disconnection and fear, also known as EGO or Edging

God Out. Or option two, from connection and love, also known as IGO or Inviting God Only. I believe we all attempt to live from EGO, until it is just too painful and we are brought to our knees. This is when people tend to extend the invitation to God and crack the door open to a different way of being.

I do not think there is a person alive who has not experienced desire motivated from the level of their ego or personality. But there is an aspect of us that is imbued with desire and motivation from a higher place. We all have the opportunity to become aware of, and align with, our higher-minded desires and intentions.

I agree with this powerful message from author and teacher James Blanchard Cisneros: "You are the vehicle God uses to express Himself on this planet. Allow Him to flow through you. It is only by allowing this that His expression can be experienced. Believe it or not, you have the final decision of what will flow through you and into the world. Not even God would force Himself through you, unless you allow Him to."

By aligning with our Higher Selves and with Spirit,

We can remember our true purpose and begin to

prosper at the deepest levels.

For much of my life I thought I wanted to be a model and actress. I focused on these goals and had a modicum of success. However, I did not find these careers to be deeply fulfilling. When

I got to the core of these desires, I realized they came from a place of wanting to be admired, to be important, seen, recognized, to be beautiful and special. I wanted other people to validate my importance, wrongly thinking that would make me feel important. These were the longings of my ego and my desire to receive the experience of happiness and value from the outside in.

As I cultivated a relationship with my Higher Self, what eventually revealed itself was that I was to write, teach, paint, become a counselor and a radio host. These were the desires of a higher nature and my soul's deeper longings. The motivation from this place was to have heart-to-heart connections with others, see the beauty of others, live in my loving, be of service, co-create with Spirit, and deeply celebrate this human experience. These revelations supported me in beginning to live from the inside out. As I began to understand and take action in this new direction, my life began to transform. My primary motivation was no longer about what I could get, but what I could give. I know, without question, I could never have manifested my soul's purpose, true happiness and prosperity, without opening to IGO, and consciously aligning with my Higher Self.

The Human Brain and Fear

The physiology of the human brain has not evolved much since we were running from dinosaurs, constantly searching for food and protecting ourselves from the elements. Fear, hyper-vigilance and the "red-alert" state has served humanity well as far as survival goes, but does not effectively support us in evolving in our consciousness.

In modern times, most of us are not in life-and-death situations on a daily basis. However, our brains are still hardwired for "fight or flight." The human brain seems to dictate fear as a natural state and anxiety as an innate propensity. In order to transcend this primal state we need to take personal responsibility and claim faith and love as our intention and priority. If we do not take personal responsibility, we can easily slip into autopilot, and fear will insidiously slide into the driver's seat.

If you experience fear, anxiety, anger, competition or aggression, know there is nothing wrong with you; fear is simply in your physiology. These emotions are not something to judge, but rather something to be cognizant of. It is also very powerful and healing to have compassion for this innate human condition. Once we understand fear as a "natural" propensity and tendency, we realize we can and/or NEED to take personal responsibility if we want to transcend the lower reptilian brain and ascend to higher states of consciousness. These higher states bring about a sense of connection, love, peace, faith, trust and happiness. Although some people naturally reside in a place of happiness, for many, it takes discipline and concerted effort. The most effective way I know to do this is through consciously choosing to align with one's Higher Self and through meditation.

Meditation

I first opened my mind to meditation because of my own personal struggle with fear and pain. I suffered intensely with anxiety and depression. I kept hearing about the benefits of meditation and thought I had nothing to lose by giving it a try. As I began a meditation practice I started to feel calmer and more peaceful. I wasn't aware of it at the time, but deciding to take a few moments a day just to focus on my breath is what supported me in opening the door to a relationship with my soul.

In retrospect, I believe my anxiety came from slipping into that innate, primal, fear-based state and from not feeling connected and aligned with my Higher Self. In other words, there was too much play in the rope of my spoke. Fear is what inspired me to turn inward, which in turn supported me in opening to a relationship with a deeper, wiser and more loving part of myself. Now I perceive fear as an invitation, as my teacher and the doorway to another way of being. I know it would have been impossible to manifest my destiny and Divine Prosperity without the motivation of my fear, the partnership of my conscious and subconscious mind and the alignment with my Higher Self.

So why does meditation work? Meditation changes our physiology and induces a host of biochemical and physical changes in the body. One way of referring to the peace that meditation produces is the "relaxation response." The relaxation response includes changes in metabolism, heart rate, respiration, blood pressure and brain chemistry. Neuroscientists have found that meditators shift brain activity to different areas of the cortex. Brain waves in the stress-prone right frontal cortex move to the calmer left frontal cortex. M.R.I. brain scans taken before and after meditation found increased activity in the hippocampus, an area important for learning and memory. The M.R.I.s also indicated a reduction of activity in the amygdala, a region connected to anxiety, stress and depression.

Benefits of meditation include better health, less stress, greater comfort in one's body, reduced fear and greater happiness. Meditation naturally helps cultivate compassion, intuition, mindfulness, awareness, calmness and clarity. Not only does meditation change and improve us physically, mentally and emotionally, it lines us up spiritually.

Swami Muktananda, the founder of Siddha Yoga, has said: "We do not meditate only to relax and experience peace, we meditate to unfold our inner being." Meditating is a way to consciously line up with our Higher Selves and connect with Spirit. It can support us in deepening our faith and living a more heart-centered, love-based, soulful life. Meditation can also help us understand who we are and what we came here to do.

Meditation helps you physically, mentally and emotionally, it also lines you up spiritually.

Meditation is a way we can hear the still small voice within and sit in the presence of God. Prosperity is simply the icing on the cake. I consistently witness those who commit to a meditation practice experience positive changes in all areas of their lives—including their financial lives. As more time is spent in an inner state of peace, a natural release of resistance occurs. When we relax our resistance, we naturally open to the receptive states of allowing and attraction. Just like a cork being held under water naturally floats upwards when let go, so do we when we release our fear and resistance through meditation.

When I meditate, synchronicity, support, opportunities, prosperity and miracles ensue. If I stop meditating, the synchronicity ceases, the anxiety returns and my life inevitably starts to go sideways. In other words, when I meditate, my life works and when I do not it does not—it is as simple and difficult as that.

Meditate to Relax into Your Authentic Shape

Life flows out from our inner state of being, and if we are not balanced, centered, peaceful and aligned, life can be confusing and challenging. By virtue of meditation, we can open to who we are on the deepest level. We access gifts we were not aware we had, we activate our ability to attract wonderful things, and we relax into the fullness and "specialness" of who we are.

> *Meditation will naturally support you in*
> *becoming who you came here to be –*
> *even if you do not know who that is yet!*

A Course in Miracles says "All of God's children are special, and none of God's children are special." All of us are made of the same spectacular "star stuff" AND every one of us has a distinct energy and an extraordinary brand of magic. Another example is that we are all snow, yet each of us is as an individual and as unique as snowflake. Like notes in a symphony, each one of us can express our incredible uniqueness, yet participate in the whole melody. Each one of us has the opportunity to use our talents to bring good to the world, to celebrate ourselves, play with others and manifest our abundance in a way no one else can.

We all come from the same singular Source of Brilliance and when we meditate, we naturally relax into the place of alignment with that Source. I strongly believe if you are consistent with your meditation practice, you align with the source of prosperity and what is yours will more naturally come to you.

The easiest and most effective way to find your unique

and authentic shape is to relax into meditation.

I have been meditating for over a decade and still feel like a novice; that is why it is called a practice—we have to just keep trying. From personal experience, I understand meditation can be hard or even impossible if you do not give your monkey mind something to do. In many spiritual traditions it is recommended that we focus on the breath. You can count numbers as you take each breath and visualize each number coming into focus in your mind's eye. Another suggestion is allowing your attention to drop from your head down into the area of your heart and viscerally feel the energy expanding. Chanting OM seven times out loud has a mind-relaxing effect and is a wonderful way to begin a meditation.

There are also "mantras" you can repeat. A mantra is a sound, syllable, word, or group of words that is considered capable of "creating transformation." This can either be done inwardly or aloud, to relax and clear the mind-chatter. You may use a mantra from a spiritual tradition, or you may want to create a personal one that really resonates for you. Some examples might include: "I am of the Light and I am prosperous," "I am a magnet for magic, miracles and money," or "I am the abundant child in whom God is well pleased." Consider the reality you would like claim for yourself and use your words, and/or prosperity mantra, as your meditation anchor. If you do this consistently for at least 20 minutes a day, and for at least 2 weeks, not only will your physiology change in a positive way, you will undoubtedly begin to experience some "beyond coincidental coincidences," and incredible winks from the Universe.

Another meditation option is to Light a candle and focus on the flame. For my prosperity support group, I created candles with my prosperity symbol on it along with this prayer:

As I light this candle I invite the energy of Divine Prosperity.

As I sit with this flame I am gently releasing all things that no longer serve me.

From this moment forward I naturally and easily attract all things that are mine by Divine Right.

Dear God/Source/ Universe/Spirit may my purpose and place in this world be made clear

and my journey be filled with support, synchronicity,
abundance and ease.

Thank you, thank you thank you. And So It Is!

After uttering this prayer, I suggest focusing on the flame with the eyes open, then eventually allowing them to gently close and visualizing the light in the third eye for 15- 20 minutes. I also recommend combining this with the inner feeling of openness, flow, gratitude, receptivity and prosperity.

Another suggestion that can help you relax and drop into a deep meditative state is a CD with ocean waves or sounds from nature. On my website I offer a free guided meditation along with others for purchase. I also offer music with Alpha and Theta toning, combined with sounds from nature and binaural beats. I like this method for a variety of reasons. The sounds and tones naturally and easily help the mind to focus and relax, which affects the brain in a positive and powerful way. Also, because the tracks are 20 minutes, I don't have to look at a clock to know how long I have been meditating. Sometimes I will allow the track to repeat a second time if I want a 40 minute session or a third time if I want an hour meditation.

Binaural beats occur when different tones are played in each ear, ostensibly causing the listener to produce a third tone as the brain's way of making sense of this. (Hearing discrete tones in each ear does not happen in nature.) Everyone hears this third tone in their own unique way. Our nervous systems respond favorably to these frequencies. According to the book *Get High Now - Without Drugs* by James Nestor, "Binaural Beats have been clinically shown to physically affect the listener's brain and body, even triggering the pituitary gland to flood the body with good-feeling hormones like dopamine." To reap the benefits, one must listen to the sounds with headphones.

If you are a visual person it can be helpful to find an object of beauty and/or prosperity to focus on as you relax your thinking mind. You may choose to inwardly imagine the color of prosperity or the most healing color for you to work with right now. Perhaps you can imagine a symbol from nature that represents abundance, such as flower, a garden, a beach, a night sky with infinite stars or a place of spiritual significance. Any of these options can be a powerful catalyst for evoking inner peace, dropping into the feeling state of Universal abundance, personal prosperity and accessing those deeper Alpha and Theta states.

There is no "right way" to meditate, it is like exercise. People respond to and enjoy different types of both physical and spiritual fitness. Just stay open and try different things. Set your meditation intentions and claim your desire to align with your Higher Self and I know you will find what works well for you.

Serena's Story

I have a client named Serena who experienced significant challenges in her relationships, in her career and with her finances. She would often call me when she was in crisis. After sharing what was going on and how she was feeling, I would ask her if she had meditated. The answer was always no. It finally got to the point where Serena would call to tell her story and when she was finished she would say: "I know I need to meditate." Serena finally made it a habit to meditate every time she felt confused, afraid, hurt or angry. She eventually realized she had the answer to every question inside herself as well as the ability to resolve her pain and challenges. As Serena became more consistent with her meditation, she became more empowered, and her life began to work with much greater grace and ease. The drama decreased and the synchronicity increased. Serena is currently in a healthy, supportive, drama-free relationship. She has also cultivated a fulfilling career making money doing what she loves. Serena will be the first to admit she would not be where she is in her life without committing to her meditation practice.

It often seems the more we need to sit down, center and connect with our Higher Selves, the more we tend to resist it. From the ego's perspective it is much more appealing to run away and distance ourselves from the discomfort. It can seem like an attractive option to look for an answer or distraction "out there." I also believe the ego thinks it might be bored if it does not have drama. However, I have found once we surrender the drama with the little "d," the "big D drama" can start to show up. This is the Drama of synchronicity, miracles, authentic heart connections and co-creation with the Universe. If you want your life to work with grace and ease, and attract your Divine Prosperity, I recommend you turn inwards towards your Self, sit down, meditate and line up with IGO. This is how you can create in cooperation with your soul and the Universe.

But I Don't Have Time!

I have heard people come up with many reasons why they cannot, or will not, meditate. One of the most common excuses is: "I do not have time!" One of the amazing advantages of meditation is when you take the time to do it, you will seem to have more time! I believe this is because when we are more relaxed and aligned, we are more efficient with our time, action steps and choices.

If time is your greatest objection, it is interesting to note the Dalai Lama has said that just five minutes of daily meditation can have profound benefits. In fact, His Holiness will recommend not practicing too long in the beginning, and has said; "Do not over-extend yourself; the maximum period is around fifteen minutes. The important thing is not the length of the session but the quality of it."

When you relax your monkey mind and come to an inner state of peace, the clutter of your random, energy-taking Alpha thoughts can go on a brief vacation. When stress and overwhelm is decreased, you reduce wasted energy, eliminate unnecessary action steps, and the "busywork" that prevents positive forward movement in your life. The Dalai Lama says meditation is the practice of allowing the mud of our thoughts to settle so we can experience the clear luminosity of our soul. From this relaxed state a bigger picture can reveal itself. Priorities, thoughts and ideas can begin to emerge in a calm, clear and open way. When you meditate consistently, you will effortlessly experience greater clarity, and naturally make more positive, productive and prosperous choices.

Meditation can put you "in the zone" and help you to become

more present, effective and efficient. When the mind is relaxed and highly focused, the experience of time is expanded. People who play sports can tell you how the ball was coming to them in slow motion. Firefighters also talk about a sense of sharpened awareness during life- saving rescues. These are extraordinary circumstances, but meditation can cultivate mental acuity which can support you in every area of your life—and the ordinary can become extraordinary.

If you start a meditation practice, and allow yourself to go on a daily "brain vacation," a natural by-product will be that your life will smooth out, and you will experience greater support, synchronicity, grace and ease. Meditation will assist you in living life aligned from your center, and more aligned with Source. Though craziness may be around you, you will be able to reside in the calm, safe space in the eye of the storm. The rewards from meditation will continue throughout your day and your life. You may find things that used to bother you no longer do. You have a greater sense of equanimity, peace, patience and faith. You will find yourself becoming more intuitive, more imaginative—and even more intelligent!

If you turn your attention to your Source through meditation,

you will find not only does Source turn to you,

but shares generously with you.

Although traditions vary on how much time is recommended for meditation, the most important thing is to do it regularly. Can you spare two minutes right now? If so, try this exercise. Relax and gently close your eyes, let go of any stress or tension in your body and your mind. Next, notice your thoughts, like clouds, floating by the clear blue sky of your inner reality. Just breathe, relax and observe. At the end of two minutes, check in with yourself and notice how you feel. If you simply take a few slow, deep breaths, relax and spend some time noticing your thoughts daily, you will find you have more time for what's important to you.

Silence and the Wisdom Within

Another common complaint I hear is: "I cannot sit and think of nothing." In meditation it is not that we try to think of nothing, it is that we simply choose to observe our thoughts. We cannot free ourselves of thoughts by simply willing them to stop. However, by virtue of being silent, still, and peaceful, our thoughts have the opportunity to slow down. It can be like potty training a puppy, whenever you notice you are thinking, bring the "thought puppy" back to the paper. Do this consistently, without judgment and with patience, and you may find your thoughts starting to slow down. After a while, you can witness your thoughts without being carried away by them. The longer you sit in silence, the more you may realize there tends to be more and more space between those thoughts and eventually the presence of a deep peace.

Once the thinking mind slows down, we have the opportunity to experience profound peace, healing, relaxation and revelations. This peaceful state is also the place where we can receive higher-minded answers to our questions. Relaxing my conscious thinking mind and then asking the deeper, quieter part of my Self for answers is when I have received some of my most important life lessons. Meditation has supported me in accessing life-altering epiphanies as well as receiving clear direction from my Soul Self.

I remember when I first started meditating I would quiet my mind and then ask my Higher Self or Source: "What should I do?" What I got back was: "Relax!" Again I would ask: "But what do I DO? I need to make MONEY!" Again, I would hear the word: "RELAX!" Especially in our Western Culture, it seems we are encouraged to be "human doings" rather than "human beings." When we relax into a "being state," we let go of the oars and surrender control, along with our insistence that we go a particular direction and pace in our lives. This is when we can be carried on the current God would prefer for us to go. Because of my meditation practice I have been carried in a direction I would not have predicted or anticipated, but that has ultimately brought me prosperity, great fulfillment and immense joy.

By relaxing and changing our inner state,
our outer reality can magically and powerfully shift
and transform.

In Psalms we are advised "To be still and know that I am God." When we are still, and when we silence our analytical thinking mind, we open to more fully to our Divine nature and naturally align more directly with our soul. A relaxed, open and receptive mind puts us in the space where we can receive insights and "ah-has." We can download profound information, have powerful epiphanies, and access divinely inspired ideas. These experiences can transform our inner reality in an instant, increase our vibration therefore naturally and positively affect our outer lives.

Your life is a reflection of your inner state. If you do no not like what you are seeing or experiencing in your life, it is far more empowering and effective to take responsibility for your inner state, and enhance your connection to your Higher Self, rather than fight or struggle with other people and the outer world. When you take responsibility for your relationship with your Inner Self, your external reality will shift in remarkable and miraculous ways.

When we quit trying to fill ourselves up,

and rather empty ourselves out,

then Source/God/Spirit can fill us up with His Essence

and give us what He wants us to have—and this is always

something WONDERFUL!

In *A Course in Miracles* we are told that miracles are the byproduct of a shift in perception. In other words, profound and lasting change can occur in an instant by virtue of seeing things from a slightly different viewpoint. This shift can occur naturally and easily when we relax our thinking mind and access awareness from within. This, in turn, can restore a more open and aligned connection with Spirit. Higher Intelligence *always* knows what we want and need for our fulfillment and truly desires to support us in living a life of deep satisfaction and great prosperity. However, the Universe cannot support and guide us if we do not make it a habit to relax, invite it in and receive it.

I have relinquished my old habits and patterns of ambition, pushing, grabbing and chasing. I have found it is much more joyful, productive and effective to relax, meditate, and allow life to bring me what is mine, and reveal to me what is mine to do. I have experienced countless miracles and have been forever transformed because of my simple meditation practice. My quiet moments in solitude, combined with my intention to surrender my limited, human, ego-based perspective to "Something Greater," has assisted me in stepping into the gracious and faithful flow of the ever-changing river of life.

Guided Meditation and Hypnosis

For those that continue to be challenged or frustrated in their attempts to meditate, guided meditations can be a wonderful tool and a great support. Guided meditations are simply "meditations with the help of a guide." It gives your analytical mind something to focus on, and is an effective way to enter into a relaxed state where your brain waves naturally shift. Guided meditations can slow down the active monkey mind and support you in sparking deeper inspiration and imagination. They can also propel you on a wonderful inner journey. These inner journeys can be designed to improve your health, well-being, confidence, relationships, finances or any other area of your life.

Meditation, guided meditations and hypnosis are similar in that they take us to the same place as far as our brain waves are concerned. However, there has been some "negative press" and mystery around the subject of hypnosis due to the entertainment value in stage hypnosis. I assure my clients that there is nothing mysterious about it and we all go in and out of hypnotic states every day. If you have ever arrived at a destination without thinking about where you are going, or remembering the details of how you got there, if you have ever misplaced your keys, or felt you have "lost time," it is very likely you were in an altered state. Finding yourself daydreaming or imagining is just another version of hypnosis. Should you wonder if hypnosis or guided meditation can work for you, I invite you to call yourself forward and fully participate in the following exercise/experiment:

The Lemon

Just now I would like you to vividly image a huge yellow, ripe, juicy lemon. See it clearly in your mind's eye. Imagine placing it on a cutting board and slicing into the firm yellow citrus skin with the pointed end of a sharp knife. You can see some of the juice spray as you make this cut. Inhale deeply, breathing in that distinct, fresh lemony scent. Now imagine some of the juice running down in cool droplets along the side of the blade of the knife and onto the cutting board. Visualize cutting the lemon into quarters. Now pick up one of the quarters and feel the uneven texture of skin in your fingers. Put that lemon quarter in your mouth. Allow your teeth to sink slowly into the cold, tart, tangy, fleshy pulp. The sour juice is pouring over your tongue, dripping down over your teeth and down the back of your throat . . . .If you are really participating in this exercise you are probably salivating by now. If your mouth is watering, or if you found yourself swallowing, your imagination was at work, your subconscious mind was engaged and your body responded.

This can also be done with other examples. If you were to imagine what it felt like to be chased by a large, scary, hungry wild bear, your heart rate would increase and adrenaline would be secreted. The energy of fear would affect your body, your brain, your physiology and your consciousness. You also have the potential and opportunity to turn inward, imagine and visualize in positive ways, which will support you in befriending your subconscious mind and partnering with your Higher Self. This in turn will influence your physiology, energy, emotions and your future in powerful, beneficial and productive ways.

As a hypnotherapist, meditation instructor, mandala facilitator and Art for Healing teacher, it is my intention and joy to turn people inward towards their own divinity so they can access their authentic power. I love assisting others in tapping into the wealth of wisdom and creativity that dwells deep within. The Universe is filled with infinite riches AND there is a bountiful treasure chest of symbols, wisdom, imagination and boundless riches inside each and every one of us. It is my desire to assist my students and clients, and you, the reader of this book, in becoming great friends with the inner realms, and in accessing the immense power of your Higher Self and the Super Conscious mind.

The Need for Sleep

It is a fact, we all need to sleep. Although lack of sleep leaves no physical marks, the psychological effects of sleep deprivation are profound. Science has proven the human body requires sleep just as it requires air, food and water. Without enough sleep the brain begins to deteriorate. In fact, a person will die from lack of sleep sooner than starvation. Death will occur in about 10 days without sleep, while starvation will take a few weeks. Going without sleep for any length of time causes a multitude of negative short-term and long-term effects. Some of these effects include reduced creativity, anxiety, irritability, a weakened immune system, slurred speech, issues with blood sugar levels, hormonal imbalances and much more.

The purpose of sleep is mysterious, magical and clearly very necessary. Human beings are unique, because, unlike most animals, we need to sleep for long periods of time. Some scientists believe this gives the body, brain, conscious and subconscious minds the ability and opportunity to communicate. Sleep is the designated time in our lives where the Beta waves stop and we heal, regenerate and integrate.

The Power of Dreams

In the mid-1950s dream researchers William Dement and Charles Fisher of New York's Mount Sinai Hospital were the first to prove that dreaming is important for both physical and psychological well-being. This was determined by having volunteers participate in "dream deprivation" experiments. In this experiment, some participants were allowed to sleep but not dream. They were hooked up to electroencephalographs, and when their brain waves indicated the onset of a dream, they were awakened. These volunteers got all of their regular sleep except for their dream time. After five nights of dreamlessness, every single participant was nervous, anxious, jittery, irritable and had trouble concentrating. One volunteer quit the project in a panic. As the experiment continued, they made more and more "bad choices." They drank more, smoked more, felt agitated, resentful and exhibited greater hostility. All experienced what was described as a general "falling apart of their personalities."

Dement and Fisher had a second control group of subjects who were also woken up during the night, but not during their dreams. This group showed no change in their personalities and did not suffer the ill effects the first group exhibited. This brought Dement and Fisher to the conclusion that "lack of dreams" rather than "lack of sleep" was what was responsible for strange behavior of the dream-deprived group. This experiment, along with other modern research, indicates that dreams are critical to our physical, emotional and psychological well-being.

Carl Jung (1875 – 1961) was a Swiss psychiatrist and the founder of analytical psychology. Jung is considered the first modern psychiatrist to view the human psyche as "by nature religious" and make it the focus of exploration. Jung is one of the best-known researchers in the field of dream analysis and symbolization and saw dreams as a doorway to our Higher Selves. He believed dreams contained all we needed to know about our questions and their answers; they could also give us remedies for our ailments. Jung was convinced that by consciously partnering with the deeper parts of ourselves through our dreams, we could access well-being on all levels, open to our potential and align with our individual destiny.

Erich Fromm (1900 – 1980) was another well-known and well-respected psychologist and humanistic philosopher. He has said "Both dreams and myths are important communications from ourselves to ourselves. If we do not understand the language in which they are written, we miss a great deal of what we know and tell ourselves in those hours when we are not busy manipulating the outside world." Fromm has also stated: "The sleep existence, it seems, is only the extreme case of a purely contemplative experience, which can be established by the waking person if he (she) focuses on his (her) inner experience . . . In sleep, we are no longer exposed to the noise of culture, we become awake to what we really feel and think. The genuine self can talk: it is often more intelligent and more decent than the pseudo self which seems to be 'we' when we are awake." Clearly Fromm, as well as many founding fathers of psychology, give great credence and credibility to the power of dreaming and our dream's connection to the soul.

We can choose to sleep through our dreams,
or we can wake up with our dreams.

In ancient times, dreams were not explained physiologically or psychologically, but were ascribed to be inspirations of the Universe. The ancient Egyptians believed deeply in the power and importance of dreams. They practiced "dream incubation" for guidance and healing at temples and sacred sites. The Egyptians believed in dreams, their spiritual eyes were open. Their word for dream was *rswt*, which can be interpreted to mean "to be awake" and symbolized with the image of an open eye. They believed by recalling and working with dreams they could develop memory, tap into knowledge that belonged to them before they incarnated as human beings and awaken to their connection with other life experiences.

There are over 200 references to dreams in the Talmud. The message from this sacred Hebrew text suggests that dreams are like "A letter unopened from a friend." The Quran places great emphasis on the value of dreams and indicates that dreams are the manner in which God converses with His followers. The Bible also shares the importance of dreams. The birth of Jesus was predicted, Joseph was instructed to wed Mary and was assured of her purity (Matthew 1:20). Joseph was warned to flee to Egypt (Matthew 2:13), return to Israel, (2:19) and to go to Galilee (2:22). The Magi, or Three Wise Men, were warned in a dream not to return to their native land along the same route they had taken (2:12) because of Herod's evil intentions. Acts 2:17 contains the prophetic verse: "And it shall come to pass in the last days saith God, I will pour out of my spirit upon all flesh; and your sons and daughters shall prophesy [preach] and your young men shall see visions, and your old men shall dream dreams." It seems that scientifically, psychologically, historically and scripturally we are encouraged to consider the importance, value and power of our dreams.

Working With Your Dreams

Dreams not only play an important part in keeping us physically, mentally and emotionally healthy, they can also support us in our spiritual growth. Dreams can function as an otherworldly advisor, counselor, problem-solver and "built-in monitoring system." Dreams can be gifts from the soul and provide insight, direction, information and concrete advice. If you chose to work with your dreams they can be powerful companions for understanding your purpose, as well as a trustworthy guide on your journey to happiness and wholeness.

If it calls to you, you may use your prosperity journal to include your dreams, or get a different journal devoted specifically to your dreams. Keep your journal by your bed and when you wake up write down the memories of the dreams you had, snippets and all. As you start to write, you may find yourself remembering more details. Do not worry if your dreams do not make sense. Dreams speak in symbols and metaphors rather than with logic and words. Sometimes reviewing dreams at a later date can be helpful in understanding their messages more clearly. You may also start to notice a theme emerging as you read them as a series.

If you have specific questions, intentions or desires, you can write them down as a request in your journal before you go to sleep at night. This is a powerful way to invite and engage your Higher Self. This is much more beneficial and powerful than dreaming at random. Making a dream request is referred to as "Dream Incubation." It is like planting a seed for the deeper parts of you to consider, nurture and work with. This exercise gives clearly identified directions to the subconscious mind and invites a particular dream topic to emerge. Dream incubation can be used for fun and entertainment, to answer specific questions or to solve problems. For example, a person may ask the question: "How can I manifest more money?" Or: "What is my life's purpose?" After the question has been asked and the invitation has been extended, the part of you that knows can reveal its answers, wisdom and creative ideas.

I rarely make an important decision without first consulting my dreams. I incubate dreams when I need clarity about saying yes or no to an opportunity. I ask my dreams to advise me whether to take action or be patient and wait. I have consulted with my dreams when I needed help making a decision about moving, going back to school and selling my art gallery. I have often found the need to be patient and faithful. I do not always get a dream or the answer on the first night of my request. However, if I am consistent and diligent, my dreams have *never failed* to steer me in the right direction.

I have explored many theories of dream interpretation and believe the most effective method to be introduced by Frederick Perls (1893-1970). Dr. Perls was a noted German-born psychiatrist and psychotherapist. Perls believed dreams contain the rejected and/or disowned aspects of the dreamer. Every character in your dreams, as well as every object, represents an aspect of you: You are the gorilla; you are the fountain in the middle of the pond; you are the pond; you are the earthquake; you are the burglar; you are the plane; you are the plane crash; you are the speeding race car; you are the multi-million dollar yacht; you are the dilapidated bridge; you are the dusty trophy on the shelf. Rather than any type of general symbology, he believed each dream, and everything in the dream, was unique to the individual who dreamt it.

In order to discover which aspect of yourself is being disowned, or needs attention, it is recommended that you retell the dream in first person and in present tense. It is important to verbalize how each and every component of the dream felt, including inanimate objects. You may also choose to reenact the dream and take on the role of the different characters and objects. Another possibility is to start a dialogue with objects in the dream, and express how you felt toward each other. By taking on different roles from the content of your dreams, you have the opportunity to acknowledge, explore and tap into feelings, thoughts and/or ideas you may have overlooked or buried. You may also continue to extend dreams in your imagination and build on them while you are awake. Through these different processes your dreams literally come alive with depth, wisdom and information.

Dreams provide you with a rich opportunity

to not only eavesdrop on your subconscious,

but to establish a direct relationship with your soul.

Although I do not believe it is *absolutely necessary* for you to pay attention to your dreams or do dream work, I am convinced that consciously working with them can accelerate your soul's growth, reveal your life's purpose and help you manifest greater prosperity. If you are open to working with your dreams, a fun, supportive and wonderful relationship can be cultivated over time. Know the more you acknowledge and pay attention to your dreams, the more your dreams will direct and guide you on your prosperity journey and on your life's path.

Exercise # 1: Meditate to Hear the Still Small Voice Within

Meditation is a way we connect more deeply to our inner world and establish a direct line of communication with Source. It has been said prayer is like talking to God and meditating is like listening. The process does not have to be hard, daunting or confusing. Just give yourself permission to relax and go on a brain vacation. Once you make meditation a habit, and become accustomed to it, you will look forward to it. Meditation is the *most important* tool I know of to empower you and line you up with your Higher Self. If you are consistent with your meditation practice, it cannot help but to change your life, in positive, productive and powerful ways.

1. I invite you to find a comfortable place in your home, where you can either sit or lie down.

2. Light a candle with the intention of connecting to Spirit.

3. Take a few deep, conscious, relaxing healing breaths, and allow your body and mind to let go of any stress or tension.

4. Once you feel peaceful, present and relaxed, say whatever you would like to say to God.

5. Once you have said all that is important to you and asked for support, focus your attention on your breath and allow your awareness to drop into your heart. Imagine a beautiful flame of light. With every breath you take imagine this light gently growing inside of you. Allow it to expand into every part of your body and mind.

6. Imagine this light extending out the top of your head and lining you up directly with your Higher Self and with Source.

7. Once your mind has completely relaxed and become silent, you are centered in one of the most powerful vortexes on the planet. You now have the opportunity to ask any questions you would like the answers to. Ask and then patiently listen for the "still small voice within." You may receive words, impressions, images, bodily sensations or a knowingness that drops into the back of your awareness. This is a powerful way of accessing profound truth and the wisdom that resides at the center of your being and from your Higher Self.

You may begin your meditation practice with five minutes a day, and if you would like, take several meditation breaks throughout the day. As you get accustomed to meditating, allow the time you spend in meditation to incrementally increase. Eventually you may find that you WANT to meditate for up to an hour. Once you get into the habit of meditating, you will find that you look forward to it because not only does it feel great, your life smoothes out and you experience much greater clarity, synchronicity, grace and ease.

Exercise #2: Write to Your Higher Self, Source or Your Soul.

All of us have the ability to have more conscious conversations with the higher aspect of ourselves. A wonderful way to do this is through writing, inviting and allowing your Higher Self to respond. You can embark on this process either by typing on your computer or writing by hand on paper or in your journal. Before you begin, open your heart, set your intentions, and then allow innate wisdom to flow to you and through you. Sincere intention is the most important quality to begin this process. When a genuine plea for growth, clarity and understanding is extended, your Higher Self, and the essence of all existence, automatically responds. Your letter or conversation can begin with something as simple as:

1. Dear Soul/Higher Self/ God/ Wise One/ Inner Counselor/ True Self (or whatever term resonates most for you), I want to open more fully to you, invite you in and have a more open connection and authentic conversation with you. I really want to hear what you have to share. Right now I would like support with _____ can you please give me some answers, clarity or suggestions?

2. Next, be still and wait for the answer to form and then drop into your awareness. When it does, start to write down what comes forward. The information may come in a few words or continue "download" and stream forth as you are writing.

3. After you receive your answer you may continue the dialogue by asking for more information or asking more specific questions. Again, be present and patient as the process unfolds.

4. Continue the dialogue for as long as you would like, or for as long as you have questions you would like the answers to.

5. When you feel complete, wrap up the exercise by expressing heart-felt gratitude.

You may be interested to know that this process is how the bestselling books *Conversations with God* came into being. Neale Donald Walsch was not unique in his ability to interact and communicate with Higher Consciousness, we can all do it. But like so many things, it takes an open mind and the commitment to do it. I have used this process with great success while struggling with my finances, in my career and with my relationships. I have consistently received prompt, powerful and helpful information. It is a simple process I will use for the rest of my life. And I hope you do too.

There is an incredibly loving, wise and wonderful aspect of you that resides in the very center of yourself and sees things from a higher and clearer place. This loving energy longs for you to experience happiness, prosperity and success. Once you have a glimpse from this higher "altitude" or perspective, your *whys* become clearer, and there is less resistance and more acceptance on your path. As you open more fully to this relationship and these conversations, you may be astonished at the wisdom that comes forward and the support you receive.

Exercise #3: Dream Incubation

1. Consider an important question you would like the answer to. Some examples may include:

   What is my life's purpose?

   How can I manifest greater prosperity?

   Should I take this job?

   Is it time to move?

   Should I go back to school?

2. In your journal, right before you go to sleep at night, write this question down as a request to your Higher Self. This invites and directs the deeper, higher and wiser parts of yourself to communicate and share its knowledge with you. It also opens our conscious mind to hear, be available and understand the wisdom. You may also add the following sentence to further empower your incubation request: "My intention is to have a vivid, healing dream that I clearly recall and easily understand."

3. When you wake up and remember a dream, lie still and review it in its entirety. Recall your dream in as much detail as possible. When you are ready, write it down. Recall and write everything you can remember, including how you felt and about any other people, activities, situations and objects that seemed important. You may choose to explore some of the symbols at this time or you may choose to do it later.

4. Later, when you are feeling fully conscious, you may reread your dreams. Then you may want to explore what it feels like to be each aspect of this dream. Do this in first person and present tense. Trust the process, as strange as it may seem, because I assure you it will be! Now be open to wonderful revelations and a newfound relationship with your dreams, your subconscious mind and your Soul.

Exercise #4: Find Your Higher Self Talisman

The word talisman come from the Greek language, "telein" which means "to initiate into the mysteries" It's an inanimate object that one "animates." This is an exercise and a tool we can use to anchor and connect with our Higher Selves in physical world reality.

1. Take a couple relaxing, cleansing breaths. Once your mind becomes still, ask your Higher Self to reveal an object, symbol or talisman to support you in more fully connecting with, aligning and merging with your Soul Self. Patiently allow it to show up in your mind's eye.

2. Once it is revealed, you can ask your Higher Self if this is your true talisman. If the answer is no, ask for your TRUE Higher Self Talisman. If the answer is yes, extend gratitude to your Higher Self.

3. You may choose to find this symbol or object in physical worldly reality. If so, you may want to put it someplace where you see it often, you may keep it with you throughout the day.

4. If you do not want to locate your talisman (or cannot because it is a spinning vortex, or a magic wand, the ocean, or something impossible to find) you may want to draw a picture of it, paint it or simply visualize it inwardly during meditation (or anytime throughout the day) to more fully connect with and align with your Soul Self.

Exercise #5: Your Prosperity Talisman

If it calls to you, you may also choose to find a "Prosperity Talisman." What comes forward may be the same or it may be different from your Higher Self Talisman.

1. Take a few cleansing breaths and ask your heart or Higher Self to reveal your ideal prosperity object, symbol or talisman.

2. If you would like, locate this object as an anchor to support you in more fully embracing, accepting, grounding and manifesting your divine prosperity in the world.

3. As you hold the object in your hands, or in your mind's eye, claim this message and really FEEL this energy: "I AM PROSPEROUS!"

Be patient with yourself, and with these exercises. Know that each time you work with your inner reality, things outside of you will shift and change in interesting, unusual, synchronistic and often unexpected ways. When you slow down your active Beta brain waves through meditating, sitting in silence, sleeping, dreaming or inwardly listening to your Higher Self, your denser, more fear based, negative and energy wasting thoughts become less prevalent. This makes room for more expansive energies to come in and help you naturally align with higher states of peace, well-being, bliss, knowingness and Cosmic Consciousness.

The primary goal with all of these exercises is to cultivate a tranquil mind and harmonize your personality and human self with your Higher Self and Source. It will support you in naturally reducing the energy of fear and increasing the energy of faith. This is the fertile ground for inner wisdom, inspiration, alignment and revelation. Even if you are simply allowing yourself to spend time in silence and relaxation, and rest in the peaceful sanctuary of your own inner realms, this will be enough catalyze and activate positive, powerful and prosperous changes in your life.

PART TWO

Deserving and Claiming Your Prosperity

Chapter 5

What Do You Deserve?

Dedicate yourself to the good you deserve and desire for yourself. Give yourself peace of mind. You deserve to be happy. You deserve delight.

~ Hannah Arendt

What do you believe you deserve? And how much do you love yourself? You may be asking yourself "What does this have to do with prosperity?" The answer is EVERYTHING! The bottom line is it *impossible* to manifest more than you believe you deserve, or out-earn your inner sense of value.

Learning to love ourselves is really about coming home to the truest part our Self. Some of the information in this chapter was derived from my learning and healings with my friend and teacher, Martia Nelson. Martia has an amazing book entitled: *Coming Home: The Return to True Self.* Years ago when I was struggling in my relationships, financially and with my health, Martia shared a radical notion with me: "Vibrant love is the essence of who you are. Love is in your body, bones, muscles, skin, organs, fingernails, cells and atoms. Love is manifested as the tangible expression of the world and is the animating energy of the Universe." When she told me this, it made my head spin. I now understand and embrace this Truth. As human beings, love is our deepest nature and the truest truth of who we are. Love is what is responsible for the beating our hearts and the energy that breathes us.

Love is your deepest nature

and the truest truth of who you are.

Love is the energy that is breathing you.

When you experience unworthiness, shame or judgment, this comes from the level of the personality and your perceived disconnection from Source. These emotions are like the grey cloud cover to the infinite, brilliant blue, sunshine-filled sky of God and love. Clouds will come and go on this human adventure, but the truth is blue sky, God, and indescribable, profound and immense love, is consistently there above it all.

If we overly identify with the limited, human and flawed aspect of ourselves, it will be challenging or impossible to manifest true prosperity. On the path of manifesting prosperity, and up-leveling in our consciousness, we eventually arrive at the place where we understand we need to love ourselves more. Once this becomes a priority and intention, true transformation can begin to take place.

Sometimes on the path to true self-love, we are still below the cloud cover, *saying* we love ourselves. Saying we love ourselves is not the same as authentically residing in the space of love within and deeply experiencing it. Living with authentic self-love is accepting love as your primary ingredient and innate essence, and allowing the warmth of that love to shine through you at all times—even while you are stressed out, afraid or in pain. True self-love is simply being settled in the place of comfort, peace and warmth within, and allowing it to radiate out through you, and into your life. I believe finally arriving at the destination of true self-love is the primary purpose of our Earthly adventure. However, the path is never without its challenges and much easier said than done.

How Much Do You Love Yourself?

While on vacation with some girl friends, I asked everyone a seemingly strange question that had dropped into my awareness during my morning meditation. "On a scale of 1 to 10, how much do you love yourself? With the number 1 signifying 'not at all' and 10 being 'completely and unconditionally.'" My answer was 8 ½, one my friend's was 8, one was 7 ½ and the other was 5. I asked my friend who had answered 5 why her number was so low. She thought about it for a moment and finally said: "I think I would love myself more if I earned more money." I responded to her by saying, "If you love yourself more, you WILL earn more money!" She was trying to attain self worth and prosperity from the outside in. I was asking her to consider the inside out method of manifesting more money. I suspected more financial woes in her future if she did not do something to change her inner climate and love number. Unfortunately I was right—she ended up having to file bankruptcy a year later.

As I contemplated my own number of 8 ½, I consciously set the intention to eventually get to 9 ½ (because I always want to leave room for improvement!). I have since accomplished that goal and my outer reality reflects my improved sense of self-love: financially, in my relationships, in my sense of fulfillment, peace and happiness.

Without self-love there is an experience of "inner barrenness," which manifests as circumstances of lack in one's outer life. If your inner experience is one of withholding love and rejecting parts of yourself, you will find life treating you the same way.

If you lack richness inside of you,

you will experience the absence of richness outside of you.

The relationship with yourself is the foundation for *everything else* in your life. If your foundation is not one of self-love and self respect, you are establishing your entire existence on a bedrock that is fractured and unstable. If your core beliefs about yourself are that you are worthless, unlovable or fear-based, it will be impossible to build anything positive and solid that will sustain itself in the long term.

A way to begin to turn the tide in the direction of prosperity is to first become consciously aware of your inner climate. Then, if this climate is not kind, loving, warm and rich, set the intention to begin to cultivate authentic kindness, love, warmth and compassion for yourself.

I now open to the unlimited love that I am made of,

I invite love to nurture, heal and guide me.

If you were to see a young child who was hurting, wounded, frightened and alone, you would naturally have compassion for that child. Every child, as well as every adult, deserves love. Love is who we are, it is where we came from and it is where we are going. Existing without self-love is a deep, soul-level wound. Now imagine reaching out to that child who is hurting and soothing their pain with words of comfort. Perhaps your healing message would be something like: "I see you are afraid and do not realize how beautiful, magnificent and important you are. I am sorry you are hurting and I am now going to send you the healing energy of love, kindness and compassion. Just let these feelings fill you up and help you understand how wonderful you are, and what a treasure you are to the world."

Now, if it resonates with you, relay this message to yourself. See you, your path and your life's story from a higher perspective. Have compassion for yourself and for the bumps and bruises that you have sustained on this Earth Walk. Acknowledge that you have temporarily lost sight of your own magic and importance. You have forgotten the love that you are and the beauty you carry within you. Then set the intention and make the commitment to rediscover your own inherent importance, worthiness and value in some way every day.

Claim What You Deserve

Each and every human being was created out of the same primary ingredient, and that ingredient is love. God did not make some of us with greater love than others, therefore, each and every one of us has access to this love. Once I became aware of this fact, accepted it, and claimed it, my life immediately began to transform in a positive and powerful way—and so can yours.

ALL of us deserve happiness, love and prosperity.

But in order to manifest it,

you have to KNOW you DESERVE IT!

Let us consider the word and the healing power of "deserve." I have created an acronym out of the word DESERVE and it can serve as a catalyst to help you claim what you desire, open more fully to your innate worthiness and manifest magnificent things. I have used the DESERVE process to help me manifest my husband, sell my art, make more money and attract more clients.

When you open to desiring and deserving on one end, you naturally open to manifesting on the other end. As you explore this exercise, you may tap into feelings that scare or overwhelm you. If this is the case, enlist the help of a good support person. You may want to consider finding a reputable therapist or counselor. Take good compassionate care of yourself. This includes reaching out for help when you want and/or need it.

Now let's delve into what you **DESERVE** by exploring these steps:

1). Desire.

2). Experience your Emotions.

3). Surrender.

4). Expectations.

5). Responsibility and Receptivity.

6). Value.

7). Express Yourself!

DESIRE: Allow yourself to yearn for what you want and CLAIM IT! Many people avoid contemplating and claiming their desires because there can be pain associated with wanting something you do not believe you can have. Ignoring or denying desire may *seem* like an effective way to avoid pain, however, the yearning, longing and desire is still locked away in the closet of your psyche, subconsciously casting a shadow in your life. Desire is still there as an uncomfortable undercurrent, beneath everything you think, feel and do. Desire doesn't go away if you ignore it, because it is woven into the fabric of your beingness - you came into your human existence with it! If you ignore or avoid your desires long enough, they may "go to sleep," and then, so do you. Without the motivation, direction and the energy of desire, you decrease your life force; you dim your wattage and you feel less vital, vibrant and alive.

Denying desire can show up in a couple of different ways in one's life. There is the "sour grapes" attitude; "I don't care, my life is fine the way it is." With this stance, there can be an underlying resentment or jealousy of others who have what you want, or are living the life you *wish* you could have. There can be the spiritual bypass or "pink paint approach," Whose message is something like: "God will give me what He wants me to have." This attitude is somewhat disempowered, and lacking the powerful magnetic energetic of claiming true desire. Of course it is great to trust Spirit, but as human beings we are powerful creators ourselves. Claiming our desire is a way we can link up with Spirit and begin to co-create our lives *in partnership* with Spirit.

Desire can be the fuel to your engine, and the activating force in manifestation. Just like a car without fuel may be nice to look at, it is still not going to take you anywhere. By consciously claiming, exploring, and experiencing your desires, it is like filling up your gas tank. It is part of the preparation that is needed to get you ready for your adventure on the open road (or wherever else you want to go!)

When I work with people who are having a problem manifesting prosperity, or anything else they want in their lives, often there is the energy of unexplored desire: a locked closet containing unfelt, unacknowledged and unclaimed longing. Not exploring your desire can be like energetically holding what you want away from yourself. It is like being hungry and saying, no I'm fine, I don't need to eat, all the while doing your best to ignore the enormous, enticing, mouthwatering buffet of culinary delights on the other side of the room.

Not considering or claiming your desires is like energetically placing an invisible barrier or glass wall between you and what you want. You can see what you want but you can't have it. When you really *allow, embrace* and *experience* your desire, it helps dissolve this barrier, and supports you in activating and embodying the life giving, vibrant energy of that desire.

There is a direct correlation between the degree to which you allow yourself to want something and what you end up manifesting. When you allow your desire to grow as large as it wants to grow, fully accepting it, feeling it and breathing it in, then the manifestation of those desires can more naturally and easily occur in your life.

EXPERIENCE YOUR EMOTIONS: Emotions are frequently referred to as "energy in motion." If you do not allow yourself to feel your feelings, it will affect you physically and mentally, it will also disconnect you spiritually. Additionally, not giving credence to your feelings will stunt or impede your ability to manifest and attract what you want. As you give yourself permission to explore your deep yearnings, longings and desires, painful emotions may come up. Allow yourself to fully feel them. These feelings may consist of anger, sadness, grief or disappointment. There can also be multiple layers of emotion. Once I gave myself permission to explore my own emotions around what I wanted and did not think I could have, I felt depressed, then angry. Beneath the anger was hurt and tears. Once my tears were released I naturally arrived at acceptance and relief.

One of the benefits of allowing and experiencing your emotions, is that beneath all of that energy is a beautiful, peaceful place of surrender, acceptance and relaxation. However, in order to authentically arrive at that location you must first take the journey through your emotions. A common experience that occurs after allowing and embracing your desires and emotions is that a nebulous undercurrent of subconscious pain is dissolved, and you are left with a liberating sense of freedom, balance and inner harmony.

A couple of exercises I have both participated in and facilitated, is allowing the frustration of not having what is wanted come up through physical movement. I have turned the music up loud and "danced out my desire." Some of those dances have been filled with the big movements of anger, frustration, hurt, doubt and confusion. I have also "moved the energy" of sadness, anguish and grief. After I have danced those energies and emotions out of myself, I felt more tranquil, calm and clear.

Another option is getting a plastic bat or a piece of rubber hose and beating the heck out of a pillow. While doing this I verbally express whatever authentically comes up during the process. Some examples of those rants have been: "I am tired of being broke! Why can't I have what I want? Where's my husband? I just want to be happy! I want to make my own money! Is there something wrong with me?" And "It's not fair!" Screaming one's confusion, hurt and disappointment into a pillow is also a way of moving and releasing locked up energy and emotion. The experience can be like a good cry with a flood of relief washing over you after its full expression. It is important to set strong intentions for healing and safety, as well as to invite the quality of compassion before, during, and after, the emotional release process.

SURRENDER: After claiming your desires and experiencing your emotions comes the peace and relief of surrender. Invite healing light to fill up these newly opened places. In the Bible we are promised that if we ask, it will be given. By fully exploring your desires and experiencing your emotions you are energetically "asking." The active work has been done. Now allow the effects of your "deserving prosperity process" to show up in your life.

Prosperity is like the sunshine, it is here for all to enjoy. By not claiming your desire and experiencing your emotions, it is like standing in the shade, saying it's not fair that others get to have sunshine and you do not. These two steps will powerfully support you in stepping out of the shadows, and into the sunbeam that has been waiting to embrace you with warmth and light. After claiming your desire, and experiencing your emotions, surrender and keep your eyes, ears, heart and mind open. You will then be able to recognize and receive the fulfillment of your desires in *whatever* forms they shows up.

EXPECTATIONS: Optimistic expectation sets the stage for wonderful situations. Where we go in our minds predicts where we will go in our lives. Feeling excited, hopeful and expectant naturally rolls out the red carpet for manifestation. Expecting great things keeps your vibration high and keeps the law of attraction working on your behalf in positive and prosperous ways. Consider what you want and how it might show up in your life. Write all of your hopes and dreams down and allow yourself to experience and embrace the powerful energy of expectation. Let the tingly, sparkly sensation of enthusiastic excitement flood through your body, mind and emotions.

Remember being a little kid before your birthday, Hanukkah or Christmas? Do you recall wondering about the wonderful presents you might receive? Think of life being like a holiday, with the Universe ready to shower you with so many fun expected and unexpected gifts. Know your prosperity may show up in expected or unexpected ways as well. You may experience a synchronistic meeting, be invited to a life-changing event or encounter a positive change in someone's attitude. You may receive a call you have been waiting for about an opportunity or an offer. You may intuitively download an "inspired idea," or have a remarkable revelation about something you want to do, or a fun way to make money. Don't place limitations on yourself about how anything *needs* to show up in your life. Set your intention to stay open, enthusiastic and optimistic.

RESPONSIBILITY AND RECEPTIVITY: A powerful shift occurs when we can look at our lives and acknowledge we are the ones who created it—the good AND the not-so- good. Until we do this we are victims waiting for someone or something to rescue us. Rejecting responsibility is a way we guarantee that what we *don't want* will continue to show up. Look at the things you do not like in your life and ask yourself what your soul is trying to learn. What are the opportunities available to you for your highest learning, healing, upliftment and growth? Consider for a moment that your soul lovingly helped you create these uncomfortable situations and/or challenges for your highest good, even if you do not understand what that is yet. When you really open your mind to taking full responsibility for *everything* in your life is when things can start to shift, transform and change for the better. This is how we move out of victim consciousness and step onto the path of authentic power.

By consciously accepting responsibility

and graciously receiving everything that represents prosperity,

you become energetically attractive and

authentically empowered.

Set the intention to be receptive to all experiences of prosperity in whatever ways they show up. Compliments, kindness, love in any and all forms are representations of true prosperity. Open your heart to receive them in a present and gracious way.

You have the opportunity to go deeper into the inner experience of empowerment and abundance by also accepting the things that you would not initially believe to be examples of prosperity. As you accept your life's challenges as opportunities for learning, you powerfully shift from the posture of victim to victor. As you receive all things graciously, you step out of the shadows of poverty consciousness and into the light of prosperity consciousness. As you take greater responsibility for your life and open your heart to yourself and others, you not only become a powerful attractor, you become a proactive, prosperous co-creator. Just as ripples form when a pebble is thrown into a pond, you are also literally affecting, shifting and healing the world around you from the inside out.

VALUE: Claim and affirm your value. Remind yourself of the love that you are. Acknowledge that you are a unique, powerful soul, and an extremely worthy aspect of the Divine. Even if you do not fully *feel* your immense value, know that there is a deeper and/ or higher part of you that does. All limiting or negative thoughts come from the level of the ego or personality. Your personality, by its very nature, buys into perceptions of lack and is prone to the feeling of being separated from love. However, your soul, or IGO self, does not.

If you are struggling to fully feel and claim your value, acknowledge your soul or Higher Self as the Truth of who you are and set your intention to align with it and hear its messages. Just like a river never experiences fatigue in flowing, your soul and Spirit never tires from supporting you and giving to you. If you open your mind, heart and inner ears, there are always messages of Truth, and acknowledgment of great value from this deeper, higher, wiser part of you.

EXPRESS YOURSELF: Celebrate and express yourself in any way that is authentic and fun for you. Did you come to planet Earth to play small? Do you want to be like a lemming and follow others? Or would you prefer to be yourself and express who you are in a wonderful, unique and creative way? If you do not know and claim your value, how can you expect someone else to? When I hear arguments and someone is trying to convince someone else of the "right way to think" I think to myself: If God wanted humans to be exactly the same, like Canadian geese, he could have made us that way. There are countless billions of humans, each of us unique, different and irreplaceable. Be the best, most wonderful and strangely unique version of yourself. Find your authentic shape, follow your bliss and joyfully express yourself. As you do, you will experience new, interesting and fun ways that the world responds to you.

You Are a Spiritual Being Having a Human Experience

Pierre Teilhard de Chardin was a French Jesuit priest and a philosopher. He famously uttered one of my favorite quotes of all times: "We are not human beings having a spiritual experience. We are spiritual beings having a human experience." At the level of Spirit (which is the truest truth of who we are) we are all wonderful, worthy, loving and prosperous. It is when we start overly identifying with our human aspect that we start buying into fear, limitation and negativity. By remembering we are spiritual in nature, we can gain higher altitude and experience a more expansive perspective.

An analogy I sometimes use to more fully comprehend this broader point of view is to think of life as going to a movie theater. Our Higher Self sits back in the big, comfy theater chair and observes what we do as our human selves play out the drama on the big screen. Where we get in trouble is when we believe we are the one-dimensional character on the movie screen, forgetting the bigger picture, and the higher aspect of ourselves that is sitting back and relaxing in a place of greater perspective. You always have the potential and ability to settle back into the audience. Take a seat next to your Higher Self and ask them what they have to say about the drama that is playing out. Try asking them if they have any words of wisdom, feedback or suggestions for you. This is another way of hearing the messages from the part of us that sees us more clearly than we see ourselves.

When people come to me in turmoil about the drama or challenges in their lives, I ask them why they go to movies. The answer is usually something like: to be amused and entertained, to be scared, to laugh, to think, to feel and to experience a range of emotions. If that is the case, why would we want less than that in our own lives? However, just like watching a movie, we do not want to become so entrenched and entangled in the experience that we forget we are in a theater AND we are the observer. Relax, enjoy yourself and don't take it all so seriously.

Sometimes I invite clients to "get out of the movie screen and back into the theater chair." Everyone has the opportunity to have a conversation with his or her Higher Selves or Source about what is really going on. What are the life lessons in your challenges? What is the Truth? Who are you REALLY? How much do you love yourself? What do you deserve? Each of us has to answer these questions for ourselves. And as you ask these questions and take responsibility for the answers, your life will undoubtedly begin to take on new meaning, greater depth and become a more joyful and prosperous adventure.

Exercise #1: What is Your Self Love Number?

1. Check inside of yourself, and ask your heart or Higher Self, on a scale of one to ten, how much do you love yourself? Allow your intuition to reveal the answer.

2. If this number is lower than you would like, consider what number you would like it to be and claim it for yourself right now.

3. Set your intention to gracefully and easily get to that higher number of self-love.

4. Imagine relaxing into the experience of being at this higher love number. How does this feel? Do you feel more confident and comfortable? Do you feel more peaceful and prosperous? Are you happier and more fulfilled? Allow yourself to explore, revel and relax in this wonderful feeling of self-acceptance and authentic self love.

5. What are some activities or kind, thoughtful or things you can do for yourself to help increase the feeling of self-love or self-worth?

6. Commit to yourself and take the actions steps to do some of these nice things you have identified for yourself. Say yes and take responsibility for the most important relationship in the world by doing small and/or large things every day that exemplify self-love. As you do, not only do you strengthen the foundation of your human experience, you transform your life from the inside out.

If you participate authentically in this exercise, and begin to increase your love number, you will soon find that life shifts around you in positive ways. We did not incarnate as human beings to be perfect, but rather to learn to be loving. True love and true prosperity begins and ends within. As you love yourself more, you create the opportunity and environment to improve the quality of your life, your relationships and your finances in many wonderful and unexpected ways.

Exercise #2: Cultivating Self Love

1. For a minute or two throughout the day stop to remember and acknowledge the love that you are. You can do this while you are driving, sitting, waiting or walking. Simply turn your attention inward and focus on the beating of your heart. As your heart beats, imagine the energy of love expanding within and then rippling outward, just as the waves made by the pebble in the pond ripple outward, eventually affecting the entire pond with its gentle vibration. This simple practice can gently and gracefully transform you, your life and the world.

2. As you relax in your bed at night, before drifting off to sleep, imagine love emanating from you. You may utter the following phrase or something else that resonates for you: "I am relaxing into the love that I am. May this love heal, direct and guide me. May my love transform and heal the world. May all other beings experience peace, prosperity and great love." Know that even if you are not feeling love, this simple practice will open the door to experiencing and accepting greater love, peace and prosperity. Done consistently over the period of a week, this will most certainly have a positive and powerful effect on your relationship with yourself, with others, with Spirit and all of life.

Exercise #3: What Do You Deserve?

This exercise is a summary of the DESERVE process I shared earlier in the chapter. Before beginning the exercise, set your intentions for healing, for your highest good and the highest good of all concerned. I would also recommend setting your intentions for safety, revelations, grace and ease. If this process brings up overwhelming emotions, confusion, or pain for you, you may want to find a health care worker, therapist or counselor to support you in navigating through the terrain.

1. **Desire:** Consciously contemplate and claim what it is you *really want*. Allow the deep longings of your heart to grow as big as they want to and as large as they can. Write about your hopes and dreams in detail in your prosperity journal. Allow them to unfold and expand as you delve into and explore your hearts deepest desires.

2. **Emotions:** If you experience emotions coming up around your desires, give yourself permission to really feel your feelings. (Remember suppressed emotions stunt the manifestation process.) Perhaps you begin to experience excitement, sadness, angry, disappointment or confusion. There is no "right" or "wrong" way to feel. You may choose to give expression to your feelings through dancing, moving, yelling into a pillow, punching a punching bag, crying, painting or drawing them out of you. Trust your inner guidance in regard to the most effective way to move, diffuse, express and use the energy of your emotions.

3. **Surrender:** After allowing and experiencing your emotions, relax and invite Spirit in, and give it all to God! The Universe knows what is for your highest good more so than you, me or any other human being. When you do your active work, then relax into the space of surrender, the veil between your will and Divine will can thin and/or dissolve. This is the powerful place of peace and non-resistance. The act of surrendering to Spirit cultivates and creates the sacred space for Universal support to show up on your behalf.

4. **Expectations:** Keep your eyes, ears and heart open with optimistic expectations. When you are not busy forcing, pushing, or banging your head against a wall, you can step back, relax, and notice the doors and windows that are opening and inviting you in that direction. When you are centered and in your equanimity you can excitedly, yet peacefully, perceive the gifts, relationships and opportunities the Universe has in store just for you.

5. **Responsibility and Receptivity:** If you can take responsibility for all the experiences of your life, you are empowered. If your heart is open in gratitude for the lessons, gifts and teachings, even the not-so-pleasant ones, you can be carried more gracefully towards the life you desire and deserve. Living a life of true prosperity does not mean things will always be easy, but it does mean things will always be positive. Be open to using *everything* that happens in your life for your learning, upliftment, evolution, expansion and growth.

6. **Value**: Acknowledge and claim your value. Even if you do not FEEL valuable, acknowledge that you ARE valuable. This keeps the door open for healing, growth and positive attraction. Treat yourself with respect and value, so the world can reflect that back to you. Consider how you would treat someone you deeply respect and value, now treat yourself that way! Know participating in this simple step *guarantees* positive changes and will attract prosperous potential in your life.

7. **Express Yourself:** You are a unique expression of the Divine, never before and never again to express in the world in your special, incredible, magnificent and unique way— so, make the most of it! What brings you joy? Dancing? Singing? Acting? Roller skating? Knitting? Fixing cars? Gardening? Consider what is fun for you, what gives you energy and what makes you happy. Open your mind and heart to exploring the unknown and undiscovered aspects within yourself, and then have fun expressing it!

Love, prosperity, deservingness and worthiness are not just feelings, but states of being. As you relax more and more into this state, you will find your authentic shape. This will help you embark on your life's truest and deepest purpose. Trust that love and prosperity is not just something you deserve, but the very essence of who you are. As you begin to explore and enjoy *who* and *what* you are, life cannot help but deliver to you amazing opportunities and adventures that you could never have made happen by virtue of working hard, pushing or "efforting."

I invite you to acknowledge your commitment to the prosperity process. This adventure is not for the faint of heart or the weak. You would not still be reading this material if you did not embody vital qualities of courage, commitment and strong intention. I commend you, acknowledge you and respect you. Know that as you hold this book, I am holding you in my heart. Take a moment to breathe this energy in and fully receive it. You are not alone. Not only are you in my prayers, there are legions of angels seen and unseen with you on this journey. My sincere intention is to empower you and energize your prosperity process with blessings of compassion, strength of heart, grace, ease and great love.

Chapter 6

How Good Can You Stand It To Get?

*Self-sabotage is when we say we want something
and then go about making sure it doesn't happen.*

~ Alyce P. Cornyn-Selby

There can be a subconscious barrier, glass ceiling or "upper limit" associated with manifesting greater prosperity. Gay Hendricks, a psychologist, writer and practitioner in the field of personal growth and the mind-body connection, describes the upper limit issue in this way: "The upper limit problem is the human tendency to put the brakes on our positive energy when we've exceeded our unconscious thermostat setting for how good we can feel, how successful we can be and how much love we can feel. The essential move we all need to master is learning to handle more positive energy, success and love."

Something I have experienced, and witnessed with many of

my clients, is the dynamic of self-sabotage when getting close to achieving a goal or when things "get too good." This can occur due to issues of worthlessness and low self-esteem, because ultimately we can only manifest what we believe we deserve. Water will always find its own level. So, if more money is coming in than one believes they are worthy of, they will find a way of ridding themselves of it. This is often the case with people who hit the lottery; they cannot maintain the outer prosperity because of the landscape of their inner climate.

At one point in my twenties I was working hard as a hairdresser and cocktail waitress. My beautiful, exquisite and generous grandmother wanted to help me purchase a home and sent me a check for $7000 as a down payment. Subconsciously I felt so unworthy and so guilty about this generous gift, that when my roommate said she needed to borrow it for a brief period I said "Sure!" You may not be surprised to hear what happened next, or rather what did not happen—my roommate did not pay me back. For many years I felt very hurt and angry. But I later came to understand, I was as responsible as she was for this unfortunate situation.

As I processed and cleared the anger I had towards my roommate, beneath it was the anger and guilt I harbored towards myself. Both the generosity of my grandmother, and the amount of money far exceeded anything I believed I was worthy of. Therefore it was energetically impossible for me to graciously receive it, maintain it and use it to purchase a home that I did not truly believe I deserved. On some level I knew it was a bad idea to lend the money, but my "inner saboteur" took hold of a pen, wrote out the check and gave it away.

If my grandmother had sent me $100 I could have handled it. Perhaps I could have even tolerated $1000, but that amount of money and profound generosity blew up my inner thermostat and melted my "worthiness mechanism." My grandmother's act of outer generosity was not a "fit" for my barren inner climate. A great deal of forgiveness, compassion and making friends with my saboteur needed to occur in order to heal my guilty conscience and increase the capacity of my worthiness barometer.

Much of what we addressed in prior chapters are buried beliefs and limiting notions about one's value and worthiness. Something else I found the saboteur wants to do is keep us safe—even if that means playing small. Unconscious fear can cause illogical behavior, which in turn blocks prosperity, undermines empowerment, and thwarts success. If you subconsciously cling to fear it may be because of the belief: "Better the devil you know than the angel you don't."

The following examples are some of the ways the saboteur can manifest in your life: If you set an intention to lose weight, but then find yourself overindulging in cookies and cake; if you're getting along really well with your beloved, and for no good reason you pick a fight; if you have ever been presented with a wonderful opportunity, and you do not explore or follow through with it; if you "accidently" oversleep for an important job interview; or if you make a commitment to get your finances in order, then go on a shopping spree, buying a bunch of items you do not need. These are situations where goals are set, intentions are claimed, actually reaching your desired destination is in sight, and the saboteur dashes the dream.

No one consciously intends to sabotage their dreams, desires and goals; nobody *purposefully* and *intentionally* avoids success and shoots themselves in the foot. However, according to Caroline Myss, internationally renowned speaker in the field of human consciousness and "archetype expert," the saboteur is an aspect within *every* human being. But WHY is this aspect within us and WHAT is its purpose? It is primarily fear-based and wants to protect us. There can be a very real fear associated with being too attractive, attaining too much success, or garnering too much attention. Some people subconsciously stop themselves from fulfilling their dreams because they believe if they are too successful it would mean their friends and family could turn on them or use them. Or perhaps they believe they would be taken advantage of, betrayed or abandoned. There can be buried fear about being out of control, fear of the unknown, fear of being alone, fear of being too visible and/or the fear of change. There can be many reasons the saboteur halts, impedes or says no to success.

My Saboteur

I have experienced my saboteur taking control on many, many occasions. Another example occurred a few years ago when I received a call back for an acting job I auditioned for. I told the casting director I was honored and excited and we set up the date and time for my second audition. The day after I was supposed to go, I remembered I had forgotten my appointment! How could I forget something so important, and something I supposedly wanted so badly? I was confused and embarrassed by my forgetfulness, and my lack of follow-through. I finally made a conscious decision to get to the bottom of this behavior; it was time to have a conversation with my saboteur.

As an archetypal hypnotherapist I know how powerful this inner work can be, I just needed to remember to do it! So I lit a candle with the intention of connecting with my inner saboteur. I imagined going to an inner garden, and invited my saboteur to join me. Once I did, I perceived a small, thin older woman slowly coming out from behind some trees. She looked like a tiny little nun, complete with a black habit and rosary beads. I asked her how she was, and she said fine but a little lonely. I asked her what her purpose or intention was. She said to keep me in my integrity, help me maintain my humility, and to keep me humble, "on my knees" and grounded. I told her I thought those were noble intentions, and I appreciated her efforts. Then buried memories and images began to unfold of receiving communion as a young girl in the Catholic Church. I recalled uttering the deeply accepted message: "I am not worthy to receive you."

I also began to recall painful memories where I watched my ex-fiancé up-level drastically in his fame, fortune and worldly success. It seemed he starting believing in his own importance and started "buying into his own press." From my perspective, as I witnessed people attain wealth, they evolved into egomaniacs; often becoming thoughtless, narcissistic, cruel and superior to other people. It hurt my heart deeply to observe this behavior, and subsequently there was a part of my psyche that vowed it would never happen to me. Subconsciously, my inner nun/saboteur took a vow of poverty and humility, choosing to be next-to-invisible so that I would never get "too big for my britches." As this bubbled up into my conscious awareness, I felt I was watching a vivid scene in a movie. It was surprising, a little sad and quite revelatory. It also made a lot of sense.

I asked my nun/saboteur if she would be open to working with me to manifest greater success. She said possibly, but there would be some important conditions to be agreed upon and met. I told her I was listening and ready to take notes. She said we must always remember to make God first. I agreed. She told me every day before I got out of bed I had to meditate, ground myself in the world, and consciously devote myself to Spirit. I told her I could do that. She said I had to stay humble and never begin to believe I was better than anyone else. I promised and crossed my heart. She also insisted we consistently tithe, and again I said yes. We did a pinky swear in my mind's eye. Then she got out of her black habit, put on a red turtleneck and some stylish black slacks. The scene made me laugh out loud. My nun said I could call her Teresa. She shared with me that she was happy we consciously connected, and thrilled to have someone to create and play with in the world.

Before I did that meditation I had no idea I had an inner nun, who (for her own very good reasons) had renounced the "stuff of the world." However, in retrospect, many of my mistakes and "bad choices" now made perfect sense. I was happy to understand her and my own deep intentions, and to have the opportunity to work together on common goals with congruent behavior. I have since made good on my promises and followed through with my commitments to Teresa, and worldly opportunities have manifested in extraordinary ways.

There has still been the rare occasion when I would hesitate, or feel a little paralyzed as soon as a large influx of money would come in, or a great opportunity would present itself. But because I had done the inner work and cultivated this inner relationship, I was more conscious of this nervous energy and the patterns of my nun/ saboteur. I also had the tools and awareness to be able to communicate, negotiate and work with her, and subsequently graciously receive the good that was coming to me.

Now anytime I feel the energy of hesitation or unworthiness starting to surface, I go inward and consciously connect with Teresa. I ask her how she is and what she needs. Then I remind her that she is worthy, that we are devoted to Spirit, and I ask her where we should tithe next. After all these issues have been addressed and questions have been answered, I then ask her: "How good can you stand it to get?" We take a deep breath, high five one another and say: "Pretty darn great!" This always provides a sense of inner relief, joy and expansion. It also gracefully raises the glass ceiling and the "prosperity bar" in my inner reality. Now it seems money can flow in, and I can follow through with my intuition, creativity and opportunities without slamming on the brakes or sabotaging my success. Teresa has been an amazing ally and good friend, and now consistently supports me in manifesting greater prosperity in the world.

In truth, the purpose of the inner saboteur

is not actually to sabotage you,

but to help you learn the ways

in which you undermine yourself,

play small and limit your potential.

The dance and dynamic with the saboteur is a way we inwardly battle ourselves to a standstill and prevent change. If you are open to cultivating a conscious relationship with this aspect of yourself, you have the opportunity to join forces with one of the most important allies you could possibly have. Once you are comfortable and familiar with the saboteur, you are able to sense their presence, work with them and heed their warnings. This can save you the pain and frustration of limiting yourself, playing small, and making the same mistakes over and over again.

Kara's Saboteur

Another example of someone making friends with her saboteur, was with my client Kara. I witnessed Kara battle herself to a standstill on more than one occasion, not following through with identified goals and action steps. I asked her if she felt she was sabotaging herself. She said yes, she clearly was, but did not know why or what do to about it. I asked her if she was ready to get congruent within herself, and get in touch with the part of her that was not on board with her intention to manifest prosperity. She said: "Absolutely!"

I did a simple guided meditation where I had Kara imagine going to an inner healing sanctuary. Then I asked her to her imagine inviting her saboteur to join her. It took a few moments, but

Kara eventually described the archetype and energy that showed up. She said she was an enormous red-haired woman, looking as if she might be 6' 5," with massive arms. Kara said: "Wow, I don't want to mess with this chick!" We both laughed, and then I had Kara ask her saboteur what she wanted to be called. She said her name was Dot. I asked Dot what her purpose or intention was, and she responded by saying "To keep Kara safe and to protect her." I told Dot that was very noble, and, of course we want Kara to be safe and protected, but also to manifest prosperity. Then I asked Dot if they could work together as a team to create more worldly success. Dot said yes, but that Kara was going to have to allow Dot to speak up on her behalf.

I asked Dot when she wanted to speak up for Kara, she said anytime she was uncomfortable, or felt like she was being taken advantage of. I asked Kara if that was something she could agree to and she said yes, as long as Dot did not beat anyone up and was socially acceptable. Dot took off her fingerless, black leather gloves and begrudgingly agreed. I suggested anytime in the future that Kara felt like she was being taken advantage of, she could invite Dot to join her and "speak through her." They both agreed this was a great plan, and the opportunity to do so was presented the very next day.

Kara was standing in line at the grocery store, patiently waiting her turn. A curmudgeonly older man cut in front of her to grab a magazine—and stayed there. Kara was confused. Her natural inclination would be to say nothing and become very small, but then she remembered our session, and her inner agreement with Dot. Kara invited Dot to speak through her. Kara cleared her throat:

"Excuse me, sir?" He ignored her. Dot got a little more aggressive: "Sir! I believe the back of the line is behind me!" He looked at her, frowned, muttered something and moved behind her. It was a small action step, but very important and powerful. Kara made good on her agreement with Dot. Now Kara and Dot could begin to work together and be on the same team, rather than be at odds and battle against one another in her inner realms.

Kara called me with the good news, and has since allowed Dot to work with her *and through her* on several occasions. Kara is now manifesting more success in the world, feeling much more congruent, confident and empowered.

Have you ever noticed yourself battling yourself to a standstill, arguing for your limitations, playing small, or behaving in some other disempowered way? Have you ever set yourself up for failure, or made mistakes that logically made no sense? Set an intention to connect with your saboteur, and learn how you can work together as powerful partners, good friends, and a congruent force in the world to manifest your magnificence and your prosperity!

Show Up and Receive!

An important lesson I have learned is we can only have what we can stand to receive. You may want great things, but if you cannot relax and receive them, you will not manifest them. This story about my sister, Tonda, exemplifies this point.

Ever since we were young children, my desire has always been to spoil and celebrate my little sister. However, I have not been able to do it as much as I've wanted in recent years. Not for lack of trying, but because she is always so busy taking care of other people. With her birthday right around the corner, I called to talk to her about her impending day, to make a plan to do something special. "Hey Sister, what do you want for your birthday?" Tonda sweetly replied: "I don't really need anything, you should spend your money on someone else." I told her if I wasn't spending her birthday money on her, I wasn't going to go out and use that money to buy presents for anyone else. Then I asked her: "Are you sure there isn't something you want?" Tonda responded: "Sure there are LOTS of things I want!" Then I said to her, "Well, if you consider what you want, and give me a hint, you are more likely to get it!" I continued: "I really want to spoil you, but you have to show up, and you have to be able to receive it." Tonda thought about it for a moment and decided she would like to be spoiled, so we made a date to celebrate.

I had so much fun treasure hunting for Tonda's presents, some of which included shoes, pajamas, stuffed animals, a bracelet, a necklace, candles, a dress, a sweater, makeup and more. We decided to meet in Los Angeles and Tonda *did* show up! I took her to dinner to one of her favorite restaurants. We had a fabulous meal complete with mango cheesecake and a birthday candle. I sang happy birthday and told her to make a wish. After our decadent dining experience, we headed home so she could open her gifts. She started tentatively, looking at me with her big green eyes, almost as if she wondered if it was really okay. She gently opened her presents, careful not tear up the wrapping paper. I was laughing, smiling and clapping my hands. After the third gift, she started to find her groove. She started to relax and began ripping her presents open with gusto.

It seemed Tonda was finally allowing herself to have fun, and gave herself permission to joyfully receive. I made her model all the clothes and admired how cute she looked. I believe she sensed how much I was enjoying her enjoyment, and so the fun and festivities continued to expand. After all the presents were opened and the fashion show was complete, I read a letter I had written to her ten years ago about how much I loved and appreciated her. It was the icing on the cake. We both had tears in our eyes from the sense of connection and love. It was a flawless, fabulous and magical evening.

The next day I asked Tonda why she had been so resistant to my spoiling and celebrating her over the years, and why she finally said yes. She was quiet for a moment and then said: "I feel I am very blessed in my life, and very grateful to have what I have. I just think there are people who need things more than I do. As I think about this more, I guess there has been an underlying issue of not deserving it." As she shared this message with me it resonated as true. It is an issue I have witnessed many people struggle with—myself included. Tonda continued, "I know how much I love to give to people, and if they don't receive, it hurts my feelings. So then I thought when you offered to spoil maybe *I am* as deserving as the next person. Once I opened my mind to it, I got excited! I allowed myself to feel special and have fun—and I am so glad I did!" I was grateful as well. That evening was so much fun and the most we had laughed in a very long time.

I wonder if God thinks about you and me in the same way as I think about my sister. "I love you and want to spoil you. I want to give you all the gifts of the Universe and everything that brings you joy . . . but you have to show up, and you have to be able to receive it." I think showing up simply means making our relationship with Spirit a priority, opening our hearts, and saying thank you when wonderful things happen in our lives.

As I meditated on this possibility, and surrendered any resistance to receiving, people began to present themselves in my life offering remarkable gifts of support and kindness. A very talented makeup artist offered to do my hair and makeup for a photo shoot. Another expert offered to help me with the design and marketing of this book gratis. I was offered the opportunity to do a radio interview, and a policeman let me out of a ticket (which has never happened before!). In all of these situations I teetered on the edge of guilt, constriction and unworthiness, but then consciously opened my heart in gracious receptivity. It seems this experiment, energy and attitude is holding the door open for more and more to show up in my life.

I refer to your worldly gifts as your "Divine Prosperity Treasure Chest." Abraham Hicks coined a term referred to as "Vibrational Escrow." Your Treasure Chest and your Vibrational Escrow contains love, relationships, prosperity, experiences and material items that are there waiting JUST FOR YOU! If you don't claim and receive them, they will simply go to waste. Your Treasures and your Escrow means what you want is THERE for you, ENCODED for you, and being HELD BY YOU and FOR YOU. No one can take what is yours away from you. It is what you have created, desired and deserve. In order to unlock the padlock to your treasure chest, and open the door to attract what is yours by Divine Right, you need to claim it, realize you deserve it, and receive it with grace and gratitude.

I invite you to take some time to consider what you want, assure yourself you deserve what you desire, and open your heart in gracious receptivity. I find relaxing into the energy of gracious receiving, humility and appreciation are like energetically rolling out the red carpet to attract unforeseen support, universal gifts, and amazing opportunities. In fact, every day can be like your birthday!

There are gifts floating around in the Universe

that are just for you,

and if you do not open your heart to receive them,

they will go to waste!

Another powerful way of opening the door to your Vibrational Escrow, and lifting the lid to your Treasure Chest, is to open your heart, and start taking the beauty and majesty of the world personally. Consider for a moment that the daffodils, tulips and pansies are blooming just for *you* to enjoy. Take the shooting star blazing across the night sky as a personal wink from God; consciously acknowledge the brilliant sunset as an artistic gesture created with you in mind; and that the waves of the ocean are rolling in to bow at your feet. Open your mind to the possibility that the leaves of the trees dancing in the breeze are waving just for you; the singing bird is serenading you; the butterfly fluttering by is celebrating you, and the full moon is glowing solely on your behalf. Take the beauty, wonder and gifts of the world very personally, and breathe

the beauty and prosperity of this incredible planet into the depth of your beingness. Open your heart in gracious receptivity, appreciation and love, and as you do, so much more will be revealed, shared and given to you.

Exercise #1: Questions for Your Saboteur

Caroline Myss suggests we answer the following questions so that we might more clearly become aware of the actions and behavior of the saboteur:

- What fears have the most authority over me?
- What happens when a fear overtakes me? Does it make me silent?
- Do I allow people to speak for me?
- Do I agree to some things out of fear that I otherwise would not agree to?
- Have I let creative opportunities pass me by?
- How conscious am I in the moment that I am sabotaging myself?
- Am I able to recognize the saboteur in others?
- Would I be able to offer others advice about how to challenge one's Saboteur? If so, what would it be?

Exercise #2: Connecting With Your Saboteur

You may want to have your journal with you to take notes from this experience. You may also choose to light a candle or play some meditative music. Open your mind and try not to have any preconceived notions or attachments about how the scene should play out. Now set your intention to connect and communicate with your inner saboteur.

1. Imagine walking down a stair case with 10 steps, with each step allow yourself to feel more relaxed, more present and more peaceful.

2. At the bottom of the staircase look around and notice that you are in a safe beautiful healing garden, or sacred inner sanctuary. Feel the ground under your feet, take in the sights, sounds, smells and the temperature of this place. Is it day or night? What season is it? Are there water, trees or any structures here? Use all of your senses to become familiar with this place and experience it in as much detail as possible.

3. Once you are familiar and comfortable with your surroundings, imagine inviting the energy of your saboteur to join you.

4. Allow whatever comes forward in your mind's eye to take shape. Be patient and really let this part of yourself know you want to have a heart to heart conversation. Tell them you truly want to connect with them and hear whatever they have to share.

5. Once they reveal themselves, thank them for coming forward. Notice everything you can about them. How tall are they, what are they wearing, how old do they look? Now,

ask them if they have a name or something they would like to be called.

6. Ask them what their purpose or intention is and listen patiently to what they have to share.

7. Thank them for their intention, knowing in truth they are on your side and want you to be safe and protected.

8. Ask them if there is some way you can work together as a team. Ask them what that might take. What do they want or need to become friends with you? What agreements, negotiations or commitments need to be made? You may want to write down what comes forward.

9. Only commit to agreements you can follow through with. If you cannot or do not, the sabotage behavior will certainly continue and possibly up-level.

10. Assure this aspect that they are safe, important, valuable, appreciated and respected. You may want to say aloud: "I am safe, important, valuable, appreciated and respected," or "We are safe, important, appreciated and respected." Allow any feeling or emotions to come up and write down what you experience.

11. Thank this aspect for the opportunity to connect, collaborate and communicate. Know in truth that this is a vital ally and important friend who can help you create inner congruence and outer success in the world.

Only you have the power and potential to connect and make friends with this inner aspect. It is entirely up to you whether they run the show from behind the scenes and battle you to a standstill OR become a helpful partner to create, play and prosper with in your life. If you listen to what this archetype has to say with an open mind and open heart, you will find they can help you manifest in the most noble, prosperous and miraculous of ways.

Exercise #3: Permission For Prosperity

We can only manifest what we can handle and what we give ourselves permission to receive. Now that you have cleared subconscious constrictions and made friends with the part of you that has kept you small, it is a great time to assure yourself you are deserving and worthy. It is time to give yourself the permission to prosper.

1. Take a few deep healing cleansing breaths allowing yourself to relax and come fully present into the moment.

2. Repeat all the following statements that resonate for you or that you would like to claim for yourself:
   - I give my conscious and subconscious minds far-reaching permission to relax and receive prosperity
   - I give myself permission to manifest success
   - I give myself permission to attract and receive money
   - I give myself deep permission to thrive
   - I give myself permission to consider and manifest all that would bring me joy
   - I give myself passionate permission to attract all I desire

and deserve for my highest good and the highest good of all concerned

- I give myself permission to live a life of prosperity, success and love
- I give myself permission to graciously receive abundant compensation for my soul level gifts
- I give myself profound permission to be authentically empowered
- I give myself permission to come into alignment of heart, mind, body and soul
- I give myself permission for vibrant, optimal physical, mental, emotional, financial and spiritual health
- I give myself permission to become congruent
- I give myself peaceful permission to receive the kindness, grace and gifts of the Universe
- I give myself permission to manifest my Divine Prosperity
- I am worthy, safe, protected, supported and adored! I give myself the permission to celebrate, to be happy and to soar!

There is nothing you need to do to *prove* your value, all you need to do is get all aspects of yourself on board and get congruent within yourself. Next, relax and give yourself deep permission to receive what you desire. Finally ask yourself: "How good can I stand it to get?" Know your answer to this question will dictate and predict *exactly* what you will attract and manifest!

Chapter 7

Weeding Your Garden

*Get rid of what you don't want
to make space for what you do want!*

A few years ago I decided wanted a garden filled with tomatoes, cucumbers, green beans, zucchini and some herbs. I had a little plot of land in my backyard, so I planted my little crop, and reaped wonderful rewards. It was so much fun to go out and witness the process of my garden growing weekly and then pick all of my fresh vegetables. What I did not know at the time were the herbs I planted were actually weeds. The following year I hacked through the hearty oregano and spearmint so I could plant my tomatoes and green beans. My crop was not nearly as successful. Each subsequent year my vegetable garden was less and less impressive. This year, once again, I attempted to hack down the tenacious jungle of annoying herbs to find space for my tomatoes. It is now the end of the season, and I have yet to pick one ripe red tomato.

Like a jungle overgrown with dense unwanted foliage, I no longer had the space in my garden, or nutrients in the soil, to sustain and nurture what I really, really want. Tomatoes!

This year I will till the land and dig deep to get rid of the roots of those pesky herbs, so next season, once again, I will have my wonderful little garden. In truth, weeding the garden and cleaning up our messes is not fun . . .but sometimes very necessary in the prosperity process. Sometimes we have to get rid of the old to make space for the new.

Life can be this way as well. It is hard to manifest prosperity and attract what we really want if we are bogged down and clogged up in our bodies, homes, hearts, minds and lives. Making friends with the subconscious mind, Higher Self and our inner saboteur are important steps in clearing and weeding our inner garden. If you want to start moving energy and preparing the space for manifesting what you want in other ways, it can be very helpful to take inventory and clear things out physically, mentally and emotionally.

On the physical level, what does your body look and feel like? Do you treat it with love and respect? Or do you abuse it and expect it to still serve you well? Every spring I do a cleanse, I like the Richard Schulze Cleanse. Here is a quote from "The Herb Doc": "For me personally, in one word, health is freedom. Disease and illness rob you of your freedom . . . and your money. Being healthy feels great, and it gives you the freedom to live your life the way you want, and the energy to do all of the things that you want to do, and the vitality to have all of the fun that you want to have, and to really, really enjoy your life to your fullest potential."

I absolutely agree with Dr. Schulze, and for me doing a cleanse is a powerful way of releasing toxins and "old stuff" that is no longer serving me. It is a way I can take responsibility for my health and my body. It is also a wonderful way to get clean and clear inside and out. Every time I do a cleanse my mind gets sharper and my vitality increases. I also experience vivid dreams, emotional healing, profound revelations and inspired creativity.

Another important area to consider: what does your home look like? What about the closets and drawers? I have found anytime I feel stuck or stagnant, cleaning out my closets, organizing and making space in my home moves the energy in other areas of my life. Creative ideas will drop in, or the phone will ring with an interesting opportunity.

If you have not worn something in 3 or 4 years, why are you still hanging onto it? Are you hoping you might fit into it again one day? Or that it might come back into fashion? Hanging to things that are not serving you can be an adherence to lack. Clinging to things that have outlived their usefulness, can be a testament to being stuck in the past, rather than enthusiastically and optimistically facing your future.

Another way we bog ourselves down energetically and prevent prosperity from showing up in our lives is on the mental and emotional levels. What thoughts do you think when you are alone with yourself? Are they negative or positive? Are the messages you share with yourself unkind or kind? Our lives go the direction of our thoughts, so it is important to become conscious and positive in our private moments and in our silent musings. *A Course of Miracles* tells us that we accomplish so little because our minds are so undisciplined. Pay close attention to the content of your mind, and if your thoughts are negative or unkind, set the intention to clean them up.

Another important area to consider is your relationships. Do the people you spend your time and energy on nurture and support you? Are you surrounded by people who respect and value you? Do you respect and value them? Are your relationships flowers or weeds? When you talk to other people do you discuss what is right with your life or what is wrong with it? Do you share uplifting, positive stories? Or do you compare, compete and complain? Do you talk about other people? And if you so, do you speak of their great qualities and what is wonderful about them? Or do you gossip, find fault and put them down? Pay close attention to your inner and outer conversations. Are your thoughts and words propelling you upward in the direction of your dreams? Or are they pulling you down and keeping you bogged down in the weeds, muck and mire? I invite you to challenge yourself and relinquish your judgement, negative thoughts and conversations about yourself and others. Pay attention! Then think and speak in ways that are positive, uplifting, optimistic and empowered!

By contemplating your relationships and conversations, and by asking yourself these questions and taking responsibility for the answers, you can consciously set the intention to weed your garden and release those things that are no longer serving you. Then you can start planting the seeds for what you really, really want in your life.

Your thoughts and your words are the greatest predictor

for what you will attract and create in your life.

You alone have the power to make the changes in regard to the thoughts you think and the things you say. This is what will determine the direction you are headed in your life, and the greatest predictor for what you will create, what you will attract and what you will manifest.

Megan's Story

Going out of our integrity to make money seems to be an unavoidable aspect of the human experience. However, as we open our hearts and minds and listen to our Higher Selves and our physical selves, we have the opportunity to make different, better and more empowered choices. Our bodies are sacred vehicles for our soul. They also are a wonderful friend and ally. Our bodies can help us attain greater clarity about what we think and feel. If we choose to consult with them and listen to them, they will *always* tell us the truth.

The following is a story about my client, Megan, and how she was able to consult with her body to make an important decision about what to do in her career. As a professional stylist, Megan is very talented, but wanted support to go to the next level of manifesting prosperity. Megan was happy to receive a call from a referral. However, when Megan told the woman her fees, the potential client began to argue about her pricing. Megan quickly excused herself from the conversation and called me. Megan told me she was feeling bad about herself and about the situation. She was also feeling conflicted. She wanted to take the client and needed the money, but felt uncomfortable speaking up for herself. She wondered if she should just accept the cut-rate fee, after all she had bills to pay and some money was better than no money. I told her she certainly could, but if she did, she was sending a message to the universe that this was acceptable.

I asked Megan to turn inward and think about saying "yes" to this client at the lower rate. I asked her to inwardly scan her body. We are holistic beings and our body is like a tuning fork, if we remember to check in with our physical selves, they will always reveal to us our deeper truth. Messages of truth come in the form of expansion and/or comfort; untruth shows up as constriction and/or pain. So, Megan closed her eyes, and checked in with her body. As she considered saying yes to this women at the lower fee, she told me her stomach felt like it was starting to tie up in knots. She also began to sense a dull throb in her temples.

Megan's body was letting her know taking this client at the lower rate was not a self-honoring choice. Then I asked Megan to take a deep breath, invite Spirit in and line up with her Higher Self. I asked her what it would look like to honor herself and reside in her authentic power in this situation. She took a moment and then shared with me that the self-honoring, empowered choice would be to tell the client she simply could not take her on at the lower price. As she did this she said the knot in her stomach unraveled, her body relaxed, she felt lighter and more comfortable within herself. I told Megan by saying no to what she did not want, she was keeping the space available in her garden for what she really did want.

Megan was nervous, but committed to speaking her truth and honoring herself. She called the prospective client and said she was sorry but she simply could not take her on at the lower rate. The client responded by telling Megan she was going to have to think about things and get back with her. Later that afternoon, Megan received a call from another referral. This time the potential client did not flinch when Megan quoted her rates, and hired her on the spot. The following day the first client called back and said she was willing to pay her full rate after all.

Megan called me, somewhat stunned about how things shifted so quickly once she honored herself and spoke up on her behalf. I reminded her if she was not comfortable and confident in her value, how could great value be reflected back to her? I also told her going against the body's wisdom is rarely a good idea. "Un-ease" in our bodies eventually manifests as "dis-ease." Megan thanked me for helping her tune into her body's wisdom, for helping her claim her value and relax into her confidence. Then Megan shared with me this additional life lesson: "We will always get what we are willing to settle for, and if we settle, not only will our bodies constrict, resentment will certainly take root. Yet another weed to contend with down the line!" After sharing this revelation, Megan proceeded to do her grateful, happy prosperity dance!

As Megan discovered, some other tenacious and insidious weeds in our garden of life include the qualities of resentment, judgment and blame. Are there people in your heart that you have not forgiven? Or that you are energetically tangled up with in a negative, unproductive or unhealthy way? At some point in time everyone has been hurt by the deeds, words, actions or inactions of another. Past hurts can leave you with toxic weeds in your garden, and the lingering energy of blame, anger, bitterness and even revenge. If you dwell on hurtful events, relationships or situations, hostility can take root. And even if you do not dwell on them consciously, this energy can take up residence in your body and subconscious mind, where it will inevitably affect your health, your life and your prosperity in various unpleasant ways.

The Power of Forgiveness

If you choose not to forgive, you are the one who will pay the biggest price. Choosing not to forgive is a toxic energy, and can leave you seeing your life through a haze, or a gray fog. It can be akin to looking at the world through a lens that is not your prescription. It can negatively affect your relationships, your health, your happiness and your wealth. Holding onto grudges and emotions of anger, judgment, resentment and hostility infect your psyche, deplete your life force, and use up precious energy that could be used in much more positive, productive and prosperous ways. They are also much lower on the vibrational scale. So if you want to move into the higher realms, and experience the higher vibrational emotions, such as joy, synchronicity, happiness, cooperation, support, love and prosperity, it is important to open your mind to the possibility of letting go of those heavy bags of rocks, garbage and unhealthy debris. You will find once you do, you will naturally start to ascend upward and "miraculously," begin to attract opportunities, relationships, experiences and abundance you could never have created, manipulated or forced into being.

Generally speaking, forgiveness is a decision to let go of resentment and judgment, thoughts of revenge and energetically release another. The act or behavior that hurt you may always remain a part of your life, but forgiveness can lessen its grip, and help you focus on the more positive aspects of your life. Although forgiveness does not generally happen all at once, by setting the intention, and consciously working on forgiveness, the healing can begin.

The process of forgiveness can lead to understanding,

empathy and eventually even compassion

for those who have hurt you

as well as for yourself.

In my book *Manifesting Love From the Inside Out*, I share the details of the deep betrayal I experienced with my famous fiancé of three years. During the final year of our relationship, he lied to me repeatedly, and finally left me for a beautiful younger woman. There was no conversation or explanation. I found out from our therapist he was not showing up for the couples' session he had scheduled for us that day . . .or showing up ever again for that matter. I was wildly confused and utterly heartbroken.

Later that evening, I stared at the television in horror as my ex gave an interview. He told the reporter, and the world, what he had failed to tell me; he had a new love and a new life. We never spoke again. It was an experience that changed me forever. My healing journey was not fun or easy. In fact, it was filled with anguish, confusion, pain, chaos and oceans of tears. The forgiveness process took years. Perhaps it could have taken less time, but in truth, I did not WANT to forgive him. I wanted to be angry and felt he did not deserve my forgiveness. After about 3 years of struggling financially, in my career and in my relationships, I sat down to meditate with the intention to gain understanding about the painful, confusing and challenging circumstances of my life.

I lit a candle, took a few deep breaths, and had an authentic conversation with God. I also made a heartfelt request for clarity and support. After I said everything I wanted to say, I focused on my breath and invited my mind to settle down. After about 20 minutes I felt my crazed monkey mind relax. Once I felt peaceful, I inwardly asked the question: "God, why aren't my relationships working, why can't I make money and why is my life *not moving forward?*" The message that dropped into my awareness was clear and succinct: "Because you are always turning around facing your past."

That message shook me to the core, because it was undeniably true. I was constantly thinking about what had gone wrong, how I could have done things differently, and how I had been victimized by that horrible, mean, monster-man. I spent a lot of time fantasizing in very non-productive ways. I was looking at my past with regret, rather than facing my future with optimism. I realized in that moment, in order to get free and move forward in my life, I needed to forgive him—not for him, but for me. So I set an intention to do just that.

Forgiveness did not happen overnight, nor was the process fun or easy. But once I opened my mind to forgiveness, things began to shift. When my ex would drop into my awareness, rather than mentally chewing on destructive thoughts, fantasies or memories, I plugged in my Forgiveness Mantra: "God bless you on your path, God bless me on my path. I forgive you, I release you, I am free." Then I would consciously "change the channel" in my mind, and visualize what I wanted for myself and my future. I had to remind myself this was a "forgiveness practice," and, like going to the gym, I had to keep working my forgiveness muscle. Just as you cannot expect to do one workout and be fit forever, and you cannot just forgive once and be done with it. So much about creating success and prosperity for ourselves is about cultivating new, positive and productive habits. And with forgiveness, it is important to know that sometimes you just have to fake it till you make it.

If you choose not to forgive, you remain in victim consciousness, and are, in fact, giving your power away. Another no-so-fun side effect of "non-forgiveness" is that you are resonating at a frequency that will inevitably attract another perpetrator. Rather than pointing fingers at another and playing the blame game, it is far more productive to ask yourself: "What is my soul trying to learn from this person or this situation?" This is an empowered stance, a "learning orientation to life." This is a much more effective way to manifest happiness, fulfillment and prosperity—perhaps the only way. The bottom line is that it does not feel good to hate another; and it is not healthy, or energetically productive to stay in anger for long periods of time.

Forgiveness puts out the fire of anger
and helps you to begin anew

Today I am happy to report I have authentically forgiven this man and now see him as a powerful teacher. Once I untangled the cords that bound us, I began to live life from a place of greater inner peace, and began to manifest greater external flow. Choosing to forgive was like hitting the reset button, which energetically cleaned up my life, inside and out. Other side effects and bonuses of that forgiveness were manifesting an incredible loving relationship and finding my own passion, purpose and prosperity.

I would not be who I am today without that painful chapter in the book of my life. Because of my ex I reached deeper into my own soul, and connected more authentically to Spirit. Additionally, because of those red-hot, painful stepping-stones on my life's path I am able to support others in making the challenging and confusing journey from anger and anguish to gratitude and grace.

Forgiving Ourselves

As we dig a little deeper and clear our garden, beneath the pain of not forgiving others, we discover the pain of not forgiving ourselves. Once we do forgiveness work with those who have hurt us, guilt and shame can come bubbling up, presenting an opportunity for forgiveness and deep healing of ourselves. Once we heal our blame and judgment of others, we can end up judging and blaming ourselves. The pendulum of judgment has a propensity of swinging from one end of the spectrum to the other; from under-responsibility, to over-responsibility. In fact, I believe many people hesitate to forgive others because they do not want to look in the mirror and reveal to themselves the deeper issues of guilt, shame and self-judgment. But until we do, life will not work easily or well, and will continue to be challenging and painful.

Remember, you manifest what you believe you deserve, so if there is shadow material of self-judgment, guilt and shame lurking in your subconscious mind, it can impede the river of your prosperity; and rather than an open, flowing, influx of clean, clear energy, it can pinch off, clog up and become a muddy trickle.

When you feel guilty, shameful, or are in judgment of yourself, it is a signal to alert you that on a deep level, you need your own compassion, forgiveness and self-love. Healing occurs when you apply love to the places inside that hurt. And though it is helpful to receive love from outside of you, the real shift occurs when you learn to do it for and within yourself. Of course this can be a challenge, and there can be many layers to reveal and heal before finally arriving at the destination of unconditional self-love and self-acceptance, but I believe it is a journey worth taking, and the truest purpose of our lives.

One of my wise and wonderful teachers said: "The whole point of being human is to learn to love ourselves no matter what!" This is certainly not what I was taught and likely a different priority than what you were brought up to believe as a child. However, until we release our judgments, forgive ourselves and love ourselves, life will hurt. Once we relax into the place of love and peace within, life naturally begins to smooth out and we experience greater equanimity, grace, ease, support and miracles.

As I mentioned earlier, I grew up going to the Catholic Church and before taking communion I would chant: "Lord, I am not worthy to receive you." Not only did I take this to heart, my subconscious mind absorbed the notion of unworthiness completely. I recall going to confession at seven years old, and dredging up all that I had done wrong for the week, and then asking for forgiveness from the priest and God. I would blubber endlessly as I admitted sticking my tongue out at my sister or dropping a plate. As I focused on my guilt, self-judgment and wrong-doing, my inner light was dimming. I was also buying into the notion of "original sin." I eventually tip-toed away from Catholicism and organized religion, but by then judgment, guilt and shame were firmly woven into the foundation of my human experience, and deeply entrenched in my subconscious mind.

As I began to cultivate a personal connection to Spirit, I came to realize and accept that not only am I a child of God, but an aspect of God. I consciously began to embrace and claim the concept of "original blessing." Once I did this my life immediately began to improve. I am happy to report, for the most part, my guilt and shame have transformed into humility and reverence. Self-judgment does occasionally make an appearance, but now I can recognize it as an opportunity for the continued practice of self-forgiveness, self-acceptance, self-compassion and self-love.

A while back I made a messy mistake and was wallowing in self-judgment. A friend, who grew tired of watching my pity party, asked me what I liked best about myself. I thought about it for a moment and then said: "The thing I like best about myself is that I would never, ever want to hurt anyone, that I love people immensely, I have a deep desire to be of service, and that I want to bring kindness and compassion to the world." As I contemplated my answer to this question, I realized these qualities, as well as my intentions, were very sincere. In that moment I knew the qualities on my list of "Pros about Tammi," far outweighed the qualities on my list of "Cons about Tammi." Identifying this helped me take a deep breath, relax, forgive myself, relinquish the self-judgment and my guilt. This helped me remember the truer truth about me; I am love, I am loved, I am good and I am worthy. In that moment I remembered my original blessing, I realigned with self-love, reclaimed my innate value and relaxed into friendly affection for myself.

Although it can hurt when others

withdraw their approval from us,

our greatest pain comes from

withdrawing our own approval of ourselves

If we forget the truth about ourselves; that we are divine and that we are love, we subconsciously identify with lack, limitation, judgment and unworthiness. If we are in self-judgment, we create a sense of smallness and separation and energetically cut ourselves off from love, abundance, kindness and flow. From this posture we will *never* be able to cultivate true and lasting prosperity. A powerful healing occurs when we forgive ourselves, relax into love, and acknowledge ourselves as priceless, incredible and wonderfully worthy.

Once you authentically forgive yourself, you clean yourself up energetically, and line yourself up spiritually. The natural byproduct of self-forgiveness is that resistance is released and the energy of flow, harmony, peace and prosperity can naturally ensue.

The following is a powerful prayer I use myself and frequently share with clients to release judgment, forgive ourselves, and restore ourselves to the Truth. It is also included in my "Deep Forgiveness" guided meditation:

> *"I forgive myself for any illusions I have placed between myself and who I truly am. I forgive myself for having placed them there. God, I bow down before you and open my heart to receive your healing grace. I release any guilt, I surrender any shame, and I give myself permission to relax and receive Your Unconditional Love. I restore myself to You wholly, holy and completely. Thank You for this healing, thank You for Your grace, thank You for Your loving. Thank You, Thank You, Thank You — And So It Is!"*

As you authentically forgive yourself, you naturally relax and move into alignment with your Higher Self and Spirit. This process opens your heart, and therefore attracts Earthly agents, and otherworldly angels, to reflect and share your worthiness and value with you. You have probably heard the sayings: as within so without; as above so below. When you take responsibility for healing your inner reality, your outer reality CANNOT HELP but to shift, transform and improve.

What I know is everyone makes mistakes. And something else I know is everyone is doing the best they can given their level of consciousness. When we know better, we do better. We did not incarnate as human beings to be perfect; we came here to learn about loving—for others and with ourselves. The act of forgiveness heals us on a very deep level and supports us in becoming more clear, conscious, loving, attractive, compassionate and prosperous human beings.

The practice of forgiveness naturally lines us up
with our soul, with Source and with our divine nature.
Forgiveness also attracts incredible grace
and remarkable good.

The visual that comes to mind is a gloomy, cloudy day. When we release our hurts, grudges, shame and judgment through forgiveness, we let go of the heavy toxic bags we have been carrying around. We start to naturally and easily ascend up through the clouds, and eventually up above the cloud line. "Miraculously" it becomes an exquisite, beautiful, sunshiny day—life is brilliant, bright and glorious. From this elevated vibration we manifest easily, and we celebrate constantly.

For others that have not done this work, they are still meandering around, stuck in the gloom and doom. They look at you and do not understand why you are so prosperous, lucky and blessed. But you do! It is because you got rid of those things that were no longer serving you and you released the bricks and boulders of judgment. You started looking at your life as a learning opportunity and an adventure, rather than something you were "at effect of." You chose to become empowered, rather than remain a victim. You took responsibility for yourself. You said yes to life! Yes to your soul! Yes to your healing! Yes to forgiveness! Yes to Love! And YES to your Divine Prosperity!

Exercise #1: Forgiveness

If you have my guided meditation "Deep Forgiveness," listen to it frequently. As long as someone appears in the meditation, or if you find yourself experience anger or challenging emotions toward another or yourself, continue to use it to support you in your healing process. Here are some additional exercises to support you in going deeper.

1. Take a deep, healing, cleansing breath and turn your attention inward. Ask your heart or Higher Self if there is anyone from your past or your present that you are still harboring negativity towards or that you have not completely forgiven.

2. After this person has revealed themselves, write a letter expressing all of your thoughts and feelings. Get any

"unsaid words" and energy out of your body, heart and mind. You may or may not choose to mail this letter to them, remember this process is more for you than the one you have not forgiven.

3. Now, open your mind and imagine them responding to you. What do they have to say? What would they like you to know? How do they feel? Finally, ask them how you can bring healing, peace, resolution and completion to this relationship and/or situation.

4. You may now choose to do a burning ceremony with the letter you have written. Set your intentions for clearing and releasing everything that is not serving you, for your highest good and the highest good of all concerned. (Of course be certain to take all necessary safety precautions.) This can be a powerful practice and ceremony that can support you in releasing them, and help heal you at a very deep level.

5. When you are complete, imagine inviting white light, compassion and love into any newly opened places. Then surround yourself with a healing, shimmering bubble. This is a bubble of protection, peace, healing, safety and boundaries. You may also send them light and imagine a bubble around them as well. Then you may choose to let them float away.

6. When this person drops into your awareness now or in the future, plug in the Forgiveness Mantra: "God bless you on your path, God bless me on my path. I forgive you, I release you, I am free."

7. You may need to do this exercise repeatedly for it to come to resolution. Know each time you do it, you should experience some relief. You may find you start to feel different, lighter, more free and be met with "winks from the Universe" letting you know you are on the right track and heading the right direction.

Exercise #2: Forgiving Yourself

1. Consider an area in your life that you are still judging yourself for.

2. Consider what you learned through the experience and how you would choose to handle things differently now.

3. Now imagine going back in time. What compassionate advice would you give to that person if you could?

4. Now open your mind to letting yourself off the hook and forgiving yourself. Remind yourself although you have made mistakes, every human has and mistakes are a powerful learning tool and an important part of this Earthy experience.

5. Share encouragement with yourself, tell yourself the positive empowering messages you want and need to hear.

6. Now I invite you to look the mirror and into your own eyes. Tell yourself that you forgive yourself. Acknowledge that it is time to be free.

7. Identify what you like best about yourself and share it with yourself.

8. Acknowledge that you are a unique, amazing, powerful, colorful, creative aspect of the Divine and whatever other accurate descriptive, positive words you want to use.

9. Finally, consider what is it you long to hear from another. Now say those things to yourself. Remind yourself you have gifts, qualities and talents no one else in the world has. Share with yourself that you are immensely, incredibly, wonderfully valuable. Remind yourself the essence of who you are is love, and that your intention is to live from that place of love more consistently every day.

Exercise #3: Free Form Writing

I sometimes call this exercise a "Mind Dump." Julia Cameron calls this technique "Morning Pages" (though I do them anytime I feel stressed or anxious). This process can also be referred to as "Stream of Consciousness Writing." Write at least 3 pages of long hand in a notebook or loose paper (I would recommend a different journal or notebook than your Prosperity Journal, this is not necessarily for the sake of keeping or rereading, though you can if you like). Write anything that pops into your awareness. This allows your mind to wander, express, purge and release. It is a powerful way of giving expression to inner disturbances and a safe way to remove negativity. This process is NOT for the purpose of writing pretty. It can be about anything and start with anything. You can begin by writing, "I don't know what to write" or "I feel tired, my head hurts." There is no right or wrong way to do this exercise. Just know that lending yourself to this simple exercise on a daily basis, will help you weed your inner garden, relinquish negativity, come into balance, heal and eventually help you experience greater comfort, peace and clarity. Do not over-think the process: just put three pages of anything on the page, and see how you feel!

Exercise #4: Surrender Negativity

Often people bond over what's bad and wrong, as well as stand in judgment of themselves or others. This can be a way of creating a limited, perceived connection or posturing as superior. However, this bad habit will make it impossible to manifest a positive, satisfying and prosperous life. Do this simple experiment for one day: Do not make a negative comment about ANYTHING or ANYONE (not your loud neighbors, your relatives, your co-worker, not the weight you gained, not the bags under your eyes, not the traffic or even your luke-warm coffee!) Find the positive and articulate what is good and right about every situation and every person. Check in with yourself at the end of the day and notice how you feel. If you can successfully participate in the powerful exercise for 28 days, you will have pulled a toxic weed out of your garden AND cultivated a great, new, healthy, manifesting habit. This in turn will help you naturally attract amazing things and propel you on the path to greater self-respect, deeper self-love and your fulfilling, abundant future!

Now set an intention to make good friends with that amazing person in the mirror, for they are truly remarkable, spectacular and one-of-a-kind. They absolutely deserve your attention, kindness, forgiveness, compassion and love. To quote the wise Buddha: "You yourself, as much as anybody in the entire universe, deserves your love and affection." Removing inner obstacles, and becoming more loving and congruent is the *only way* to create real and lasting change and to move in the direction of your purpose, your prosperity and manifest the life of your dreams.

Chapter 8

Tending Your Garden

You have brains in your head. You have feet in your shoes.
You can steer yourself any direction you choose. You're on
your own. And you know what you know. And YOU are
the one who'll decide where to go . . .

~Dr. Seuss, Oh, the Places You'll Go!

After your garden has been cleared out, it needs to be tended, nurtured, watered and fed. This ensures it—and you—continue to expand, grow and prosper in the direction you desire. Some important ways we can do this is to take responsibility for our relationship with ourselves and our inner world. Then we need to think and speak positive thoughts and words. It is also vital to implement the qualities of loving, respecting and honoring ourselves and others.

A basic premise of spiritual psychology is that our outer reality is a reflection of our inner reality. What that means is our relationships, our finances, our experiences and our lives are simply feedback and a reflection of our inner realms, our beliefs and how we treat ourselves. So if you notice painful patterns in your life, there is a powerful opportunity to explore the ways you are imposing these patterns on yourself.

You alter your patterns of outer manifestation

by altering your inner experience of yourself.

What Are You Trying to Prove and to Whom?

Recently I complained about life being harsh with me, so I posed the question: "How am I harsh with myself?" Although I had been working on cultivating self-love for some time, it seemed there was still room for improvement. After considering this question for a bit, I had to admit, I WAS still harsh with myself. I would often work long hours and push myself through fatigue and hunger. I also did not take the time to acknowledge or be proud of myself as I completed goals, I would whip myself and just keep on going.

One day, as I was sitting in front of my computer for the 14th hour in a row, a girlfriend of mine came by to say hello. She knew I had been there all day and into the night. She sat there and patiently observed me as I furiously pounded away at the keyboard. "You're a workaholic," she said. "Thanks" I said, responding as if it were a compliment. I was working on my dissertation and was determined to get it finished in record time. Then my girlfriend asked me a question that stopped me dead in my tracks. "What are you trying to prove and to whom?" With my fingers suspended in mid keystroke, I turned and looked at her. Before I consciously chose my words, or processed what they might mean, I listened to a deeply buried belief escape from my mouth. "I'm trying to prove to my father I am not stupid, and prove to my stepfather I'm not lazy." A completely insane notion, especially considering my stepfather had passed away over thirty years ago.

After listening to those buried subconscious beliefs come to life through my spoken words, I shut off my computer, got a glass of wine and sat down on my favorite chair. I continued to ponder what I had just said. How could I possibly win in this scenario? I wasn't even trying to prove I *was* smart and ambitious - I was trying to prove I *was not* stupid and lazy! In those precious and powerful few moments, I was becoming aware that it was going be *impossible* for me to create success for myself, while still harboring self-judgment and those toxic weeds in the corner of my psyche. This was all made worse because it was combined with an underlying motivation to prove myself to others who weren't even asking for it - and who may never approve of me anyway!

I had a habit, unbeknownst to me, of jumping through invisible hoops for the illusion of a reward from others. All the while never offering rewards of any kind to myself for my accomplishments, just continued self-flagellation. I was so grateful to my friend for asking me such a direct question and for helping me come to terms with my inner conflict. Her question created the opportunity for the answer to be brought up from the recesses of my subconscious realms and into my conscious awareness. Once this belief and habit was revealed, it was then released and healed. I was thrilled to be removing that *huge tenacious weed* from my garden!

It came clearly into focus that day that I was *still* trying to work hard to prove my value and worthiness. By doing so I could convince myself that I deserved love, success and prosperity. Consciously, I knew there was nothing I needed to do, or prove to anyone. However, unconsciously I was on autopilot and still struggling. Now that this buried belief had been ushered out of the shadows and into the light, it helped me boldly claim that I deserved success simply because I existed; simply because I was a child of God. I recalled the message from T. Harv Ekar: "You must acquire the mindset that you can be wealthy without having to prove anything. It is important to adopt the belief "*I AM WORTHY*."

I knew something significant had just happened and I had just made space in my garden to plant and claim what I wanted. I got up, went to the mirror, looked in my eyes and said the very thing I wanted hear, believe and receive: "*YOU ARE WORTHY!* You are worthy of success, you are worthy of making money, you are worthy of love!" I also shared with myself the message I wished I could have heard from both of my fathers: "You are doing good, you are hard worker and you are smart." And most importantly: "*I AM SO PROUD OF YOU TAMMI.*" My eyes stung with tears as I took the deepest breath my lungs could contain. I took a few moments to marinate in this message, receive this truth and allow my newly claimed reality to sink into every crack, crevice and corner of my being.

The very next day, out of the blue, I received a phone call from my father in Norway (it was quite unusual for him to touch base). Dad said he just wanted to call to tell me he was proud of me—something he had never done before. I almost fell off my perch! And even though I *know* the power of this work, and I *know* outer reality is a reflection of inner reality, I am still astonished by the synchronicity, miracles, feedback and support from my father . . . and my Universal Father.

The truest Truth is that

you do not have to prove anything to anyone

(including yourself) to be worthy of

immense prosperity and success!

So just now I invite you to go inside and consider the question: "What do you think you need to prove and to whom? What do you need to *do*, and who do you need to *be* to deserve money, prosperity, success and/or love?" Take some time and allow the answer to bubble up from deep inside of you. Now I invite you to go to a mirror and look into your own eyes. Share the messages and plant the seeds you would like to hear and claim for yourself right now. Perhaps you want to repeat the message a few times, and allow it to sink in deeply so it can really take root. Know this simple process can dissolve limiting content, transform buried beliefs, and change your life radically and powerfully in an instant.

The truest Truth is *YOU ARE GOOD! YOU ARE WONDER-FUL! YOU ARE AMAZING!* And *YOU ARE WORTHY!* You do not have to prove anything to anyone to deserve all you desire. Claim it for yourself, share this with yourself, and then be open to the feedback, messages, support and kindness from the world.

Susan's Story

Another example of observing outer patterns as a reflection of one's inner environment was with my client Susan. Susan told me she was experiencing a pattern of people "nickeling and diming her." Clients were not paying for her services in a timely fashion. They also often attempted to get her to lower her fee after the price had been negotiated and after her services had been rendered. So I posed the question: "How do you nickel and dime yourself?" Susan had to sit with the question for a moment, and then experienced a powerful AHA. She responded by saying: "I nickel and dime myself when I go to a discount store, when I would really rather go to Nordstrom. I nickel and dime myself when I buy the dress that is on sale I really don't like, rather than buying the dress that is not on sale that I love. I nickel and dime myself when I order the less expensive chicken entree when I really want the steak!" This was a powerful revelation indeed.

Susan had a habit and pattern of frugality, which was fine. She did not have to give that up, but I invited her to relax and check in with herself about what really honored her before making a purchase. She had the opportunity to up-level her discernment and find the balance between what she could afford and what really honored her, rather than her old habit and pattern of automatically settling for what was cheapest. I predicted soon she would find life and other people starting to honor her more. Later that week Susan went to Nordstrom and bought a beautiful dress, then she met a friend at a nice restaurant and ordered filet minion. Not surprisingly, Susan found the pattern of people trying to nickel and dime her "miraculously disappeared!" She was shocked, but not surprised, at how people were starting to honor her talent and her services. As a bonus, she started making more money almost immediately.

The Physical Journey Versus the Emotional Journey

Abraham-Hicks talks about taking the physical journey versus the emotional journey. The physical journey is one that entails hard work and taking the action steps, which I think can be a piece of the puzzle, but can be a waste of time and energy until one has taken the emotional journey, which is about getting into a good feeling state. As I sat in front of the computer pushing myself and unconsciously beating myself up, I was taking the physical journey. It is a habit and something I have done a great deal in my life . . . it was what I was taught do. But as I refine what I want, and nurture the garden of my life, my intention now is to do things with greater sweetness, kindness, grace and ease. This happens through being conscious of the emotional journey. This includes releasing resistance and cultivating the qualities of openness, gentleness and receptivity, especially for myself.

As we do this for ourselves we naturally, authentically and easily do it for others. As I have relaxed into this good feeling state, and shared the messages with myself that I want to hear, the world has responded in kind.

Yes, treat others the way you want to be treated,

additionally, treat yourself the way you want to be treated.

Treating yourself the way you want to be treated is a powerful way of tending your inner garden and taking responsibility for the very foundation of your life. As you nurture, care for and are kind to yourself, your life will absolutely shift, transform and improve. If you want roses, don't plant dandelions! Consider what you really want and how you want to be treated. Now plant those seeds and treat yourself that way! If you want to be treated with value; treat yourself with value. If you want to be treated with respect; treat yourself with respect. If you wanted to be treated gently; treat yourself gently. If you want to be appreciated; appreciate yourself. Consider how you want to be treated—now consider how you can treat yourself that way.

Gratitude

Another powerful and important practice that nurtures and sustains a healthy beautiful garden the practice of gratitude. Gratitude is one of the most powerful energies in the universe and every teacher of prosperity affirms the importance of this practice. In the Bible, Paul recommends we make known our requests with praise and thanksgiving. Paul was sharing what he knew about the secret to rise above one's challenges and come into the presence of Spirit.

When we reside in the energy of praise, gratitude, and thanksgiving, we are naturally lifted into the higher realms of joy and peace. The attitude of gratitude keeps our hearts open and minds receptive. This, in turn, provides a channel for God to bless with us incredible gifts, support, guidance and miracles.

A thankful heart is always close

to the creative flow of the Universe,

causing countless blessings to ensue

by the law of cosmic law of action and reaction.

Often people will say something like: "When I get what I want, *then* I will be happy." If you are ready to manifest, you will find it much more effective to be grateful first, then you will be happy and *then* you will attract what you want. Happiness and gratitude are not *outside of you*. They are qualities that reside as seeds of fulfillment, and manifestation, *inside of you*. They are just waiting for you to activate them. How do you do that? I will give you some examples. My friend, Mark, was really on an upward trajectory with the money he was manifesting. I asked him what he was doing differently and he shared his powerful secret—gratitude.

Mark shared with me that he had recently created a "Gratitude Box," a shoebox covered with images, symbols, crystals, and all the things that represented gratitude and prosperity to him. Every bit of money that showed up in his life, he put it in his gratitude box. Then, every Friday afternoon, he would do a "Gratitude Ceremony," a simple ceremony where he would light a candle, acknowledge God, and give heartfelt thanks to the Universe for all the money he manifested. The subconscious mind LOVES ceremony and I KNOW how powerful gratitude is, so it is understandable how effective and powerful this simple practice could be.

Gary, a cab driver, is another wonderful example of shifting into a life of prosperity, gratitude and grace. Gary picked me up and was driving me to the airport. He was so upbeat, cheerful and kind, so I asked him if he liked his job. He said to me: "What's not to like? I get to connect with wonderful people, have great conversations, and I make good money." I told Gary I loved his attitude. Then he told me it was a conscious choice, and not always this way. I asked him what he meant, so he shared his story: "When I first started this job, I hated it. Every day felt like an execution, it was so horrible and painful. The people were awful and more often than not I got stiffed. But then I read about the power of gratitude. I figured I had nothing to lose, so I decided to give gratitude a try for 30 days. Every day before I went to work, I would think about everything I was grateful for. Then, every night, I would do it again. Within one month, I started to genuinely like my job. As a bonus I started meeting some really amazing people and started making a lot more money." Then Gary shared with me his powerful happiness secret: "My 30-day gratitude practice completely transformed every aspect of my life—now I will never stop being grateful!"

Mark and Gary are both living examples of this truth: When you are grateful and appreciative, you tend to get more of what you want in life. Why? Again, it comes back to the Law of Attraction—because we get what we focus on. And when you pay attention to and give thanks for what you are grateful for, you are facing the direction you want to go in your life, not the direction you do not want to go. Prosperity will never be drawn to somebody who is consistently negative or a whiner or complainer. To achieve real prosperity, we must learn to focus on what we have and are grateful for, rather than what we do not have and long for.

When you long for something outside of you and think you need it to be happy, you are vibrating in a frequency of "not enoughness" and lack. This prevents what you want from being naturally attracted to you. When you relax into gratitude for what you have, this creates a powerful energy and a magnetic state of attraction. This invites what you desire to naturally and gracefully be drawn to you. Imaging the energetic difference between being grouchy and greedily grabbing at something you want, versus being open, peaceful, grateful and graciously receiving something you want. Can you feel the difference? The Universe can too.

Cultivating a consistent attitude of gratitude

guarantees we will attract more and more to be grateful for.

Cultivating conscious gratitude is a choice. Practicing gratitude daily can become a natural habit. When we consciously practice being grateful for the people, situations, blessings and resources in our lives, we begin to cultivate better relationships, more positive results, more blessings and greater prosperity. When you complain and bemoan your lot in life, you are facing the direction you do not want to go and spiral downward. Instead, choose to cultivate a daily habit of gratitude, and you will find you attract more positive people, experiences and begin to spiral upward in your life.

Gratitude is one of the highest emotional vibrations available to us, in fact, some spiritual teachers have shared that Universal Energy is really more like gratitude and appreciation than even love. So it could be said when our heart is authentically open, and while we are residing in gratitude, we are aligned with the Creative Source of our physical world reality.

Author Melody Beattie has a powerful and beautiful quote (Gratitude, 2007), "Gratitude unlocks the fullness of life. It turns what we have into enough, and more. It turns denial into acceptance, chaos to order, confusion to clarity. It can turn a meal into a feast, a house into a home, a stranger into a friend. Gratitude makes sense of our past, brings peace for today, and creates a vision for tomorrow."

Gratitude creates a powerful vortex of co-creation and directly aligns you with the Creator of all things.

Gratitude and prosperity may be viewed as interconnected states of being. When your heart is open in gratitude and thanksgiving, it opens the doors to heaven and the floodgates to prosperity. When you are grateful, you are at peace, and vibrating at a very high frequency. This state of being is magnetic, attractive and encourages more prosperity. Residing in gratitude, literally defined as "grace and that which is pleasing" connects and aligns you with the Divine. This, in turn, opens you to otherworldly support, inner guidance, inspired creativity, well-being, peace and ease.

Karen's Attitude of Gratitude

I have worked on my gratitude practice for several years and know it has supported me in many ways. However, I recently witnessed a good friend exemplify gratitude in such an extraordinary way she inspired me to up-level my own appreciation.

My friend Karen is an actress, and was up for a sizable role in a film. I was with her when she received a phone call from her agent. I heard her say: "That is great news!" I assumed she got the part. When she hung up the phone I congratulated her. Then Karen told me that, in fact, she was not booked for the part. I was confused. I did not understand how she could feel grateful after receiving a call I would consider disappointing. So, I asked her why the information was great news. She said she knew if she did not get something she thought she wanted it was God's way of protecting her, keeping her safe, and available for whatever He really *did* want for her. It reminded me of something I once heard Marianne Williamson say: "If a train doesn't stop at your station, it's not your train." I shared this with Karen, she smiled and said "EXACTLY!" Then she proceeded to share an analogy with me. She told me how much she loved her little dog Twinky. She feeds Twinky, cares for him, keeps him warm, safe and dry. And as much as she loves her little dog, she knows God loves her even more.

Karen has such consistent faith and deep trust in a Universe that adores her that she maintains a very relaxed posture and abides in a very consistent state of appreciation and gratitude. I have never witnessed Karen go into a victim state, complain or whine "Why me?" or "Why not me?" Rather than spending time contemplating

"What is *wrong* with this picture" she is immediately looking at "What is *right* with this picture!"

I am astonished at Karen's practice of faith and gratitude exemplified in ways that would defy most people's comprehension. When her little dog Twinky was bitten by a much larger dog, she immediately started praying and focusing on what she was grateful for. She picked up Twinky, and, while they were both still covered in blood, she uttered words of gratitude that he was alive. She rushed her dog to the vet. Twinky had suffered significant internal injuries and Karen was told he may not survive. When I told her she might need to surrender her little doggie to the Universe She said she'd already done that. Then she shared with me that she was so very grateful to have been his caretaker for the last several years.

Twinky was in the ICU for several days. On the fourth day, Karen learned his organs were failing. I really believed Twinky would be an angel before nightfall. I called Karen the following day, astonished to hear that Twinky was not just still hanging in there, but that things seemed to be turning around; he was eating. The following day he was playing with his favorite stuffed hotdog toy. Twinky continued to get stronger and stronger and is now fully recovered. That three pound Chihuahua is a living breathing miracle according to the vet! Did Karen's attitude of faith and gratitude contribute to Twinky's miraculous recovery? Perhaps we will never know. However, I am utterly convinced it did.

Karen experiences challenges and disappointment as we all do, but consciously and consistently directs her attention to what she is grateful for, what she happy about, what is good and what is right in every situation. Therefore, she naturally maintains her open, aligned connection to Source. I constantly witness miracles happening around her. She easily attracts wonderful people and amazing opportunities. She is financially secure and very prosperous on all levels. Karen is a great friend, profound teacher and an amazing example of living gratitude and true prosperity consciousness.

Shutting Doors/Opening Doors

You have probably heard the saying, "when one door shuts another door opens." But we often spend so much time staring at the closed door, we do not see all the doors around us opening. I know I have personally spent years sitting in front of a shut door, woefully and longingly staring at it. As I did this, I would ask questions like: "Why am I not worthy? Why doesn't God like me? Why do other people get what they want but I can't have what I want? What is *wrong* with me?" And one of my most frequently used phrases during my whine fests: "IT'S NOT FAIR!" I would mope, brew and stew in the low vibration of victim consciousness. It took me quite some time to figure out how to do things differently and from a more empowered posture.

A teacher once told me "No matter *WHAT* is happening in your life, it is for your highest good." When I first heard this I found it hard to believe. How could it be for my highest good to have a friend die from cancer, or from suicide, or for me to lose my job, have a car accident or for my fiancé to leave me? However, I now know this statement to be a profound truth. There are soul lessons in *everything* we experience, and we are created, loved and adored by a benevolent God.

Those experiences, relationships and obstacles that no matter how you try to look at them are "not good" can support you in honing skills that can help you be of service to others one day. Resolving challenges and growing beyond suffering is how we cultivate compassion, expand in our consciousness, learn significant life lessons and evolve spiritually.

Now when something happens that is "bad," or is confusing or painful, I immediately surrender it to Spirit and ask my soul what it is trying to learn. Powerful information floods into my consciousness. Then I ask for any "open doors" to reveal themselves—and amazingly they do. People sometimes ask me how I manifest so quickly and I know this is an important part of the prosperity process. Our pain and our "stuckness" comes from our resistance. My intention is to keep my mind and heart open and go with the flow of life rather than fight against the tide.

Self-Pity Versus Self-Compassion

There is an enormous difference between self-pity and self-compassion. If you have ever indulged in a pity party, you know how unpleasant and painful it can be. You become entrenched in the energy-depleting emotion of fear, while residing in the low vibration of victim consciousness. Self-pity comes from buying into the belief that you are small and powerless. When you are "in pity," you are not taking responsibility for the experiences in your life, but rather pointing to outer circumstances as the source of your disempowerment and problems.

The pain from pity comes not only from feeling sorry for yourself, but also because your heart is closed to the love and wisdom that is within you and all around you. It is impossible to manifest your dreams or step into authentic power from the position and stance of self-pity. Energetically pity is closed and tight. It also represents unprocessed pain.

Self-compassion, on the other hand, is a very different energy. It allows you to feel open and vulnerable; allowing the process and experience of your feelings to move through you unobstructed. It includes the capacity to extend kindness, love and empathy to yourself, acknowledging that sometimes this human experience hurts. The energy of self-compassion comes from maintaining your connection to Source, and flying in the higher realms of love and connection. Cultivating compassion for yourself is an empowered perspective that can support you by taking time out for self care and nurturance, all the while getting ready to stand up, take responsibility, and continue to move forward on your path.

When you consciously choose to be kind, compassionate

and gentle with yourself, your heart is open to love,

wisdom, assistance from others and the support of Spirit.

If you decide you would prefer self-compassion rather than self-pity, sharing some of the following messages with yourself, your inner child, or the part inside of you that is hurting, can be very helpful, deeply healing and incredibly powerful:

- I know this is very hard, and I'm here for you. You are not alone.
- The challenges of life can be very confusing and painful. I'm so sorry you have to go through this. I love you and everything is going to be okay.
- I know you are hurting right now, just know this situation has nothing to do with you being bad, not good enough or not being loved.
- Life sometimes hurts. You are not being punished. You are deeply loved and unconditionally adored.
- It is okay to let your tears flow. Let's invite our guardian angel's wings to embrace us, and/or allow God to comfort us right now.

If you are in self-pity, you have abandoned yourself. If you are in self-compassion, you are keeping your heart open to yourself, to others and to Source. An additional bonus of cultivating compassion is the capacity to authentically extend empathy and compassion to another.

It is also important to know that your life's purpose can be hinted at, or revealed by virtue of the hurts you have endured and the challenges you have overcome. Loss and heartache can support us in being the most effective kind of healer there is; the "wounded healer." No one can support someone struggling in the throes of addiction more than a recovered addict; no one will have the care and compassion for someone dealing with cancer than a cancer survivor; no one will have the same level of understanding for someone being abused than someone who has lived through the anguish of abuse but has since become empowered; no one can help another process the heartbreak and agony of suicide like someone who has lived through that kind of loss. When we know this, understand it, and take the empowered orientation to learn from life, we don't spend as much time feeling sorry for ourselves and living in pity. Consciously choosing self-compassion energetically keeps the door open so we can attract support from other people, as well as synchronicity, divine guidance and divine prosperity.

To quote one of my wonderful teachers "Use everything that happens in your life for your learning, upliftment and growth." That means *everything*, even (and maybe *especially),* the tough, challenging, painful and confusing times. Allow these experiences to teach you and help you expand, rather than constrict you and shut you down.

Goal Setting

Another important aspect of tending the garden of prosperity is setting long term and short term goals. When we consciously contemplate and set goals for ourselves, it helps us claim an ideal future. It can also help us get really clear about what we want and the action steps that need to be taken to move in the direction of our ideal future.

Focused intention combined with goals and action steps

is how we can effectively manifest prosperity,

success and our divine purpose.

A set of specific goals is much easier to achieve than a vague end result such as "I want more money." Cultivating intentions, combined with small do-able, clearly identified action steps, is how we ultimately achieve success. It is also important to remember to celebrate those small accomplishments and small steps, knowing that is how we will eventually achieve our bigger-picture end result.

Consider what would you like to accomplish in your lifetime. Now work backwards, what about in 10 years? 5 years? 1 year? 6 months? Now ask which small goals and little steps you can take now to support you in reaching your bigger dreams. Sometimes contemplating the big goals can be so overwhelming we become paralyzed and give up before we even get started. When we break things down into bite-sized pieces we can start to have more fun with the process.

Have you seen a Ring Toss game at a carnival? Imagine holding a ring in your hand with the intention of hooking it around the dowel. The further away you stand from the dowel, the more challenging it is to achieve that goal. Often, with a really big goal, it is like standing far away from the dowel, hoping and praying you will get the ring around it— and it usually doesn't work. Not only is this frustrating, after a few misses it can undermine your confidence. Now imagine walking up closer to the dowel, in fact, imagine being arm's length from it. Now imaging dropping your ring around the dowel, isn't that easier? You can easily and effortlessly achieve the goal of getting the dowel around the ring each and every time. Creating goals can be like playing ring toss. Create small attainable goals and get closer to the dowel. Not only is this a way of creating consistent success, it creates positive momentum and cultivates confidence.

When I "got" that I needed to write my first book, I was so overwhelmed I did nothing for quite a while. Then, as I sat with my anxiety, I finally realized I could start the process by breaking things down into smaller steps so I could move closer to the dowel. I decided to first identify the sections of the book; then the chapters. After that I focused on one chapter at a time. My goal became to play an easy game of ring toss and write for two hours a day. Once I identified the goal, broke it down into smaller pieces, and got closer with my rings, the process of reaching my big goals no longer freaked me out. I started to feel more motivated, excited and optimistic. I started writing lists at night identifying the things I wanted to accomplish the next day. As I crossed my little goals off the list throughout the day, I would acknowledge myself, and add new goals to the list. I started to enjoy the momentum. I also started to witness and acknowledge the journey towards my desired destination.

Some areas to consider in the arena of goal setting may include:

Career or Life Purpose: What level do you want to reach in your career, or what do you want to achieve by the end of your life?

Education: Is there any education you want to acquire or classes you need to take to support you with your other goals? What information and skills will you need to have in order to achieve these other goals?

Creative: Can you identify any goals regarding writing, art, music, or sharing your gifts by creating a website, a blog or manifesting your creativity in some other way?

Attitude: As you monitor your thoughts, attitude and actions, do you find any part of your mindset, beliefs or behavior that is holding you back? (If so, create a goal or set an intention to improve your behavior or change your beliefs or to find solutions to the problems.)

Service: Do you want to make the world a better place? If so, what does that look like and how can you do it?

It can also be very powerful and helpful to connect with an "Accountability Partner," a friend you can chat with once a week to go over your goals and the action steps you have taken to cross those goals off your list.

Michael's Goals

I worked with a client name Michael. He wanted to move away from his job as a salesperson at a gym and do something "more meaningful." After some soul-searching and meditating, he came to the conclusion that the word meaningful, for him, meant supporting people in attaining physical, mental, emotional and spiritual fitness. I asked Michael to write down his lifetime goals. This is what he claimed for himself:

Career/Life Purpose: To support others in manifesting a healthy body, mind and spirit. To feel fulfilled and to be of service

Financial: To make a six-figure income per year, and to feel prosperous, fulfilled and free.

Education: Complete my education and become certified as a life coach and trainer.

Creative: To create a logo, flyer, brochure, blog and website describing the services I offer as well as helpful tools, tips and techniques.

Attitude: To be positive, optimistic and excited about my life and my new career as it continues to form, evolve and come into being

Physical: To be optimally healthy physically, mentally, emotionally and spiritually so I am the living example of my fitness philosophies and practice.

Once Michael listed his lifetime goals, I had him break down his goals on a timeline.

Five-year goal: Have a thriving coaching and fitness program making $100,000 a year.

One-year goal: My certification program and education is complete. I am ready to take clients, my website is ready, I am able to participate in interviews and speaking engagements.

Six-month goal: Create a website, blog, flyers, brochures and newsletter about fitness.

One-month goal: Be enrolled for my certification program.

One-week goal: Research certification programs.

As you can see from this example, breaking big goals down into smaller, more manageable goals makes it far easier to see how the bigger picture can come into being. Together Michael and I worked as a team and broke down his goals. Through this process I witnessed him go from being utterly overwhelmed and paralyzed, to excitement, taking small action steps and movement. Together each week we would create his "homework" for that week, then he would diligently chip away at it. He used me as his coach and accountability partner, but, after the first 2 months, he was adding his own goals and marking them off the list. He no longer needed me to support and encourage him. Michael cultivated and established great goal habits. His confidence had grown and taken root and his follow-through became impeccable—he was off to the races! Michael continued to hit his goals and now has a fulfilling and lucrative career as a "Fit for Life Coach."

Visualization

Another great way to create and tend your garden is through the practice of visualization. I know in the past I would use my imagination in counterproductive ways. I would recall past relationships that had not gone well, contemplate missed opportunities and bemoan my unfair lot in life—then would I wonder why my life was not working. To quote a wonderful teacher: "It is silly not to win in your own fantasies!"

I decided to create a new habit, and rather than focus on the negative, I decided to focus on the positive. I started imagining and visualizing my future in more enjoyable, positive and productive ways: I imagined a great relationship and what a true heart connection would feel like; I imagined easily maintaining my optimal weight and enjoying vibrant health; I imagined creative pursuits, work I enjoyed and being well-compensated for it.

Athletes often use the process of imagining and visualizing to enhance their performance. The subconscious mind does not differentiate between actual experiences and imagined ones, so often the best way to go someplace in our lives is to fully create and experience the desired reality in our imagination and in our inner world.

One way we can do this is by creating an "Ideal Scene." An Ideal Scene is a way we can identify, in detail, the things we want to manifest. One way I like to create an Ideal Scene is to get a piece of blank paper and put a symbol in the middle of it. It can be a circle, a diamond, a heart, an image from a magazine, or anything else that calls to you. This symbol represents you centered in your authentic power. Next draw spokes or lines emanating from the symbol. On those lines write down and claim some of the details you want to attract, manifest and/or experience. For example, some of Michael's spokes on one of his ideal scenes said:

- I am creating an informative brochure
- I am creating an educational and attractive website
- I am completing my certification in fitness
- I am naturally and easily attracting the right clients for me
- I am teaching Fit for Life classes
- I am gracefully and easily supporting and empowering my clients
- I am being asked to do radio interviews and speaking engagements

- I am gracefully and easily manifesting $2,500 a week doing
  what I love
- I am writing helpful, information-filled monthly blogs and
  magazine articles
- I am vibrantly physically healthy
- I am productive, profitable and fulfilled
- I am of great service doing what I enjoy
- I am mentally sharp
- I am emotionally stable, in my equanimity, joyful, centered
  and peaceful.
- I am spiritually aligned
- I am experiencing synchronicity, miracles and Divine support

After you have completed your own ideal scene, allow yourself
to feel it and see it in your mind's eye. Imagine living from this place
in as much detail as you can: see, feel, smell, hear and experience
all you have claimed as a living vision. By getting into the feeling
state, you are taking the emotional journey. This will support you in
further identifying and claiming your goals as well as strengthening
your ability to manifest them. Know you can continue to revise,
refine and recreate your ideal scene as often as you would like.

Prosperity, Happiness, Fulfillment, Success!

Another fun class I sometimes offer is simply repeating the words
"prosperity, happiness, fulfillment, success." As images and scenes
come forward, I invite my students to write a living vision about
what they see, sense, experience and feel. A few months after partici-

pating in this exercise, one of my students shared what came forward for her with this exercise: "I saw myself dressed beautifully and going to the airport. I got on a plane, sat down in first class and was flying to New York City. When I landed, I was met by a limo driver with my name on a sign, chauffeured to a lovely hotel and later enjoyed a wonderful restaurant and a Broadway play. I didn't tell anyone about my vision because I thought it might seem silly. Well, a couple weeks later I found out my boyfriend had planned a trip to New York for us; first class, with fine dining and a Broadway play! The experience was so surreal and so similar to my visualization, I was stunned by the uncanny synchronicity of it all! I am now using this technique and having great fun with it, because I know it works!"

Visualization brings order to one's mind and the Universe.

The use of vivid imagination invites

and allows this order to be expressed.

"There is nothing unusual or mysterious in the idea of your pictured desire coming into material evidence. It is the working of a Universal Law. Everything in the whole world, from the hat on your head to the boots on your feet, has its beginning in mind and comes into existence in exactly the same manner. All are projected thoughts solidified." (*Your Invisible Power*, 1921)

If you tell your subconscious what you want in positive, clear terms, this is a mental reality. As you explore and allow yourself to experience what you want to feel this is an emotional reality.

Now visualize what you want to be doing and seeing, this is the physical reality. If you spend time in your inner world vividly experiencing all three of these realties, you are powerful affecting your outer reality and are taking responsibility for consciously co-creating your life.

Bill Gates's Big Vision

Bill Gates effectively used the power of intention, goal setting and visioning to create Microsoft, the largest software maker and one of the world's most valuable companies. Back when computers filled entire rooms and were so expensive only corporations and the military could afford them, Gates had an enormous, powerful, clear vision that one day almost everybody would have their own personal computer. When his little software company began to expand and gain momentum, he confessed to a fellow programmer his two large goals: "To design software that would make a computer easy enough for my mother to use and to build a company bigger than my dad's law firm." His journey was often tumultuous, and there were many obstacles to overcome, but he maintained his vision and eventually manifested his intentions. Bill Gates' inner vision years ago has now become an outer reality with his software powering 90 percent of the world's personal computers.

What really set Gates apart on the path to prosperity was the boldness and clarity of his vision: "A computer on every desk and Microsoft software in every computer." Now Bill Gates and his wife Melinda are using that same power of visioning and intention in their philanthropic endeavors, to be of service to others and help heal the world. In a letter on their website www.gatesfoundation.org, the Gates's shared this:

> *"Our friend and co-trustee Warren Buffett once gave us some great advice about philanthropy: "Don't just go for safe projects," he said. "Take on the really tough problems." We couldn't agree more. Our foundation is teaming up with partners around the world to take on some tough problems: extreme poverty and poor health in developing countries, the failures of America's education system. We focus on only a few issues because we think that's the best way to have great impact, and we focus on these issues in particular because we think they are the biggest barriers that prevent people from making the most of their lives.*
>
> *For each issue we work on, we fund innovative ideas that could help remove these barriers: new techniques to help farmers in developing countries grow more food and earn more money; new tools to prevent and treat deadly diseases; new methods to help students and teachers in the classroom. Some of the projects we fund will fail. We not only accept that, we expect it— because we think an essential role of philanthropy is to make bets on promising solutions that governments and businesses can't afford to make. As we learn which bets pay off, we have to adjust our strategies and share the results so everyone can benefit.*

We're both optimists. We believe by doing these things—focusing on a few big goals and working with our partners on innovative solutions—we can help every person get the chance to live a healthy, productive life."

What a wonderful, positive and powerful message they are envisioning for themselves and sharing with the world! Bill and Melinda embody and exemplify many prosperity principles: imagination, service, preference vs. attachment, balance, persistence, diligence, confidence, big thinking and generosity—all important ingredients and aspects of authentic prosperity consciousness.

Exercise #1: How Do You Want To Be Treated?

1. Consider a pattern in your life that you would like to shift, transform or heal. Are you treated in an unpleasant way by others? Do you often feel unappreciated or disrespected? Do you feel life is stingy with you? Can you pinpoint a behavior, pattern or experience you would like to be different?

2. As you identify and observe this pattern, ask yourself: "How do I *treat myself* this way?"

3. Take some time to process this information. Write down any revelations and allow any emotions that start to come up to fully express.

4. Now consider what you would prefer instead. What would

you like more of? How do you want others to treat you? How would you like life to show up for you?

5. Consider how can you take responsibility for treating yourself that way now. How can you treat yourself the way you want others and the world to treat you? What are some action steps you can take or messages you can share with yourself to change your internal climate and relationship with yourself?

6. Remember outer reality is a reflection of inner reality, so keep your eyes and ears open for immediate feedback from the Universe that an important shift and significant healing is underway.

Exercise #2: Gratitude

1. Take a moment and go inward and consider five things you are grateful for *right now*. It could be as simple as a stranger smiling at you today, the joy of having your family around you or that someone held the door open for you this morning. It can be your home, your friends, your car, that you are safe and warm, that there is enough food in your refrigerator or that you have good health. Nothing is too large or too small to be grateful for.

2. Commit to your gratitude practice! Every evening before you go to bed claim at least 5 to 10 things (and more if you are on a roll!) that you are grateful for and write them down in your journal. Cultivating a habit of gratitude can support

you in programming your subconscious mind, ensure great dreams and assist you in miraculous unexpected ways in the days and weeks to come. It can be fun and very rewarding to watch this list grow as you pay attention to it. To up the ante in your gratitude practice you may also want to start your day contemplating and claiming what you are grateful for. This can set the tone for the day. Before you know it your outdated, blurry and cloudy prescription lenses will turn into clean, clear, rose-colored glasses. And not only will your glass start to look half full rather than half empty, it will start looking ¾ full, 7/8 full and eventually your cup "shall runneth over!" Expand your attitude of gratitude and prepare to attract and graciously receive your prosperity!

3. Consider the challenging things in your life, the circumstances and relationships that have been hard or painful. Can you open your mind and find anything to be grateful for? Ask yourself: "What was (or is) my soul trying to learn from these situations?" Listen to the still small voice and the wisdom that bubbles up from within.

4. Thank God and the Universe for all the miracles, blessings and prosperity that is on the way to you now. Appreciation in advance keeps the doors open and energy flowing in the direction of positive attraction and prosperity. Imagine all the things you desire one by one, place them in a pink bubble of gratitude, then send it off to the heavens and into God's hands. Know that you will receive your gifts and all that is yours by Divine Right in the perfect time and in the perfect way.

Exercise #3: Goal Setting

It is important to set your goals on a number of levels:

1. First you create the "big picture." What would you like to accomplish in your lifetime? Those goals can include, but not be limited to: Career; Relationships; Finances; Education; Creativity; Attitude; Service.

2. Break the big picture down into the smaller and smaller goals. Where are you and what are you doing in ten years?

3. What about five years?

4. What would you like to accomplish by the end of this year?

5. What would you like to do in 6 months?

6. What can you do this week?

7. What are some small action steps you can take tomorrow? What about today? What about NOW?

It has been proven the greatest predictor for success is WRITING THINGS DOWN! Create your lists, write your goals and intentions down and mark things off when you achieve them. When you achieve your goals, even the very small ones, it is important to take the time to acknowledge yourself, be proud of yourself and enjoy the satisfaction of what you have accomplished. Enjoy the process and absorb the implications of your goal achievement. Also take the time to observe and acknowledge the progress you are making on your journey towards your larger goals. If the goal was a significant one, reward yourself appropriately. All of this helps you create a solid foundation for prosperity, supports you in cultivating momentum in the "right direction" and assists you in establishing the self-confidence and self-esteem that will serve you for the rest of your life.

For additional support, consider connecting with a friend who wants to grow and expand in the direction of their dreams as well. Find an "Accountability Partner" so you can both cheerlead for one another. Lift each other up, give one another feedback and hold each other's feet to the fire if need be. Set up weekly appointments to review your lists, acknowledge the goals that have been achieved, as well as contemplate any additional short term and/or long term goals that can be added.

Exercise #4: Create an Ideal Prosperity Scene

Get a blank piece of paper and put a symbol in the center of it. This symbol can be a circle, a butterfly, a heart, a diamond or anything else that represents you in your authentically empowered state. Then, draw spokes or lines emanating out from this symbol. On these spokes write down the all the qualities, experiences and/or goals you want to manifest in your life. Somewhere on this ideal scene write "This or something better for the highest good of all concerned." After you are complete, imagine this ideal scene in as much detail as you can. Have fun with it, and be open to new thoughts and inspired ideas. You can recreate, revise or update your ideal scene as often as you would like.

Exercise #5: Visualization

Consider these words: "prosperity, happiness, fulfillment, success!" Repeat them in your mind several times then allow it to express through your imagination. Allow yourself the feeling experience of embodying those qualities as the inner scene emerges. Let it unfold in great detail in your mind's eye and be open to things that you have not consciously considered before, including unexpected scenarios and amazing adventures. Have fun with the process and then write down what comes forward as a living vision.

You have more power than you think and you are more precious than you know. When you take responsibility for tending the garden of your life by treating yourself the way you want to be treated; cultivating conscious gratitude; practicing self-compassion; creating (and following through with) long-term and short-term goals; and by identifying and visualizing your empowered ideal future, you are doing the work necessary to plant the seeds for what you want to grow in your garden for your fabulous future! These practices and exercises will support you in cultivating and manifesting the empowered, prosperous life you really want and deserve. If you DO NOT take responsibility in these areas, you give away your power and create your life by default. This is when you will energetically be swept along on the wave of mass consciousness, which, unfortunately, is primarily fear-based. If more people were willing to take personal responsibility, there would be more prosperity. There is an abundance of money and opportunity in the world, and by taking personal responsibility you can attract and manifest more of it for yourself.

Take a hold of the reigns, take responsibility, say yes to your power. Commit yourself and DO THE WORK. Beautiful gardens do not just happen, and prosperity consciousness is not an accident. You CAN have what you want, you CAN manifest the life of your dreams, but it won't happen if you do not take the time, assume responsibility and expend the energy. The process does not have to be hard, torturous or arduous, it can be filled with grace, ease, joy and fun. Make friends with this journey and keep setting your intentions. I assure you the rewards for this work will be glorious and the harvest from the garden of your life will be abundant!

PART THREE

Getting Real With Money

Chapter 9

Your Relationship with Money

Master money so it doesn't master you.

How is your relationship with Money? Often people find this concept to be revelatory, but our relationship with money is, in fact, a literal relationship—and for many it can be a confusing, fear-based, co-dependant and unhealthy one. As I mentioned earlier, money is not prosperity, but money *is* an aspect of prosperity. We all have an inner relationship with money and an outer relationship with it. If you want more money in your life, it is important to take responsibility for both of these realities.

So what is money? What does money mean to you? What do you think you need to do to deserve money? When I first consciously considered these questions, I was surprised at what bubbled up. Deep down I thought I had to suffer and struggle to deserve money. I believed money was a double-edged sword, the root of evil; a way to manipulate people and have power over others. On some level I did not want to participate in these realities, but I did want to pay my bills. So eventually I realized I needed to change my beliefs, feelings, attitude and relationship with "the almighty dollar." I knew it was time to open my mind and take responsibility for getting congruent in thought, action and deed around my dysfunctional dynamic with cash. It was time to heal my love-hate relationship with money.

Over the centuries people have killed and died for money. Many have made it their savior and their god. However, this is a fear-based reality and rarely works out well. If someone is willing to go out of integrity to "get" money, it is because they are buying into a Universe of scarcity and unworthiness. Their very existence is built on the fractured foundation of fear. If one understands the Truth, that the Universe is unlimited, and if they know their importance and value, money can become a good friend, an ally and something easily attracted.

Money is energy, a tool and medium of exchange. To quote my good friend, author and teacher Bob Burnham: "Money is a thought backed by confidence."

If you are confident and balanced in your inner world,

your outer world and your financial life will reflect it.

Money in and of itself cannot buy happiness, that has to come from having a love- based relationship with yourself and from doing your inner work. But having more money *can* support you in doing, being and having more in your life. Something I have found fairly consistently: having more money allows people to be more of who they are. If they are generous and kind by nature, they become more kind and generous. If they are egotistical and arrogant, they become more so. So, who are you? And are you ready to be, do and have more?

People who struggle financially believe there is a scarcity of cash. In truth, money is everywhere. The amount floating around in the world is staggering and beyond most people's comprehension. One way we attract and receive more of it is to be positive, responsible, appreciative and respectful of money.

A common quality of the super rich

is that they truly respect,

appreciate, enjoy and love money.

If you want, you can cultivate these qualities as well!

A vital step to attract more money in your life is to acknowledge that you are 100% responsible for the amount of money you manifest—or do not manifest. Until you do, you are in a victim stance and nothing can change. What you attract is created by your thoughts, feelings and good and/or bad habits. I will share some tips about how turn the steering wheel in the direction of financial responsibility, and cultivate positive, healthy money habits.

Getting Real with Money

Getting real with money entails keeping track of what you earn spend, save, invest and pay in interest. Perhaps this seems scary or overwhelming, but if you want to manifest more money, it is vital to confront the "realness" of it. This is a way you can heal fear, get out of debt and release any judgment you may have for making "past mistakes" with your finances. This will also support you to make better choices in the future. There is not one person alive who does not feel they have made a mistake with money at one time or another. It can be so powerful to consciously forgive any mistakes you think you have made, learn from them and claim that there is a lot more where that came from!

What we put our attention on grows, and attention to your budget can support you in feeling more grounded, more aware of prosperity principles at work in your life, and more confident of yourself as you deal with money in the world. Dealing with the actual numbers can make you feel that money is a game and help you lighten up about it. Another advantage to paying attention to the concrete data of "what comes in" and "what goes out" is that you need to know these numbers to figure out how much more you need to earn. In other words, you need to know where you are, in order to get where you want to go. You want to be clear, centered, calm and focused on the additional amount you need to manifest each month.

Dealing with money can be tricky, and it is a rare day we don't deal with it. So it is important to be aware of the energy you're emitting emotionally when dealing with money, while making a purchase or paying your bills. Don't beat yourself up if you have some conflicting and confusing emotions around this loaded topic when you are face to face with bills, bank statements and spreadsheets!

Many people feel "negative emotions" while paying their bills. Consider how you feel as you write out a check to pay your taxes, make a car payment, house payment, water or heating bill. If your emotions are not positive, think about how many people in the world are without these blessings. Additionally, remember that a bill represents that you have been trusted in advance for a product or service. If you really think about this, it is a really big deal! Claiming and residing in gratitude while paying your bills or buying anything energetically keeps you open and in a space to attract more abundance.

Pay attention to the energy in your body while considering making a purchase. For example, if you're in debt and saying, "Oh what the heck, I'll just buy this," when you see a shiny object, or you've got a knot in the pit of your stomach when you push a "buy" button on Amazon, it's probably not a good idea to purchase these items. The same holds true for situations where you're resentful of spending the money or feeling pressured by a salesperson. Check in with yourself, take responsibility and set the strong intention to make mature, healthy and positive purchasing decisions.

The issue of whether to buy or not also comes up when people consider investing in themselves, their ideas or a new business. There may come a time when you want to learn, expand or grow by taking a seminar, hiring a business coach or earning a degree. This can entail spending a large amount of money and making a big commitment. It may be out of your budget and you may have to take out a loan, but it also might enhance your earning power relatively quickly and could be worth it if it shaves years off your big goals.

When I decided I wanted to go back to school for my masters in Spiritual Psychology, I felt dizzy as I contemplated the large numbers I would need for tuition. But something in my heart strongly prompted me to sign on the dotted line. Two days after taking that leap of faith, a large amount of money came to me that covered my tuition for the next two years. It was a situation where I chose to listen to my heart over my head. Today my career is built on the foundation of that education.

When contemplating bigger purchases like education or investing in yourself, trust your instincts and listen to your inner voice. Meditate, listen to the still small voice within and/or ask for signs or answers in your dreams. You may want to hold your choices and decisions close to your vest and until you're clear within yourself. Others may attempt to talk you out of something that may enhance your future and be in alignment with your larger life purpose. It may bring fear up as you stand on the precipice of expanding, because it is outside of your comfort zone and the ego likes to keep us safe. Be prepared to feel a mixture of emotions. But if and when you do put the money down and feel excited, expansive, optimistic or relieved, that's a signal that you did the right thing.

Financial Responsibility

One important way we can begin to take greater financial responsibility is to set the intention to become good friends with money. Like any good relationship, this includes the important qualities of respect, honesty, admiration, gratitude and responsibility. Responsibility can also be defined as accountability, reliability and dependability. Another way to describe the act of responsibility is simply the "ability to respond."

There is often a negative connotation associated with the word responsibility. It can be confused with such things as obligation, requirement or duty. Some may sense heaviness or negativity around these words. The word "should" also seems to come up a lot when it comes to financial responsibility. For example "I *should* pay my bills, I *should* live within my means, I *should* create a budget."

I love something I heard Louise Hay once say: "Stop shoulding on yourself!" When you tell yourself you *should* do something, you are in essence shaming yourself. By saying you should do something you are saying you are bad or wrong: You are wrong for not doing what you say you *should* be doing! It is a sneaky and covert way we disempower ourselves, stay limited and keep ourselves playing small. Using the word "should" is a way we unconsciously create resentment. Nobody likes to be told they *should* do anything . . . even if it is us telling ourselves! It is also a way we energetically buy into the notion that we are not free. Why? Because it is based on a belief there is no choice.

One of the most powerful and effective ways to manifest a happy, empowered, financially rewarding and prosperous life is through knowing we ALWAYS have a choice!

Part of my process in taking greater financial responsibility included choosing to consciously contemplate what I was shoulding on myself about:

- I *should* live within my means
- I *should* take responsibility and spend less money than I make
- I *should* clip coupons
- I *should* create a budget.
- I *should* not have a Starbucks cappuccino every day!

Then I changed my shoulds to coulds.

- I *could* choose to live within my means
- I *could* take responsibility to spend less than I make
- I *could* have fun with coupons
- I *could* create a budget
- I *could* give up my daily Starbuck cappuccino habit

Once I completed this simple process, I immediately felt better. Now, take a moment to consider some of your "shoulds." What are some of the things you think you *should* be doing in order to be more financially responsible? Now take your shoulds and make them coulds.

How do you feel when you replace should with could? Doesn't it feel a lot different? Much lighter? Doesn't it feel more inviting and joyful? For me it also created a greater possibility for action as I considered I *could* create a budget, rather than I *should* create a budget. The word *could* is invitational and suggests freedom as well as the opportunity to make positive, healthy and empowered choices.

On the surface this might appear to be a simple exercise, and it is, but it is also another way to release self-criticism and negative self-talk and move in a more positive and prosperous direction.

Rather than barking orders by using the word "should,"

the word "could" gives us the opportunity

and permission to succeed.

It feels much better to know we can say

yes to the invitation and stay open to possibilities.

Implementing "coulds" around creating budgets and increasing financial responsibility does not have to be hard or unpleasant, it can actually be fun and empowering. Just make the conscious decision that it *could* be, *can* be and *WILL* be! This small step invites natural, graceful and positive movement and helps you to energetically pivot in the direction of your authentic power and your dreams.

Freedom

If someone has a habit of overspending and is out of balance with their finances, it is an indication they are also internally out of balance. If you are financially overextended, a question to consider is: "How am I internally overextended or in a state of lack?" Also: "Why do I buy what I buy?" Are you spending on needs or wants? And if you are purchasing too many wants, are you looking for something outside of you to fill up something that is missing inside of you? Are you looking for something material to validate you, distract you or temporarily make you feel better?

What feels *really good* is being responsible, respectful, on solid internal ground and in integrity with yourself—and this includes spending habits. When I ask people why they want money and what it represents to them, it usually boils down to one of three things; power, respect and freedom. However, the qualities of authentic power, genuine respect and true freedom have nothing to do with anything outside of us. They are inner experiences and something that is available to anyone at anytime.

Life is full of circumstances where choices are seemingly limited, and few options can be found. But even in situations that seem out of your hands, you still hold the key to true freedom because you are never left without choice. Even if that choice is how to choose to *feel* about something.

After the dissolution of my relationship with my wealthy fiancé, I plummeted into an experience of financial fear and poverty. I admit I was very afraid, but I finally chose to change my mind. Yes, I had to tighten up my belt . . . a lot. Yes, I had to change my lifestyle significantly. However, I eventually decided to consciously claim that this reality was temporary; it was only for a limited period of time. You have probably heard the saying: "What you resist persists." I finally realized being upset about my situation was not going to change it. I stopped resisting my circumstances and made peace with what was present.

I decided to explore what it meant to feel internally free. I chose to love and respect myself through this process. I relaxed into a state of connection with the Universe and the experience of authentic power. Once I relaxed and surrendered my resistance and moved into acceptance, I made a few more decisions. I decided to have fun clipping coupons. I decided to plan all my meals for an entire week and buy all of my groceries on my tiny budget. I chose to make it like a sport to see how little I could spend each week.

Once I made the conscious decision that my financial plight was temporary, I realized I could relax and have more fun with it. This helped me to feel more empowered and even a little amused. I relaxed into a liberating sense of inner freedom. And though I had less money than I wanted, I set my intentions to eventually manifest greater prosperity. Then I visualized what I wanted, and got into the feeling state of what it was going to be like when I could easily purchase those fabulous boots, or that shiny black convertible. I was just careful not to put the cart in front of the horse, and chose to happily, respectfully and patiently live within my means, while planting the seeds for my prosperous future.

The first step in experiencing power, respect and freedom is to start responding to life's situations in ways that are optimistic, empowered and congruent with what you want. I knew I wanted to eventually have immense prosperity again one day, and so I started being more consistent in my thoughts, actions and deeds. I decided my lack of money was not a life sentence . . . I started looking at it as a temporary adventure. Rather than feeling bleak, mad, discouraged or like a victim, I decided to feel curious, entertained and amused. I started to ask what my soul was trying to learn through this challenging experience. What I got was "personal responsibility" and "getting on solid ground within myself."

When you stop resisting what is present,

is when the circumstances of your outer life

can began to shift.

Once I processed and released my anger about my limited finances and the current situation, life began to show up differently for me. I have no doubt choosing to change my mind and feelings around money (or the lack of it) started to turn the tide in the direction I wanted to go, and laid the groundwork to manifest what I really wanted—more money and greater prosperity!

I recently witnessed one of my great teachers, my husband Steve, teaching responsibility to his kids. As he slowly gave them more freedom, they took a little more responsibility, so in turn he gave them more freedom. As they continued to take more and more responsibility, the leash got longer, a little at a time, and the rewards became greater. I think Spirit does this for us as well. Spirit is like a good parent—in fact, God is the BEST parent we could ever imagine. He is not going to give us more than we can handle, and no matter what, we are completely and unconditionally adored.

As we take greater responsibility, we naturally cultivate

a sense of confidence, pride, self-respect and self-esteem.

And our outer reality will always reflect this back to us in

positive, powerful and prosperous ways.

Creating a Budget!

Here is another great quote from Calvin Coolidge: "There is no dignity quite so impressive, and no one independence quite so important, as living within your means." This can support you in finding solid ground within yourself and from there you will likely find your means beginning to expand. This quote brings to mind something a wise friend said to me: "If you watch your pennies, you won't have to worry about your dollars." This advice is the essence of financial responsibility. It means if you care enough about the change in your pocket, then the paper in your wallet will take care of itself. If you take good care of the small things, they will grow, expand and evolve into bigger things, creating a stable foundation on which to build a solid structure. As you are fiscally responsible, you will find it natural and easy to attract and create more money and greater prosperity.

Living within your means simply means creating a workable budget. Creating a budget may not sound like the most fun thing in the world to do, but it will help put you on solid ground financially and help you keep your finances in order. A budget is a guideline to help you spend your money responsibly and wisely. A budget allows you to see what is coming in every week, and what is going out; bills, personal necessities, leisure, tithing, saving and/ or investments. A budget is a comprehensive plan for how to spend your money, which can help you stay on track.

The basic premise of creating a workable budget is making sure that income matches obligation. It is a very simple formula; your income should cover your expenses. And if you do not have it, do not spend it. Creating a budget generally requires four basic steps:

1. Determine how much money you are making right now.

2. Identify how you are spending money and your current spending habits.

3. Total your income and expenses.

4. Track and review your habits every month and make sure you stay within those guidelines.

I go over these four steps in more detail in the exercise portion of this chapter. To give yourself the greatest chance for success, it is important to gather as much detailed information as possible. The end result will provide you with information about where your money is coming from, how much there is and where it is going. A budget can be a very important part of helping you claim financial freedom, and assist you in moving in the direction you really want to go.

The qualities of discipline and discernment are also important with regard to financial responsibility. It is taking the time to get very clear about needs versus wants. As I tell my stepsons, eat your vegetables before you have dessert. My husband also says: "Do what you have to do so you get to do what you want to do." Prioritizing is vital if you want to create stable financial growth and manifest greater prosperity.

As I mentioned earlier in the book, it rarely goes well when someone who has struggled for a lifetime suddenly hits the lottery. There is too much play in the leash, they are not on solid ground and will find it very challenging (if not impossible) to take responsibility. The ones who do well, and maintain their prosperity, are the ones who hire a professional money manager or financial advisor. Perhaps that is something you may want to consider if you are challenged by creating a budget, or feel you could benefit from some professional advice or input from an expert.

If you do not want or need a money advisor, but want more "nuts and bolts" information about money and financial responsibility, there are many great resources available to support you. Some areas to consider or explore include: how to improve your credit, debt management, investments and record keeping. Do your research and get some recommendations from people you respect.

Credit

No conversation about financial responsibility is complete without mentioning the wise use of credit. Far too many people assume as long as they make the minimum payment on credit card balances, they are being financially responsible. This is not the case. Credit is an area that can cause a great deal of headache and heartache. I have had several girlfriends end up with tens of thousands of dollars in credit card debt and no actual plan to reduce it or pay it off. The ostrich head in the sand is not the most responsible way of dealing with debt.

One of my girlfriends argued with me: "Tammi, you told me to get into the feeling state of prosperity. Well, these Christian Louboutin shoes make me feel prosperous." Her explanation seemed childlike, immature and irresponsible. She was manipulating prosperity theory for the purpose of instant gratification. There is nothing wrong with Louboutins or any other designer shoes. However, there *is* a problem if you are overextending yourself, going into debt, and living beyond your current means to acquire material items. It indicates that you may be overextending yourself within. Internal balance will always support your external decisions. Financial responsibility means prioritizing, getting grounded, solid, and clear, and then expanding from there.

Credit cards can be tempting, and can evolve into a problem if you are not careful. It is important to limit the number of credit card accounts you have and pay attention to your interest rates. You certainly can use credit cards providing you have the money to pay for what you want as if you did not have a credit card. Credit and debit cards have become replacements for writing checks or using cash. Pay credit cards on time, and pay them off completely every month if you can. If you pay them off in their entirety, not only does this keep you out of debt, it keeps more money in your pocket (rather than giving it in interest to the credit card company). It also really improves your credit score. In my early 20s I looked into buying a car and found my credit score was very high. The sales person was shocked and wondered how I had done it. It wasn't that I made a lot of money, but I did consistently pay my bills on time, as well as pay my credit cards off every month. My mother taught me early on to make certain to take care of my financial obligations and responsibilities so that I would have good credit. I am so glad I listened.

Resisting impulse buying is also key to financial responsibility. We are bombarded by constant visual and audio stimuli to entice people to purchase items they do not need, and in some cases, cannot comfortably afford. Choosing to create a list of needs vs. wants can cut down on impulse buying to some degree. Another way to reduce impulsive purchases is to set aside a fixed amount in the budget that is considered "free" money—money that can be spent on any type of whim. But once the free money is gone, there is no more impulse buying for the remainder of the budget period.

Lastly, I suggest saving a portion of your income to begin building up your reserves. By doing so you not only strengthen your financial situation, you also gain confidence in your self-discipline.

Once you believe YOU CAN and then YOU DO,

the Universe will respond by

rewarding you in countless ways.

Financial responsibility isn't something that comes naturally for most. Often people have to change the way they think about money and how they spend it. You will want to learn as much as you can about debt, credit and credit scores so you understand how your actions and habits may affect your future. Bad old habits with money can keep you spending. New good habits with money can help you start saving. If you need help getting organized, talk to a financial advisor. Staying on top of your finances can help prevent you from going into debt, help you raise and/or keep your credit score high and support you in attracting more money.

My Money My Friend!

As an archetypal hypnotherapist, I sometimes do sessions for people and ask their subconscious mind to reveal a person, character or archetype around different qualities or aspects. This works well in astrology, and to cultivate different aspects of one's personality. I have personally asked for the archetype of business to reveal itself and share its suggestions and teachings with me. I have also worked with the archetype of the artist, the teacher, the wise one, the inner child, the saboteur, the Higher Self, the healer and more. This process is yet another way to tap into our inner resources and partner with the innate wisdom within.

As an experiment I did a session with a client who struggled in her relationship with money. We asked to have the "Archetype of Money" reveal itself as a person. She was open to it and described this person as a good-looking man. She told me she felt suspicious of him. She wondered what he wanted from her and if he was going to take anything from her. Immediately there was important information revealing itself. I had ask her "Mr. Money Man" a series of questions: What did he want? What would it take to become better friends? How could they become more trusting and respectful of one another? As this inner relationship was being explored and revealed, she found that Mr. Money was really very funny. She began to like him, enjoy him and trust him. I suggested she connect with him often, continue the dialogue, and be open to how things might shift and change in her outer reality with money.

I did this again with a friend who has a good relationship with money and never really struggled financially. I asked her to consider money as a person, how did he or she show up in her imagination? She told me she looked like Glinda the Good Witch from the "Wizard of Oz." She told me she was beautiful, loving, very familiar and friendly. She told me they had an open-hearted connection with each other and an innate sense of respect and trust. I was not surprised by this information, but did find it very interesting.

I too have personally worked with my money archetype. Money showed up as a very tall man, and when I first connected with him, he was wearing a very stiff looking, shiny, strange emerald green suit. As we hung out, talked and began to cultivate a friendship, he began to transform. I have been consulting with him for a while and now he appears very differently to me. He is more relaxed and has a beautiful expensive olive green suit. Sometimes he takes off his jacket and we sit on a blanket on the ground and have a lovely picnic. We converse, I ask him questions and I listen. I also request advice, suggestions and wisdom and I take notes. Not surprisingly, as I have done this, I have had epiphanies, experienced deep healing, and my outer experience with money has relaxed, shifted and up-leveled. This is a fun exercise and yet another way we can take responsibility for our relationship with money.

Painting for Prosperity

A class I offer to understand and heal one's inner relationship with money is called "Painting for Prosperity." Through this creative process, participants experience powerful revelations; this, in turn, shifts their attitude, perspective and vibration. I frequently witness immediate and miraculous results occur in my students' lives after taking this class. This is because a small shift in one's inner reality can create a significant difference in their outer reality. An analogy would be like hearing static while listening to the radio, then moving the tuner one or two degrees and then the station comes in loud and clear.

In my Painting for Prosperity class, I support students in using color and abstract art as a language for emotions. One does not have to be an artist for this work to be powerful and have a positive impact. Color, symbols and creativity are just another tool to open the door to inner resources and inner wisdom. This class is *not* about creating a masterpiece or something beautiful to hang on your wall; it is about revelation, awareness and healing. Painting for Prosperity is *process* oriented, not *product* oriented.

The first part of the Painting for Prosperity class consists of asking my students simple questions like:

1. What is the color and shape of anger?

2. What is the color and shape of fear?

3. What is the color and shape of happiness?

4. What is the color and shape of love?

After each question I give them a moment to paint their answer on a canvas with sponges, brushes, paper towels, their fingers and/or Q-tips. After this warm-up exercise, the next questions I ask are around the subject of money and prosperity. I will ask my students to scan their body inwardly as I say the word "money." Is there any discomfort or constriction? Where is it located? What color is it? What shape is it? Is there a symbol associated with it? Then I will give them a few minutes to paint what they receive on the canvas. Then I have them consider the color, shape and symbol of compassion and place it on the canvas. Next I have them breathe compassion into the place of discomfort. What does the discomfort have to say? What is its message and what does it want or need to relax? I will ask them to consider the color, shape and symbol of prosperity and give them some time to paint it. Finally, I will do a brief guided meditation to support them in relaxing into their open, healthy "Money Rhythm" and invite them to complete their painting.

In my last Painting for Prosperity class, every student experienced profound revelations around their buried, unconscious beliefs about money. The following week one of my students told me she received an unexpected raise. Another student told me she was invited to put the jewelry she was designing in an upscale shop and immediately started selling her pendants. Yet another student told me she refinanced her home and was receiving an additional $600 per month without doing anything differently at all. Coincidence? Perhaps. But I don't think so!

Choosing to consciously consider and take responsibility for your inner relationship with money is a powerful way to change your thoughts, feelings and energy around it. This, in turn, will change how it shows up in your life. Explore and accept money as your friend. Get into the feeling state of an open, flowing abundant life in your mind, body and inner realms, and it will eventually manifest in your life. The mental expectancy and energetic receptivity of prosperity sets the stage for it to become your outer reality. I whole-heartedly agree with Napoleon Hill's well-known quote: "Whatever the mind can conceive and believe, it can achieve." *(Think and Grow Rich, 1960).*

Exercise #1: Your Outer Relationship With Money

1. **Pay Attention to Your Money and Manage it Well.** Being responsible with the money you have will put you on solid ground to manifest more. When you manage what you have effectively, the more effectively you will manage greater amounts of money. Keep track of your daily, weekly and monthly income and expenses. Document what you earn, what you spend and where. By making this a consistent habit, your finances are less likely to get out of control and you are more likely to make responsible and positive choices. Creating a budget simply means "Live within your means." Creating a budget includes setting aside a portion of your income for savings and tithing. Get in the habit of diverting a percentage of your income into a wealth-building account, even if you are paying down debt.

Creating a Budget:

1. Record all of your sources of income. If you are self-employed or have any outside sources of income be sure to include this. If your income is a regular paycheck where taxes are automatically deducted, then using the net income, or take-home pay amount is fine. Record this total income as a monthly amount.

2. Create a list of monthly expenses. List of all the expected expenses you plan on incurring over the course of a month. This includes a mortgage payment, rent, taxes, car payments, auto insurance, groceries, utilities, entertainment, auto insurance, etc. This list should include everything you spend money on.

3. Total your monthly income and monthly expenses. Subtract the total expenses from the total income, and if your end result shows more income than expenses, you are off to a good start. This means you can prioritize the excess to areas of your budget such as retirement savings or paying more on credit cards to eliminate debt faster. If you are showing a higher expense column than income it means some changes may need to happen.

4. Review your budget monthly. It is important to review your budget on a regular basis to make sure you are staying on track. After the first month, take a minute to sit down and compare the actual expenses versus what you had created in the budget. This will show you how

you are doing and reveal the areas that need improvement.

Be sure to consult with a tax or investment professional to answer questions and provide additional advice. Managing money wisely takes intention, education, skill, responsibility, endurance as well as the qualities of patience and faith. What makes a person's future prosperous is not the amount of money itself, but rather making the relationship with money positive, respectful and healthy. Although this can take some work, in the end it is worth it. The ultimate reward for financial responsibility includes immeasurable power, freedom and *more money.*

2. **Strengthen Your Boundaries.** Have the courage to say "yes" to what you want and "no" to what you don't want. Also consider *wants* versus *needs.* Boundaries and discernment around money can help you prioritize and build self-esteem. Focus on what is most important to you and if you don't have it, don't spend it. If you can't afford something, it's not your time to buy it right now. Patience is a powerful virtue when it comes to spending and manifesting more money. Patience can also support you in your practices of attracting greater prosperity.

3. **Brainstorm Every Week.** Consider creative ideas to generate more wealth in your business or personal finances. Remember, when you start asking the questions, inspired answers can start showing up.

4. **Surround Yourself With Positive People.** You take on traits of the people you spend the most time with. If you want to be financially free, spend your time with positive and financially successful people who share your values. Connect with others who are responsible and prosperous in their thoughts, actions, words and deeds. Support each other in any way that serves, share ideas and opportunities for up-leveling your financial responsibility.

Exercise #2: Your Inner Relationship With Money

This exercise may or may not be one that works for you. But know that your current financial situation is a *direct reflection* of your inner relationship with Money. I have witnessed profound healing by virtue of this process. So I invite you to grab your journal and open your mind. You may be surprised at what you find!

1. Take a deep healing breath and center your awareness in your heart. Now invite your subconscious mind to reveal money to you as an archetype, character or an actual person.

2. How does money show up as a human being? Are they male or female? What do they look like? How are they dressed? Ask them if they if there is a name they would like to be called.

3. How do you feel about this "Money Person?" Do you trust them? Do you like them? Do they trust you? Do they like you? Would you have a relationship with this person if you did not have to?

4. Ask your Money Person the following questions and listen to his/her response.

   - Are there any limiting thoughts or ideas I could release, reframe or change about you?
   - How can we become better friends?
   - What do you want or need from me for us to have a more abundant, respectful, positive, prosperous and healthy relationship?

5. Do you have any other questions for Money? Does Money have any requests for you? How do you want things to be different? What is something you can do to make these changes real?

6. Now imagine taking a step back and looking at this relationship between yourself and Money from the outside. Is this relationship love-based or fear-based? How does the energy flow? What needs to happen to bring greater openness, balance, peace, joy, fun, attraction and celebration into this relationship?

Our relationship with money is like any other relationship; it comes where it's invited, appreciated, respected and loved. It rarely responds positively when threatened, hated, resented, grabbed at, manipulated or chased. Money *can* be your good friend *if* you listen to it and genuinely like it. The more you care for this relationship, the more you will find it showing up and supporting you in your life. The process of inner and outer financial responsibility begins with the simple understanding that you have the choice and ability to improve your situation. Make commitments to the choices that are congruent and consistent with what you really want. As you shift your thoughts and beliefs around money, and start to view it as a good friend and vital partner in your life, money can show up and bring incredible good in many forms—both *to you* and *through you!*

Chapter 10

To Tithe or Not to Tithe?

Give, and it will be given to you.
Good measure, pressed down, shaken together,
running over, will be put into your lap.
For with the measure you use it will be measured back to you.

~ Luke 6:38

The Law of Attraction dictates that what we put out we get back. It is a flawless system that can also be referred to as: Reaping What You Sow, the Boomerang Effect, the Law of Resonance, Karma, Cause and Effect, or "Water finding its own level." When we get to the essence of this principle, it is really very simple: what you do, will come back to you. If you give more love, you receive more love; if you are judgmental and competitive, you will attract judgmental and competitive people. So, if you are ready to manifest positive things, think about what you want to attract, and then give those things to others.

The more freely you give,

the more abundantly you shall receive.

Years ago I decided I was ready to take greater responsibility for consciously creating my life. I took some time to consider what I really wanted to manifest. The qualities that came to mind were peace, happiness, prosperity, freedom, respect and love. I decided to embark on a practice of energetically tithing to others. I chose to consciously treat others with these qualities. I also prayed for others to manifest the very same things I longed for myself.

When you pray for others,

the by product is greater good for everyone –

this includes you!

Every morning I uttered a heartfelt request for prosperity and peace for my family and my friends. The power of this practice is confirmed in Job 42:10: "After Job had prayed for his friends, the LORD restored his fortunes and gave him twice as much as he had before." When we pray for others, the energetic side effect is that we naturally attract and manifest good things for ourselves.

Metta for Manifesting

My "peaceful prosperity prayer" eventually expanded to include everyone I ever met, ever would meet, and you, the reader of this book. My prayer practice has continued to ripple out and now includes all human beings and sentient beings, including those who have hurt or betrayed me. In Buddhism, this loving kindness practice is called "metta." The literal translation of the word is "friendship." Practicing metta supports us in becoming a better friend to ourselves, to other people and to all of life. It is the foundation of connection. What I have experienced from participating in this practice is an increased sense of compassion, greater prosperity and a more consistent state of equanimity.

If it calls to you, consider what you really want, utter a prayer requesting these things for yourself, then make the very same request for others. An example would be: "May I be peaceful, may I be prosperous, may I live with ease of heart." You can use this phrase, or change it to whatever feels good for you. Repeat it gently and kindly to yourself. You can do this either silently or aloud. Next, one by one, call to mind your family members and friends as you continue your prayer: "May you be peaceful, may you be prosperous, may you live with ease of heart." Allow the energy of your request to gently ripple out to include everyone in your community, your state, your nation and the world. The final step is to include all beings everywhere without distinction or exception. After practicing this simple prayer for a few short days, you will undoubtedly notice an increased sense of peace, well-being, and very likely, greater prosperity.

Being of Service

Another powerful practice in the process of manifesting, is tithing our energy and/or the act of service. Years ago while in the throes of my depression, I prayed and asked for relief. What dropped into my awareness was that I needed to give more generously of myself. After considering different options, I chose to volunteer with hospice. Although initially I was uncomfortable and a little bit afraid, I took my action steps to be of service. Not only did the experience eradicate my depression, but blew my heart wide open in love and compassion, the very qualities I asked to cultivate for and within myself.

Recently a friend came to me and told me of her depression and financial woes. I invited her to consider doing some volunteer work as an "offering to the Universe." She thought it was an odd suggestion since she didn't seem to have enough energy or money for herself, but she opened her mind to the prospect. She researched a few options, and found something that sparked excitement in her heart. She decided she would devote a little of her time to the food coalition in her area. She found as she gave love and compassion to those in need, her depression lifted. As she fed others, her soul was fed. As a bonus, she connected with another volunteer who needed to hire someone with her skill set. The compensation for this position was much more than anything she had ever made before and included benefits. When she called to tell me the story, she was astonished. I just smiled.

There are many ways to move energy and manifest miracles. Consider what you want, then give generously. As you take the action steps, the natural byproduct is to attract miracles. For every action, there is an equal and opposite reaction. This is Newton's third law of motion, the uncompromising boomerang effect of energy and the guaranteed consequence of karma. I am certain you have heard the proverb: "As you sow, so shall you reap." There is no way of getting around it --You will ALWAYS harvest what you plant!

Manifesting More Money

If you are really ready to up-level your financial prosperity and manifest more money, then it is time to plant seeds of money. In other words, it is time to tithe. This is the biggest sticking point for most people who want to attract more abundance, often stating something like: "I don't even have enough money for me, I can't afford to give any away!" The energy of hoarding and clinging will *never* create prosperity and will *always* produce lack and "not enoughness." If we hold tightly to the things that we possess, including our money, then we are a prisoner of those very things. When we surrender every area of our lives-- including our finances--to God, we relax into the space of true freedom, an abiding faith in a Higher Power and authentic prosperity.

Let's look closer at the word tithe. In Hebrew, "maaser" or "maasrah," translates into *tenth*, or *tenth part*, and in Greek "apodekatoo." In both, it means a *payment or giving or receiving of the tenth*. A tithe is one tenth of our income that we give to God or Spirit. This energetically invites God to move on our behalf in the area of prosperous blessings. The Bible records numerous accounts of man tithing to God. God is the creator of everything and owner of all that exists and we are simply stewards of what we have been entrusted with. The tithing principle is this: "He gives unto us, we give back to Him one-tenth of all that He has blessed us with."

Tithing isn't really giving, it is returning

Tithing is a powerful healing practice that comes up frequently in spiritual teachings. It is also a subject that comes up frequently when talking to those who have acquired great wealth. Robert Kiyosaki has been quoted as saying: "Over the years I have found that many of the richest people in the world began their lives with the habit of tithing." John Rockefeller, the man often regarded as the richest person in history, has said: "I never would have been able to tithe the first million dollars I ever made if I had not tithed my first salary, which was $1.50 per week."

Most people want to receive, yet they hesitate to give.

However, in order to receive we must first give.

To Whom Much is Given Much is Expected

Another very wealthy person who shared the importance of giving back was Andrew Carnegie (*The Gospel of Wealth*, 2006).

Carnegie was a Scottish-American industrialist, businessman, entrepreneur and a major philanthropist. He is regarded as the second-richest man in history after John D. Rockefeller. Carnegie started as a telegrapher and by the 1860s had investments in railroads, railroad sleeping cars, bridges and oil derricks. He built further wealth as a bond salesman raising money for American enterprise in Europe.

Carnegie earned most of his fortune in the steel industry. In the 1870s he founded the Carnegie Steel Company. By the 1890s, the company was the largest and most profitable industrial enterprise in the world. Carnegie sold it in 1901 for $480 million to J.P. Morgan. He spent the remainder of his life the living example of his belief: "The wealth creator has a moral obligation to enrich the lives of others in whatever way they can." Carnegie thought it important to distribute one's fortune with the same diligence used to create it. He erected noble institutions and facilities, including universities, libraries, parks, museums, art galleries, hospitals, concert halls and churches. Carnegie touched and enlightened millions of people with his attitude, his prosperity, and his immense generosity. Carnegie played big and embodied the saying: "To whom much is given much is expected."

Spiraling Down and Getting Back Up

In my late 20s and early 30s I lived a "big life" filled with lots of money, private jets, limos and red carpets. I was engaged to, and drafted in the wake of, a very famous and financially successful man. I did not consider tithing or giving back. I was consumed and tangled up in a world of materialism and ego. I also experienced significant fear and anxiety. Although I was immersed in a reality of material wealth, I was not living a prosperous life. People would often tell me I was lucky, but in truth I cried and was terribly depressed much of the time. I experienced firsthand the old adage: "Money does not buy happiness." When that relationship dissolved, I spiraled down to a place of even deeper depression and poverty.

I spent a great deal of time praying and asking for help. The prospect of tithing came up for me a few times in different ways: as a suggestion from spiritual teachers, when I would read books about prosperity, and inwardly when I would meditate. I have to admit, as is true for many people, tithing was an ENORMOUS sticking point for me. I had lived an opulent, affluent, decadent life and was now working at jobs I did not enjoy in order to survive. I was also trying to put myself through school, so giving away 10% of what I earned seemed daunting, and quite frankly, stupid. I had a budget, I even clipped coupons. Every nickel and dime was accounted for. I thought maybe someday when I had a lot of money again, I would begin a practice of tithing. Sure, I wanted to put God first, but not until I was financially stable!

Something that seemed to happen rather consistently through those "lean years" were unfortunate situations such as receiving speeding tickets, parking tickets, losing valuable items, car problems, sitting on my sunglasses, and accidently throwing away a book I needed for school and had to replace. "Ridiculous things" frequently happened that separated me from my money. All the more reason to hold on tightly to it, I would argue! But as I meditated I really "got" that God wanted me to trust him and put my money where my mouth was, so to speak. Talk is cheap, writing out a check and giving it away is so much more difficult.

Despite my desire to cultivate a personal relationship with Spirit, I was not a religious person and did not go to church regularly. I would meditate, read sacred text, walk around in nature or sit at the beach in order to connect with Source. One day, while sitting in the warm sun-soaked sand in Marina del Rey, California. I stared out at the ocean. I eventually turned my attention inward and asked Spirit what He would have me do. I was prompted to trust God as my Source and to tithe. So I asked inwardly, "Where?" I realized and understood I was to tithe wherever I was spiritually nourished.

Although I was afraid, I finally said yes and committed to tithe . . . for a while . . . as an experiment. Just then off the coast a whale breached and I noticed the diamond-like sparkles dancing across the surface of the water. A wave of goose bumps washed over me and I took it as a sign. In that moment I felt safe, supported and profoundly connected to God. Later that day I got out my checkbook, and, with my hand shaking, I wrote out my meager tithe and sent it to the non-profit organization Save the Whales. I had made a commitment, so I kept my eyes, ears and heart open to receive and acknowledge Divine nurturance and inspiration. A couple of weeks later a friend reminded me fear was an illusion, and that I was safe, supported and loved. It was exactly what I needed to hear, exactly when I needed to hear it, so I decided to tithe to her then and there. The following month, I was reading a book, and the author's words author spoke directly to my soul, so I found her and tithed to her.

There is no right or wrong place to tithe,

it is simply suggested we give 10% of all we receive

to a person, place or institution where we have

received spiritual sustenance.

My first tithes were small, but little by little, they consistently increased. The great news was it seemed *almost instantly* the parking tickets and ridiculous situations subsided. Additionally, interesting opportunities to make money presented themselves. For instance, I was asked to draw a picture of an angel for a fellow student and she gave me $50. A modeling job showed up out of thin air. Then I was asked to create a logo for an acquaintance. When he paid me $150 for this creative endeavor, I was ecstatic!

After tithing for a short while, money started showing up in the strangest and most miraculous of ways: twice in one week I found a twenty dollar bill on the ground; I received a refund I was not expecting; a friend I had loaned money to years ago paid me back. Was this all a coincidence? I was not sure. As I meditated and asked this question inwardly, I got the impression God was smiling at me. Today I have beautiful homes, nice cars, money in the bank and a clear sense of purpose, freedom and peace. I am absolutely convinced I could not be where I am financially or otherwise, without initiating and participating in my tithing practice.

Edwene's Story

On occasion people have asked me: "Tammi, why do I need to give my money to God? He doesn't need it!" We do not tithe because God needs our money but rather to let God know energetically that He is number one in our lives. According to Edwene Gaines, tithing is the *number one, most important* principle of prosperity.

As a young mother, working two jobs, Edwene struggled financially and lived in abject poverty. In fact, sometimes there was not enough food for her and her daughter to eat. Crying on her knees one day, desperate about her financial plight, Edwene was inspired to pick up her Bible. It fell open to Malachi 3: 10 – 12, where it says: "Bring the whole tithe into the storehouse, that there may be food in my house. Test me in this and see if I will not throw open the floodgates of heaven and pour out so much blessing that there will not be room enough to store it. I will prevent pests from devouring your crops, and the vines in your fields will not drop their fruit before it is ripe. Then all the nations will call you blessed, for yours will be a delightful land, says the LORD Almighty."

Edwene read this verse repeatedly looking for a loophole. She tried to convince herself this message about tithing was not meant for her. When she couldn't find a way out, she got mad. Then, after an angry conversation with God, she ended up making a deal. She would tithe . . . but only for six months. If something did not radically change in her life, she was going to stop. And so Edwene wrote out a check for her little tithe later that week and made good on her agreement. After three months of tithing, her income doubled, and within six months it had tripled. This was 30 years ago and today Edwene is a prosperous, successful businesswoman.

Edwene currently owns a beautiful retreat center, travels first class all over the world and teaches others about the power and practice of tithing. Needless to say, Edwene is absolutely devoted to her tithing practice and has never considered quitting. For more about Edwene's incredible story and the power of tithing, please listen to my archived interview with her dated dated March 20, 2014 on Journey to Center, at www.Empoweradio.com.

Give Generously and Receive Graciously

I had been tithing for a few years and am constantly surprised by how, when and where money shows up. As I have learned to relax and generously give, I have also had to stretch out of my comfort zone and learn to graciously receive.

One day I was talking to my good friend, Marion, about prosperity. She wondered about my relationship with money, and how I had created this abundant life for myself. She asked a lot of questions, listened to my answers, and seemed intrigued by my stories. Then, she quietly went into the other room, got her wallet and proceeded to write me a check for $200. When I asked her what it was for, she told me she had not made any money in a couple of months, but it was her intention to make $2000 the following month, so she was tithing to me in advance.

As Marion handed me the check, I could feel my face begin to twitch. I started sweating, my stomach knotted up and I felt a little dizzy. I was conflicted about receiving her money; I thought to myself: "What if this doesn't work?" I reminded myself this was not my law but God's law. Then I thought: "Well, maybe I won't cash the check, and we will just see what happens. If she manifests her intention and makes her $2000, *then* I will cash it." As if Marion could read my mind she said, "Now I want you to go and cash that check right away, so that I can start expecting my miracles and my money." In a great deal of discomfort and doubt, and what felt like a good-sized rock in my stomach, I promised her I would cash the check the next day.

Marion called me a week later with good news, she just booked a gig and was going to make $1200! I laughed and then breathed a deep sigh of relief. Two weeks later I got another "Marion Money Update." A friend of a friend wanted to hire her for weekly piano lessons. Then she got an editing job. She was now up to $2,400 for the month. Wow, I thought, as I continued to receive Marion's updates, this really *does* work! The final day of the month, Marion called and informed me she made another $300 that day, for a grand total of $4100 for the entire month—over *twice* what she had set her intention to manifest and tithed for! Marion thanked me for starting her prosperity engine in earnest, and for helping her make this newfound relationship with money possible.

Marion also shared with me how being able to give money away made it more acceptable to receive it. She realized she had harbored subconscious guilt associated with money and deep-seated issues of unworthiness. However, she found as she focused on sharing her good fortune with others, she relaxed, and her guilt, questions and doubts naturally dissipated.

Marion continues to keep me updated about her abundant,

miraculous and prosperous adventures. In the last eight months she has more than doubled her most successful year ever. Amazing opportunities seem to come out of nowhere. Almost every week we compare notes, laugh and celebrate our good fortune and synchronistic stories. Marion told me just about every day she gets paid to play. Her professional life has gracefully evolved, and she now works a great deal as writer and actress. She also teaches classes about art and grant writing, and manifests a great deal of money (and joy) doing this.

Marion's tithing practice opened her heart and mind to a more gracious, grateful, fun and healthy relationship with money. It has also opened unexpected doors and moved energy in a positive direction with her career and in her life. Marion has been an A-plus prosperity student as well as an incredible teacher. We have so much fun talking about where we are going to tithe next, being one another's cheerleaders and spiritual prosperity partners.

The true purpose of tithing is to acknowledge God as the source of our good, and that we are consciously aware and grateful for this good.

Why does tithing work? There are two levels activated when we make God financially first in our lives—a worldly level and a mystical invisible level. The worldly level is activated when we look at our abundance and contribute joyfully by paying it forward. The mystical is an energetic communication saying, "You are abundant, responsible and handle abundance so well, so here is some more." The action of tithing sets up a countenance that is a form of glory in the human being and that glory attracts more abundance. God/Spirit/The Universe by Its very nature is made of grace and generosity. If you begin to tithe in earnest, you will eventually find when you give to God you cannot out-give Him.

Tithing versus Charity

An important distinction to make is that a tithe is *not* the same thing as giving money to the homeless person standing on the corner or giving to a charity, although it is wonderful to do those things as well. A tithe is different because we are giving to whom and what feeds our soul, the person or institution giving us spiritual nourishment, not just giving out of kindness and compassion. All giving is good, but when our intention is to "Give to God" we find God gives to us.

Tithing is law that cannot fail, and the surest way to move in the direction of prosperity. The *only place* in the Bible where God asks us to put Him to the test, and prove him wrong, is in the area of tithing: "Bring all the tithes into the storehouse so there will be enough food in my Temple. If you do, I will open the windows of heaven for you. I will pour out a blessing so great you won't have enough room to take it in! *Try it! Put me to the test!*" Saying yes, and putting both feet solidly on the path of prosperity, takes courage and commitment. Nobody said this would be easy—if it were easy everyone would be doing it!

You have probably heard the saying: "If you do what you have always done, you will get what you've always gotten." If you want to raise your consciousness and achieve higher altitudes of abundance, you will need to do things differently than you ever have before. The process can be akin to being a spiritual rock climber. You will need new tools and the courage to go where you have never gone, doing things you have never done. For periods of time, you might feel disoriented and dizzy from the new heights. There can be fear associated with the prosperity journey; you may feel at times you are your reaching your "upper limits." But with a backpack filled with positive intentions, faith, courage and commitment, you can break through the glass ceiling of fear, and rise to higher and higher levels of prosperity, connection, creativity and co-creation. As you do, God *promises* you *will* experience life in a whole new, wonderful and abundant way.

Are you ready to commit to your relationship with Spirit and prosperity? Are you ready to take a leap of faith and to move in the direction of your dreams? Take this small, yet enormous step, and be prepared to manifest profound miracles!

Exercise #1: Rooting Out Fear

1. Do you have fear and resistance associated with tithing? If so, spend some time getting to the root of that fear. Allow the fear or resistance to have a voice and to speak; what does it have to say and to whom? If you have sadness, let the tears flow. If there is anger, scream into a pillow or find another safe way to get the energy out of your body.

2. After you have allowed the fear to express itself, then invite Spirit in to support you in transforming your fear to faith. With faith the size of a mustard seed, and a commitment to yourself and Spirit, mountains can be moved and miracles will be manifested.

3. Relax into the energy of compassion. Allow yourself to be soothed and comforted either by a guardian angel, Spirit or your Higher Self. The human experience CAN be really painful and scary. However, once we transcend our fear and heal our hurts, otherworldly support can show up naturally, gracefully and easily. Fear and hurt is healed through the qualities of love and compassion.

4. I invite you to inwardly ask yourself: What is the color of love? What is the color of compassion? Now allow yourself to bask in the colors, and healing energy, that reveals itself to you.

Exercise #2: Is it Time to Tithe?

1. Turn your attention inward and ask yourself: "When was I the happiest this week? Where did I feel spiritually nourished, aligned and connected? When, where, and with whom has my soul been nurtured?" Listen to the still small voice within, what comes forward?

2. Now ask yourself:

   a. Am I really ready to manifest more prosperity in my life?

b. Do I have the courage to commit to Spirit and begin my practice of tithing?

3. If your answers to the questions in number two are no, know your prosperity process will be limited and challenging. If your answers are yes, determine how much money you have made this week (or this month if you really want to go for it) and write a check for 10% of what you have made to the person, organization or establishment that came forward. If you do not know where to tithe you can still write out the check and wait for the right opportunity to reveal itself to "give your money to God." Set your intention and keep your ears, eyes and heart open to where you are spiritually fed, and be ready to tithe when the opportunity presents itself. Even if you are afraid, and even if you do not believe it will work, your tithes WILL start to open up the floodgates and start moving the energy in your life in a positive, powerful and prosperous direction. This is Spiritual Law.

Exercise #3: Document Your Prosperity

Pay attention to all the money you manifest: every penny you find on the sidewalk; every gift you receive; even the money you found in the jacket pocket you forgot about. Do not discount anything. Pay attention, open your heart, receive with gratitude, thank Spirit and write it down. Then tithe 10% of what you receive to any place, person, organization that supports you in deepening your faith and your relationship to Source. Tithing is like going to the gym. You wouldn't just work out once and think you are ready for the Olympics, would you? In order to get spiritually fit and move energy in the upward direction of prosperity, tithing needs to be a consistent practice.

As you continue to tithe, your life and your income will expand, up-level and increase. Make your relationship with Spirit a priority and you will be made a priority in the world. Pay attention to all the money you manifest: graciously acknowledge, receive, document, and tithe on it. Next, put on your seatbelt and prepare for prosperity!

PART FOUR

Prosperity and Your Purpose

Chapter 11

Surrender

Once we surrender our mind to God completely, He will take care of us in every way.

~ Sri Sathyha Sai Baba

As I have shared with you, there was as time in my life when I struggled financially; a financial blueprint had been handed down to me from my parents. As a young person, the most important people in my life all had deep-seated beliefs that money was hard to come by, and that unpleasant work was necessary to survive. With this programming firmly in place as an adult, I constantly struggled in my relationship with money—even while engaged to a multi-millionaire.

Supporting others in releasing unconscious constrictions, dueling intentions and limiting beliefs around money and prosperity has been a passion of mine for several years. However, before I could teach it effectively, I really had to learn it. Tithing, gratitude, clearing my subconscious mind of limiting beliefs, making friends with my inner child, positive visualization, combined with claiming my value and treating myself well, supported me in healing my fear-based relationship with money. Over time, I created some breathing room and accumulated a nice little nest egg. I was feeling pretty good about myself and my relationship with money, when a seemingly wonderful opportunity as a spokesperson for a large corporation presented itself to me. I was thrilled when I was hired, and shortly thereafter I decided it was time to buy a condominium.

The first place I looked at I fell in love with; it really felt like home. I negotiated what I thought to be a great deal. I was extremely grateful and very optimistic about my new job and my new home. Life was good. However, several days after we closed escrow on my wonderful little condo, my job fell through. I was panic-stricken! What was I going to do? I had depleted my savings for the down payment on my condo AND my bills were going to be much higher now because of this purchase. It seemed the Universe was really upping the ante in my reality.

In my fear-based state, I sat down with the intention of having a heart-to-heart conversation with God. I laid it all on the line: "God, here's the deal, I just bought this beautiful place and my job fell through, I am really scared and not sure what to do." As I focused on my breath, I started to relax. In that moment I decided to surrender this situation, and my condo, to God. I let Spirit know I was willing to work hard and do whatever I needed to do, but if it was for my highest good to relinquish my new home, I would.

A couple of weeks prior to this situation I was feeling creative and painted a little wooden box, then I put butterflies and crystals on it. It was really very pretty and it made my heart smile every time I looked at it. I called this decorative box my "God Box." I set it on my dresser and put jewelry in it, but now I was going to use it for something far more important. I removed my bracelets and rings and set it down in front of me. I imagined putting my condominium, my fear, my stress and this whole situation in the God Box. I took a deep breath and placed everything in God's hands. In that moment I consciously chose faith over fear. I contemplated and counted my many blessings: I had my health, my mind, my friends, a very nice boyfriend, my car and condo (for now) and this beautiful sunshiny day.

After expressing my gratitude, I continued my conversation with Spirit: "God, I KNOW you love me and everything happening is for my highest good, so I am going to relax and give this whole situation to you. I am requesting clarity and grace. And since I don't know what else to do, I am going to be nice to myself and go get a pedicure." I immediately felt an inner shift and a sense of peace. For about 20 minutes I relaxed into an inner state of openness, safety and free-flowing energy. Then I walked out to my car, put the convertible top down and went to go treat my feet.

The next afternoon I got a call from a peripheral friend, Jenny. I had done business with her and the company she worked for as a model years ago. She said: "Tammi, I am so overwhelmed, we are so busy selling these air purifiers, I cannot process all the orders, can you help me?" I said "Sure Jenny, I happen to have some extra time on my hands, what can I do to support you?" She asked if I had the ability to process credit cards and I told her I did. She suggested I purchase some air purifiers wholesale then sell them retail to the people calling in wanting them.

Jenny proceeded to give me the names and numbers of several customers. I immediately got busy returning calls and processing orders. Before the day was over I had made $300! I was astonished by this "miracle." I had an instant and direct experience of choosing faith over fear. Faith immediately put the universal wheels into motion on my behalf. I continued with my practice of gratitude, surrender and faith, and the orders kept coming in. I ended up making more money in the next six months than I ever made in my life—and over twice the money I would have made from the spokesperson job if it had come through! Shocking but not surprising. The principles of prosperity really do work!

When we consciously choose faith over fear,

our lives transform in miraculous ways!

Lawrence's Story of Surrender

Another example of prosperity consciousness and the power of surrender, occurred with my client "Lawrence." Lawrence was a successful businessman. He worked very hard to create prosperity and did a pretty good job. However, it seemed with the downturn of the economy, the old ways of doing things were not as effective as they used to be. It seemed the rules of the game were changing. His competitive edge and work ethic alone were no longer supporting him in the process of manifestation. Lawrence felt the world shifting under his feet and fear was becoming more and more prevalent in his reality.

During a session one day, I suggested we do a guided meditation and a surrender process. Lawrence hesitated, he was not quite ready to relinquish control just yet and decided to do it his way a little longer. About a month later, Lawrence came back to see me. When he showed up I was shocked at his appearance. He looked as if he had aged 10 years, disheveled, drawn and exhausted. All his hard work was not working at all; his business was in serious decline. There were indications that perhaps it was time to consider bankruptcy. Lawrence told me he had "no fight left in him" and was now ready to try anything—including surrender.

Before we began, Lawrence shared with me his feelings of "being a failure" and making "so many mistakes." He told me if he could go back in time and do things differently, everything would be so much better. He was judging himself and beating himself up for trusting the wrong people and making some bad choices. I told Lawrence there really is no "wrong," only lessons and learning. I reminded Lawrence: "We are here to learn soul lessons, and those lessons don't always come easy." I also told him judging himself was not going to help him move in the right direction, and, in fact, this posture would *ensure* that things *would not* get better.

We live in world where course correction and healing are *always available* to us and the Universe *wants* to support us. It's like cutting our hand or breaking a bone, there is innate wisdom within us that can heal us and get us back on track. However, unlike a broken bone which innately heals on its own, with our soul lessons, we need to INVITE the healing, surrender to it and be open to receiving it.

I told Lawrence by virtue of relinquishing his judgment, forgiving himself, surrendering to a Higher Authority and being open to learning his soul lessons, he would be supported in getting back on the right track, realign and start moving in a better direction. Then I shared this simple truth: "There is no such thing as failure, only feedback." When things don't go the way we want them to, or think they should, it can be because we are either supposed to be learning something, we are heading the wrong direction, or we are being invited to ask for help from a wiser authority. Lawrence took a deep breath and we both knew it was finally time for him to turn inward, surrender to Source and access his inner guidance.

I started our session with a centering and invited Spirit in for the highest good of all concerned. I requested blessings of revelation, clarity and healing. Next, I facilitated a guided meditation and supported Lawrence in turning inward. I took him through a process where he shared with me the experience of an "inner earthquake." He told me he felt the foundation was cracking beneath him. I told him to allow it to crack, crumble and fall apart beneath his feet. I asked Lawrence to share with me what was happening through this process. Lawrence shed tears as he experienced intense fear and frantically attempted to hold all the pieces of his fractured foundation together. I assured him he was safe and asked him to breathe, relax and trust the process. As Lawrence allowed his inner experience to unfold, he found himself falling through the shattered floor and into another realm.

Lawrence stopped resisting and relaxed into what was present.

He described his new surroundings as more spacious, more free-flowing and more peaceful. He told me he sensed someone or something was with him, and, for the first time, realized maybe he was not all alone. I asked who was with him, and he identified the energy as his Guardian Angel. I encouraged Lawrence to ask this being for some words of wisdom or advice.

His Guardian Angel assured him that all was well, that he could relax, be patient and give everything to God. Lawrence took the advice of this inner teacher and uttered a heartfelt prayer of surrender. I was touched by how raw and real his request was. He told God if it was for his highest good to release his company, he would. He articulated his preference to have it survive and thrive, but was now relinquishing his attachment to how things were "supposed" to look and what was going to happen. Rather than continuing to try to control the circumstances, Lawrence offered his company to the Creator and held it in his open hands.

Lawrence then shared an inner vision of desperately clutching a fistful of golden sand, and watching it escape through his tightly gripped fingers. Then after his prayer, a softening occurred. He imagined his hand opening up and relaxing, with the sand staying in place. Soon more and more sand began piling up. As he described his vision the verse from Matthew 13:12 dropped into my awareness: "Whoever has will be given more, and he will have an abundance. Whoever does not have, even what he has will be taken from him." Where the clenched fist is ungenerous, unreceptive and closes things down, the open hand is vulnerable, generous, invitational and welcoming.

After we were complete with his guided meditation I asked

Lawrence how he felt. He indicated he was peaceful, calm and much better. His fear had dissipated significantly and for the first time in a very long time, he felt optimistic. It looked like the light was back in his eyes. He thanked me for my help and I reminded him that he was doing the work; it was his intention to surrender control and partner with Spirit that created this shift. Lawrence told me he was now committed to the process and booked weekly appointments. Lawrence was diligent with his inner work and through his counseling sessions we identified and cleared deepseated limiting beliefs around success, refined what he desired, cultivated a gratitude practice and invited God into every aspect of his business and his life.

Lawrence's circumstances did not change overnight, but there were some immediate winks from the Universe that he was on the right track and heading in the right direction. Within four months everything completely shifted. A short year later his company was in the best shape it had ever been in; more profitable, productive and efficient than ever before in its 20-year history.

Recently I asked Lawrence what he learned though this intense period. Here is the incredible wisdom he shared with me: "Be willing to release everything; surrender but don't give up. It is vital to invite God in and trust He will help you sort things out. Identify your priorities, look for 'signs' from Spirit and be willing to act on them." When he shared his message and soul lessons with me, I got thousands of goose bumps and felt incredibly proud of him and so honored to know him.

As Lawrence shared his insights with me, a saying from Ernest Holmes and Religious Science came to mind (*Science of Mind*,

1927): "Treat and move your feet." Do the inner work: prayer and meditation, then take the actions steps in the outer world. One without the other is incomplete and ineffective. Lawrence had been very willing to do the "move the feet" part but was light on the "treat." Now Lawrence had come into a wonderful and effective balance. Not only is he now thriving in his business and in all other areas of his life, he is currently consulting with other entrepreneurs and supporting them in working through the unique challenges presenting themselves at this time.

When we choose to relax and surrender

we move into a direct relationship with God.

In a state of surrender we relax and take a break from needing to know or understand anything. When we surrender, we open the clenched fist that desperately clings to our attachments and offer them up to a power much greater than ourselves. I enjoyed something a student said to me: "We want God to fix our toys, but He can't unless we really let go of them." When we surrender, we let go of our toys, give them to God, we relax into faith and we trust. That is when God can fix our toys and give them back to us as good as new—or even better!

It is ironic that ambition, pushing and working hard can actually keep our prosperity from us. Think about the energy of the ocean and surfing. Rather than trying to create the wave, it is much more effective to relax and be prepared to ride a wave when it arrives.

A vital ingredient to manifesting true prosperity is the conscious act of surrender. Surrender is the act of being patient, faithful and receptive. Not 50%, or 80 %, but 100%. It is comforting, liberating and so powerful to know God hears your prayers, understands your intentions and is lining the waves up on your behalf.

The truest truth is God is *ALWAYS ON YOUR SIDE!* The simple act of surrender and abiding faith creates the magical dynamic that will support you in attracting the people, circumstances and events that will lift you to the next level of your life. Surrendering to Spirit invites miracles, attracts prosperity and is a *vital* ingredient in co-creating the life of your dreams.

Exercise #1: Create a God Box

Perhaps you want to create your own God Box. It can be a wooden box, a shoe box or any other container. Decorate it with paint, fabric, buttons, crystals, items from nature or anything else that appeals to you. If this is not something that resonates for you, you can create a God Box in your imagination. Allow yourself to see it clearly and vividly. Once you have your God Box, imagine placing any stress, tension, situations, any and all relationships, fear, uncomfortable emotions, your health, your career, your finances, your purpose, along with anything and everything you would like support with, clarity about and/or help with. Now relax, knowing it is in God's hands and be nice to yourself. Finally, set your intention to keep your eyes and ears open for signs from the Universe about any action steps you should take.

Exercise #2: Breathe, Relax and Receive

The following is a very simple and relaxing surrender exercise. You may use it in combination with your God Box as it sits in front of you, or may use it alone. With a soft smile on your face, inhale gently to the count of four, and then slowly exhale, while claiming your intention.

For example:

Breathe in two, three, four,
Breathe out: I am peaceful and relaxed,
Breathe in two, three, four,
Breathe out, I am prosperous and calm.
Breathe in, two, three four,
Breathe out, I am gracious and receptive.

You can use the same affirmation for each exhale, or claim different ones. You will find after 15-20 minutes of gentle breathing, surrendering and intending, your state of being "smoothes out," softens up and shifts in a peaceful and positive way.

Exercise #3: What Do You Want? Why? And How?

1. Consider for a moment what you really, really want.

2. Now identify WHY do you want it? Do you want more money because it will give you greater freedom? Do you want greater prosperity and more vibrant health so you can experience greater joy and deeper connections?

3. Once you have identified the WHAT and WHY portion of this exercise, consider HOW can you to get into that feeling state NOW?

For example, if freedom is what you want, what can you do now to get into the free feeling state now? Consider and explore how it feels to have what you really, really want, and get into that feeling state. Take a deep breath, allow the feeling of freedom to flow through you. Revel in it, enjoy it, celebrate it and spend time there. Now consider how you can empower and experience this feeling state in your life: Maybe ride a bike with the wind in your hair? Go for a swim? Or perhaps you would like to take a day off and go to the museum or have a picnic in the park. Whatever helps you create and experience the feeling state that you desire will help you manifest and attract it. This is the powerful practice of creating prosperity from the inside out.

Exercise #4: What Brings You Joy?

Consider what brings you joy. What makes your heart sing? Are there things you can do in your life right now that can lift you to a high, energized vibrational state? If you can do something every day, even something small to support you in getting into this feeling state, it will inspire, uplift and empower you. It will put you into a magnetic state and attract opportunities to you, as well as help you step more fully into your power, productivity and prosperity. Trust your joy as your compass and know that it will lead you in the direction of your soul's purpose and greatest contribution to the world.

Chapter 12

Creativity and Prosperity

All prosperity begins in the mind and is
dependent only upon the full use of our creative
imagination.

~ Ruth Ross

When I mention that I am an Art for Healing instructor or a sacred art facilitator, often people take it as an opportunity to tell me they are not creative. It is my belief, if you are breathing, you are an aspect of Creative Intelligence, therefore innately creative and intelligent. Our greatest opportunity for creativity is the medium and expression of our lives.

Creativity does not have to look like painting, drawing, music or sculpting, although it can. These are some of the tools and opportunities we have available to get us out of our linear, logical, thinking mind, and delve deeper into our subconscious and super conscious mind. One of my husband's favorite creative mediums is business and spread sheets. My stepsons enjoy playing sports.

One of my sisters likes taking pictures, the other enjoys dancing. Creativity can take an infinite number of forms.

In order to attract Divine Prosperity,

you must sow your seeds of creativity.

Your life will not feel satisfying or complete until you explore and express your gifts. I have seen it happen repeatedly; when one discovers and claims their inner creative resources, it supports them in manifesting their prosperity. I like the saying: "Money is always out there looking for creative ideas." A creative mind has no limitations. The only limitations any of us have are the ones we impose upon ourselves.

Although I have had access to a great deal of money during certain periods of my life, it did not bring me peace or happiness. Activating my happiness happened by virtue of accessing my creativity and discovering my inner gifts. Money will not bring fulfillment. Fulfillment occurs when one is aligned with their soul and channels their higher nature. As one taps into their creative nature, they often find money showing up as a wonderful side effect and added bonus.

True wealth is a manifestation of activating your

inner treasures and then sharing them with the world.

I feel it is important to mention money may or may not show up as a direct result of the art classes or the jewelry making courses you take, although it might. Opening to your creativity supports you in opening your mind and heart to higher realms of imagination, inspiration, ideas and new ways of thinking. This, in turn, can positively influence every other area of your life, including your finances.

Invention Through Imagination

Some of the greatest inventions of mankind did not come into being by virtue of logic, knowledge, intellect or reason; they came to be by virtue of imagination and creativity. One of the most brilliant minds of our time, Albert Einstein, said: "Imagination is more important than knowledge. For knowledge is limited to all we now know and understand, while imagination embraces the entire world, and all there ever will be to know and understand."

When you open your mind to going on a vacation from common sense, you open the door to the realms of mystery and uncommon sense. "Common sense" is what the world regards as normal or average. If inventors like Da Vinci or Edison had maintained a common sense mindset, our lives would be very different, and likely much more mundane.

Leonardo Da Vinci lived from 1452 until 1519. This famous and very talented Italian was perhaps best known for painting the Mona Lisa and the Last Supper, but his creativity did not stop there. He was also a sculptor, architect, musician, scientist, mathematician, engineer, inventor, anatomist, geologist, cartographer, botanist and writer. Da Vinci was a profoundly curious man and a creative genius. He was self-taught (or better yet, Self-taught) and kept the door wide open to his imagination. He was not afraid of seeing what most would dismiss as insane or impossible. Some of his drawings and ideas included the helicopter, the military tank, scuba diving equipment, the alarm clock, the airplane, solar power, the calculator, the machine gun, submarines, parachutes and the "horseless carriage." Many of his "crazy creative ideas" are now a reality in our modern world.

Thomas Edison is another example of a man with uncommon sense. In a 1910 interview, he was quoted as saying: "Someday some fellow will invent a way of concentrating and storing up sunshine to use instead of this old, absurd Prometheus scheme of fire. I'll do the trick myself if someone else doesn't get at it." If people of that era were to eavesdrop on this conversation, I am certain most would have thought him completely off his rocker! In fact, after it had became public knowledge that this was something he was attempting, a reporter asked Edison, "How many times are you going to fail at creating the light bulb?" Mr. Edison replied, "Son, I haven't failed! I've simply discovered another way not to invent the light bulb!"

"Genius is 1 percent inspiration and 99 percent perspiration."

~Thomas Edison

It took Thomas Edison two years and many "failures" before successfully manifesting his inner vision in the outer world. It has been estimated that Edison experienced over 10,000 unsuccessful attempts at creating the light bulb. Fortunately for us, Mr. Edison possessed persistent determination and uncommon sense, which allowed his creativity and imagination to light up the world.

The Magic of a Mouse

Just as a world without electricity and light bulbs would be hard to imagine, can you imagine a world without animation, Tinkerbelle, Mickey Mouse and Disneyland? I for one would not even want to! However, if not for the creative genius, courage, commitment and uncommon sense of Walt Disney, that would be our unfortunate reality.

Though Mr. Disney came from humble and unremarkable beginnings, he was a pioneer and innovator and possessed of one of the most fertile and unique imaginations the world has ever known. Disney was born and raised in the Midwest, the fourth of five children, with a strict father and little money. As a young boy, his imagination and purpose was hinted at through his sketches. On occasion he sold his art to supplement the family's income. As a teenager, Walt joined the Red Cross and was sent overseas to France, where he spent a year driving an ambulance and chauffeuring Red Cross officials. His vehicle was not like others painted in camouflage, but instead covered from bumper to bumper with his cartoons.

When Walt returned from France, he began to pursue a career

in commercial art and created a small company called Laugh-O-Grams, which eventually went bankrupt. With several failed business attempts beneath his belt, Walt decided to head to Hollywood with just a suitcase in hand, and forty dollars in his pocket. At his self- proclaimed "rock bottom," while riding on the back of a bus, Walt got out his drawing pad and sketched a little mouse. And Mickey Mouse was born.

Walt experienced many setbacks and "failures," but maintained his imagination, determination, courage and optimism. He started to gain a little momentum with the world's first animated cartoon featuring Mickey Mouse and the subsequent success of the "Alice Comedies." He continued to build on that success, and, in 1937, the first full-length animated musical "Snow White and the Seven Dwarfs" was released. This occurred during the Depression and the cost of nearly $1,500,000, making it nothing less than a miracle by most people's standards. The original "Snow White" is still considered one of the greatest feats in the motion picture industry. During the next five years, Walt completed other full-length animated classics including "Pinocchio," "Fantasia," "Dumbo," and "Bambi."

In addition to animation and film, Walt was a pioneer in television. "The Mickey Mouse Club" and "Zorro" become popular favorites in the 1950s. By this time, Walt had manifested great success and was quoted saying: "You reach a point where you don't work for money." Though he no longer NEEDED to do anything for financial reasons, he WANTED to continue imagining, expanding, playing, thinking and creating. In 1955 his dream for a fabulous amusement park came true. Disneyland was launched as the $17 million Magic Kingdom.

Walt brought many of our favorite fairy tales to life and accomplished remarkable feats in the world of entertainment, but he still had more he wanted to do. Next he turned his attention toward the problem of improving the quality of life in urban America. He directed the design of an Experimental Prototype Community of Tomorrow (EPCOT) and the purchase of 43 square miles of virgin land in the center of the state of Florida. He master planned a whole new "Disney World" of entertainment, which included a new amusement park, motel-hotel resort vacation center and his experimental community. After more than seven years of planning and preparation, the Walt Disney World Resort opened on October 1, 1971. EPCOT Center opened on October 1, 1982, and on May 1, 1989, the Disney-MGM Studios Theme Park was unveiled.

Though Mr. Disney passed away in 1966, the ripple effect of his remarkable and otherworldly inner vision lives on, and continues to bring magic and joy to the world. Walt Disney is a legend, a creative genius and a folk hero of the 20th century. Many believe that Walt Disney did more to touch our hearts, minds and emotions than any other person in the past century. To quote the wisdom of Walt: "All our dreams can come true, if we have the courage to pursue them."

Walt encountered many setbacks, disappointments and failures, but realized they were important in the overall scheme of things. He was once quoted as saying: "All the adversity I've had in my life, all my troubles and obstacles have strengthened me . . . You may not realize it when it happens, but a kick in the teeth may be the best thing in the world for you."

Thankfully for all us, Walt embodied the qualities of courage and commitment. He also maintained the important connection to his inner realms of fantasy, curiosity and imagination. Through all of his success he also maintained his humility and was the first to remind his employees, fans, family and friends, "Remember this all began with a mouse!"

I believe *everyone* is born with gifts, talent and other worldly magic, and *everyone* has the capacity to bring their vision to life. I often wonder how many millions of geniuses and remarkable humans have been born, but did not have the courage to go for their dreams and the wherewithal to just keep trying. Now for a really important question: Do YOU have the courage, and commitment to bring your unique brand of brilliance to the world? I sincerely hope you say YES!

Be Like Little Children

In a previous chapter I discussed working with your inner child, reprogramming limiting beliefs and healing childhood wounds. Once we do this we have the ability to connect with the True Inner Child. Carl Jung called it the "Divine Child" and Emmet Fox called it the "Wonder Child." Some psychotherapists call it the "True Self" or the "Eternal Child." The Inner Child refers to the part inside each of us that is alive, energetic, creative, joyful and fulfilled; it is our "Genuine Authentic Self." It is who we are at the deepest level. In the Bible, Matthew shares with us in order to get into the kingdom of heaven we need to be like little children. I personally believe this means coming full circle, reconnecting and partnering with the Divine Child residing within.

Do you know any young children? Have you witnessed them

at play? Everything is an adventure. A box and blanket can become a fort, an empty wrapping paper tube a sword. Young children are adventurous, creative and immersed in the present moment. They are in awe of things we adults take for granted. Children are filled with optimism, excitement and enthusiasm. The word "enthusiasm" comes from the Greek word *enthousiasmos* which means inspiration or possession by the presence of a god. Can you recall what it felt like to be a child and how magical life seemed to be? Do you remember feeling so excited about life that you hated to go to bed at night and couldn't wait to get up in the morning? It is amazing to experience magic and wonder as a child, but even more incredible to experience as an adult ALIGNED and CONNECTED with their Divine Child.

Kindergarten classrooms are filled with joy and genius. It is not until children get older do they start to buy into the notion they are not creative or are not artists. This can happen for a number of reasons: perhaps their projects were not chosen for an art fair, maybe a teacher told them they were not good at art, perhaps another sibling received the title of "the artistic one," or maybe a parent did not acknowledge or value the endeavors of their young ones' creativity. If you are one of those people who put the creative part of yourself in the closet, it really doesn't matter why, just invite this part of you out of the shadows and allow it to explore, express, create and play.

Relinquish the need to control, understand or know anything, and open your mind to uncommon sense and not knowing. Do you think Leonardo Da Vinci, Thomas Edison or Walt Disney believed they knew anything for sure? They trusted their intuition, kept an open mind and continued to experiment, practice, learn, explore and expand. This in turn made them magnets and conduits for creative genius, sparks of magic and miracles to be downloaded and manifested through them.

Choosing to become like a child,

means leaving your preconceived notions

and old beliefs behind, and opening to the awe, mystery

and wonder of the magical present moment.

Consider the following scenario: A mother and very young child sit down to eat breakfast. Dad enters the room, then slowly lifts up off the ground and starts floating around the kitchen. The child says, "WOW, COOL!" She is excited and filled with joy! The mom faints dead away. The mother thinks she knows everything and knows this is impossible! It is likely, if she is like most adults on planet Earth, that she is bored, tired, agitated and has put a lid on her curiosity and wonder. The child still has an open "beginner's mind" and to her everything is magical and wondrous; every day is a brand- new adventure filled with miracles. Opening ourselves to become like a child again invites the experience of joy. It also creates the space in our hearts and minds for new ideas, inspiration and opportunities to show up in our lives.

If you would like, close your eyes for a moment. When you open them, say to yourself, or out loud: WOW! Look around with fresh, new, curious eyes. Pretend you are from another planet and seeing this world for the very first time. Witness this Earth in wonder. Marvel in enchantment at the exquisite beauty of nature. Imagine being from a long ago time in history, and observe in awe, the mind-blowing phenomena of our modern day technology. Allow yourself to be astonished and amazed at your surroundings. Consider with an inquiring mind everything it took to create the material items in your immediate environment. How did the fabric or furniture come into being? Who are the people who created these things and what are their stories? It is easy to take life, other people and our physical world for granted. But we can choose to consciously open to a more inquisitive, curious and appreciative state. And as we do, not only does life become more fun, it can deepen our fulfillment, increase our satisfaction and help us attract more magic, miracles and magnificence!

Self-Acceptance

If you want to step into the creative process and manifest greater prosperity, it is important to accept yourself just as you are. Give yourself permission to make mistakes, be vulnerable and look silly. Relinquish your need to know, to be right, to be perfect, as well as your fear of failure. If you want to open to the deeper part of yourself, it is best not to "know" anything. Being right and knowing keeps you very limited, as does the desire to be perfect. In fact, I believe being perfect is one of the most toxic desires we can have.

When did you last start something new? Was it a long time ago? As children we are always starting something new. Then, as we get older we become more hesitant about being a beginner again. Why? Maybe it's because we don't want to be embarrassed or feel ashamed if someone sees us fall or fail. Fear can keep us playing small and prevent us from manifesting, creating and attracting what is ours by Divine right.

We did not come to planet Earth to be perfect,

we came here to learn, explore, express,

to be creative and to be loving!

Open your mind to the possibility of stepping out of your comfort zone and relinquishing control. When we attempt to appear a certain way in the world, to know everything or to be in control (in other words living in ego) is when we lose our connection to the deeper, wiser, creative and brilliant parts of ourselves. In order to access creative genius, we need to cultivate curiosity and enthusiasm. Be willing to explore and "not know." Be willing to look silly and laugh at yourself. Authenticity and being able to laugh at yourself is much more attractive than trying to be in control, look smart or appear in any particular way. Do not worry about what other people think. Choose to be amused with yourself—after all, you are adorable! If you want to manifest your divine prosperity, it is important to respect yourself, appreciate yourself, give yourself permission to make mistakes, live with an open heart and love yourself no matter what.

The Beginner's Mind

A beginner's mind is a wonderful quality to have while opening more fully to creativity. Give yourself permission to fail gloriously and have fun with it! There is something referred to as the "Don't Know Mind" in martial arts. The *Don't Know* Mind is the wisdom of the warrior. If we think we know, we are closed to all other possibilities. "I *Don't Know*" means staying energetically open, flexible and able to respond in the moment according to whatever presents itself. To not know keeps us open and available for wonder, inspiration, intuition, joy, learning, amusement and excitement. The beginner's mind is about staying in the spirit of enquiry without getting trapped into notions of logic, limitations or past lessons.

Here is a Zen story about this:

> *A student once visited a Japanese master to inquire about Zen. The master served tea. When the visitor's cup was full, the master kept pouring. Tea spilled out of the cup and over the table.*
>
> *"What are you doing? The cup is full!" uttered the student. "No more will go in!"*
>
> *"Like this cup," said the master, "You are full of your own opinions and speculations. How can I show you Zen unless you first empty your cup?"*

You can see how this story applies not only to learning about Zen, but to learning about anything at all. The spirit of enquiry is a mind that is accessible, available, open to the unknown and empty of pre-conceived ideas.

Being Right is Playing Small

The need to be right and to know is a notion of the ego, it keeps us rigid and makes us brittle. When we hang on for dear life to our viewpoints and perspectives it keeps us limited and playing small. This posture not only destroys relationships, it can keep you broke. I think beneath the desire to be right is the unconscious belief that being right somehow makes us worthy of love, of life and of success. The willingness to be wrong is not only more attractive in our relationships, but also more energetically attractive in the world. It keeps us flowing, flexible and able to implement course corrections more quickly. It also keeps us spiritually open, peaceful and aligned.

One of the biggest problems I see in my counseling practice is my clients' attachment to being right. I know I used to be guilty of this unhealthy habit myself. I would fight to the bitter end in my relationships, intent on proving my viewpoint, rather than being curious about another's perspective. When we fight to be right, not only do we miss the opportunity to listen, learn and understand, we also make others feel bad by trying to prove them wrong. We pinch off the vital life-giving energy of connection, acceptance, approval and love.

Being willing to be wrong and not know anything was one of the most liberating experiences of my life. I also believe it is a significant contributing factor in the success in my marriage and my career. Now, when someone does not agree with me, rather than defend or explain myself, I open to my curiosity and ask them about their thoughts, perspective and reality. Getting into another person's heart and mind can be like going to visit another planet and tends to reveal deeper lessons and profound revelations, for both myself and for others. Rather than the exhausting posture of knowing, defending, fighting, explaining and "against-ness" it is like relaxing into the open, flowing, energetic of aikido. Once my students and clients relax into the powerful posture of curiosity and the "willingness to be wrong," I witness miracles and often a complete transformation of their relationships, their careers, their productivity, their purpose and their prosperity.

The willingness to be wrong takes courage, self-acceptance and self-confidence. It is also a necessary ingredient to step more fully into our higher potential and our inspired creative nature. I have heard many people *say* they want to go to the next level in their lives, but then slam on the brakes for fear of what that might look like, their fear of making mistakes or "getting it wrong." Once you are willing to be wrong, you can then courageously step into the river of life, relax into the mystery, connect with others more deeply and be carried the direction the Universe would have you go.

Creativity as Spiritual Connection

We are all born to be creators. It is an innate compulsion for us to express our Selves by bringing thoughts, feelings, messages, images, ideas, stories and symbols into being. It is also a deeply ingrained human desire to prosper. We are all linked up to the same Creator and Source of Brilliance and I believe we can all manifest fulfilling, prosperous, expressive lives. Exploring creativity is a way you can delve deeper into Self-discovery. If you go deep enough inside of yourself, you have the capacity to merge more fully with your soul and open the doorway to the Divine. When you accept that you are a being imbued with unlimited creative potential, you can activate and access the creative urge within you, as well as discover your hidden gifts and priceless treasures.

After some of my creativity classes, I asked my students what their experiences were like. Here are some of their responses:

> "I was afraid of what I was going to create, that it was going to be ugly and that I was not going to get it 'right.' I was also worried about what other people would think. Then I realized I feel that way in all areas of my life. When I reminded myself it was just a canvas and I could paint over it, I didn't take it so seriously. That is when I decided to just have fun. Now I don't care what anybody else thinks, I love what I created! This process has been so liberating. This learning, and my new attitude, has helped me relax and have more fun in every other area of my life!"

> "It was scary to open to the unknown within myself, but once I did, I felt I opened the doorway to the Divine."

"After feeling numbed out, dried up, bored and exhausted for years (as well as broke!) creativity has brought me back to life. I feel my inner light has been turned on and my wattage turned up. I now feel energized, excited and optimistic. I am also attracting more opportunities, more amazing people and more money!"

"Although at first it was scary, embarking on this path of creativity has helped me cultivate my faith. Now, rather than fighting a current of fear, I am joyfully riding a wave of faith into the mystery!"

"Getting involved in some of Tammi's classes helped me know myself on a deeper level. It helped me not take myself so seriously. I have heard we are spiritual beings having a human experience, but exploring my creativity help me really feel it, rather than just intellectually know it."

"Initially, I thought taking this class would be frivolous, a waste of money and silly. But after giving myself permission to play, I realize that THIS was the missing piece of the puzzle in my life. I now find fun translating into all other areas of my life, including my work. Now I feel rather than working to make money, I get paid to play!"

"I learned not only am I creative, I learned I AM CREATIVY! It's incredible to realize this after all the years of believing I am 'just a wife and mother.'"

"Uncorking my creativity has given me a reason to live. After my bout with cancer, I really don't believe I am exaggerating when I say creativity saved my life."

"Making collages, painting, writing and the crystal classes have helped me know myself in a deeper way. They have also helped me cultivate confidence. I now realize there is much more to me than meets the eye. I am not what I see in the mirror, I am not just my body, my feelings or my thoughts. I am a spark of creativity; I am a splinter of God."

One student shared with me that when she opened to her creativity she found there was more and more within herself to explore and express. "Not only did I lose weight, I found the real me!" She continued, "Creativity IS my life" and "Creativity is inevitable." For one artist, creativity is "a reason to live" and for another "It helps me live." Creativity is being aligned with our TRUE selves, and invites our inner light to shine through our physical selves. Another artist commented: "Creativity is a release, a relief and way to experience heaven on Earth!"

Some of the words I have heard repeatedly after people have been immersed in creativity are: rewarding, satisfying, gratitude, appreciation, transformational, liberating, expansive, fulfilling, soulful, exquisite, compassion, sweet, reverence, connection, respect, mysterious, fun, peace, joy and bliss. These are clearly high-vibration emotions and energies, and if water finds its own level (which it always does), increasing our vibration by virtue of cultivating our creativity, *guarantees* our lives will up-level and improve in all areas . . . and this includes our income!

Creativity Heals

Creativity has been a powerful catalyst for authentic transformation in my life and something I witness consistently with others. Tapping into our creative nature can heal us physically, mentally, emotionally, spiritually and financially. Some of the therapeutic benefits of creativity are relaxation, centeredness, hope, understanding, clarity, peace, possibility and alignment with your soul self. Tapping into inspired creativity can give you an endorphin rush and usher in energy and new life. It can uplift, inspire and motivate, as well as provide the impetus to push further, delve deeper and reach higher.

Creativity can ignite passion and invite courageous action. Creativity can evoke the qualities of exploration, spontaneity and adventure. It can help us access the ability to solve problems and cultivate new ways of thinking and being. When we get comfortable opening ourselves to our inner worlds in partnership with our creativity, we can begin to apply these skills to other areas of our lives. The process can help us learn to trust, explore and experience our Selves on a very deep level. I have also found opening to creativity can open our hearts and bring more vitality and love to our relationships. Most importantly for me, I have discovered creativity is my lifeline to the Creator.

When you are immersed in creativity,

you are held in the heart of the Creator

For more about the healing power of art and creativity, I invite you to go to my website. I offer a free eBook: *The Healing Power of Art and Creativity*. To review or download it please go to "articles and papers" at www.journeytocenter.com.

Poverty as a Catalyst to Creativity

After having access to a great deal of money which did not make me happy, I then got to experience poverty and *really* felt unhappy! However, in retrospect, I understand how everything that happened was perfect for my soul's growth. Being broke supported me in setting the intention to dig deep and pull myself up by my bootstraps. If I would have ended up with a big settlement from my relationship, or if money had come easily to me, I never would have developed my creativity. Nor would I have deepened in my connection to my soul and developed the tools, character and strength of heart to become the teacher, artist, writer and counselor I am today.

I can now look back with understanding, appreciation and compassion for my life's path, as well as my painful dance with poverty. To quote Helen Keller: "Character cannot be developed in ease and quiet. Only through experience of trial and suffering can the soul be strengthened, ambition inspired and success achieved." Success and prosperity would not have been so gratifying, or maybe even possible, if I had not taken personal responsibility to dig myself out of the trenches. I also would not have the ability and tools to support others in making the same journey.

Fred's Path to Prosperity

An example of fighting the flow of creativity and true self-expression because they "had to make a living," is my good friend and artist, Fred Choate. When the economy took a turn for the worse, Fred's financial crisis demanded he get creative. Doing what he was *supposed* to do to make money was slowly being eliminated, so Fred decided to explore what he *wanted* to do, and that was to paint. Fred took some art classes and started painting walls, and eventually murals, around town. For a while life was good. Then, the economy tanked again and wiped Fred out for a second time.

Confused and depressed, Fred found himself at church. The message he received in the sermon that day changed his life forever. The minister presented an opportunity to consider "the facts of your life," vs. "the truth of your life." The *facts* were Fred was broke. The *truth* was he now had the freedom to follow his vision. Fred opened his heart and mind to doing what he really loved, and started to put brushes to oils and canvas on a daily basis. He began furiously painting landscapes and nature scenes. Delving deeply into creativity shifted Fred's inner reality; it changed the way he saw things and the way he felt.

For Fred, the creative process was a wild ride into the mystery and a powerful catalyst for transformation. Slowly, his artwork filtered out into the community, then the state of Idaho. His work continued to ripple out into galleries across the nation and he was then picked up by an art publisher. Fred is now an award-winning artist and making more money than he ever has. Fred is a living example that it is not only possible, but probable, that if you do what you love the money will follow. He will admit the journey has not always been fun or easy. But because of his loss of income, the Universe seemed to force his hand and insist he do what he always wanted but was afraid to do. Fred has said: "I don't want to sound glib, but thank goodness the economy fell apart, because otherwise I never would have had the courage to go for my dreams."

Fred shares his wisdom about the four steps involved in the creative process:

1. Unconscious incompetence: You don't know what you are doing.

2. Conscious incompetence: You start to learn what you do not know.

3. Conscious competence: You get better but you have to think about everything.

4. Unconscious competence: You go with the flow. You are no longer using your mind, but channeling and flowing with the creative process.

Fred's 4-step creative process has been true for me in many areas of my life, including: painting, writing, doing my radio program and counseling. Sometimes it takes work, practice and diligence and to make things look and feel effortless!

Pamela's Prosperity

Another example of creativity supporting prosperity is a story about Pamela. Pamela was a client of mine who was struggling financially. She was considering taking some classes to help her cultivate a new career. One day she showed up for her session with me holding a local continuing education pamphlet, open to the page "Introduction to Computers." I was a little surprised, knowing technology was not something she enjoyed. I told Pamela I thought it was great that she was willing to stretch out of her comfort zone and the class was probably a good idea, but as far as a new career was concerned, perhaps something else might be a better fit. I asked her how she felt as she imagined going into the classroom filled with computers on that first day of class. She said she felt queasy. I asked her to explain more about the energy of queasy. Was it excitement? Fear of the unknown? Her answer was, "No, just plain sick." I told her Spirit did not want her embarking on a career that she did not enjoy or much less made her sick. Then I asked Pamela what would be fun for her. What would she enjoy? We said a prayer of intention and invited her heart to be her guide. Pamela went through the magazine again.

Pamela mulled over all the classes, one at a time, until she reached a pottery making class. A huge smile brightened her face and the light went on in her eyes. Pamela joyfully exclaimed: "That's it! That is what would be *really fun* for me." A few seconds later her smile disappeared as she energetically put on the brakes: "But I don't know anything about making pottery or even why I want to do it." I shared with Pamela needing to know and "intellectually understand" were traits of the mind, and this was a "heart process." Then I reminded her the most important reason to take the class was to explore, create, play and experience joy. This was about partnering with her Divine Child and aligning with Higher Self. I encouraged Pamela to trust her happiness and go into the mystery of "not knowing." Armed with courage, unanswered questions and a commitment to her soul, Pamela signed up for the class later that day.

A couple of weeks later when Pamela brought several of her colorful pots to a class, the students began clamoring over them. Everyone wanted to buy one! This gave her the courage and confidence to create more and take some of her bowls and pots to a local shop. They placed an order on the spot. As Pamela continued to trust and explore her creativity, her work and her prosperity expanded. Her creativity has exploded and she now makes mosaics, frames, vases, jewelry and much more. Pamela now has a website where she offers her wares and teaches classes. Pamela's joy and creativity have now become a lucrative career. Just the other day she said to me: "Thank goodness you talked me out of the computer class!" (Which of course I did not, I simply encouraged her to explore her creativity and have fun.) I wanted her to do as Joseph Campbell suggests: "Follow your bliss." Everyone who knows Pamela is so grateful she listened to her heart and her joy, and heeded the wisdom from within!

The Healing Power of the Mandala

A class I offer to support students in tapping into inspired creativity is the process of creating a mandala. The word mandala comes from the ancient language of Sanskrit and can be translated to mean "sacred circle" or "container of essence." Mandalas have been used for centuries to heal physically, mentally, emotionally and spiritually. They have also been used to attain insight and even enlightenment.

Carl Jung said that a mandala symbolizes "a safe refuge of inner reconciliation" and "a synthesis of distinctive elements in a unified scheme representing the basic nature of existence." Jung referred to the mandala as "the archetype of wholeness" and used them for his own personal healing and growth. Mandalas can be used as a vehicle to explore science, religion, art, creativity and the nature of life itself. The mandala has been said to contain an encyclopedia of the finite and is a roadmap to the infinite.

Mandalas have often been referred to as "a painted prayer" or "a spiritual path disguised as art." By creating mandalas we heal on a very deep level and call all parts of ourselves home. Even if you do not consider yourself an artist, this process can stimulate creativity, evoke intuition and assist you in lining up with your soul. You can print them out on your computer and color them, find a mandala coloring book, get a mandala drawing kit, or simply get some newsprint, a selection of different sized plates and either magic markers, colored pencils and/or crayons. Before you begin, turn inward and ask for the perfect healing symbol for you right now. You may also ask your heart or Higher Self to reveal a quality, characteristic or intention that would be most beneficial for you to claim at this time. If you are going to color a mandala that has been already drawn, you can ask for the most healing colors for you to use. There really is no right or wrong way to create a mandala.

The powerful activating ingredient
for creating a mandala (and your life) is INTENTION!

Mandalas can be created for virtually any intention, a few examples may include: improving physical health, attracting a new career, attaining balance, healing a relationship, forgiveness, expanding in love, discovering one's life purpose, inviting creativity, manifesting greater prosperity and more. In fact, the healing opportunities for mandala making are infinite.

Why is the mandala so powerful? Much of this remains a mystery, but if you consider the microcosm and the macrocosm, we constantly observe patterns of circles; from the atom, the building block of all physical world reality, to the spiral formation in the creation of new galaxies. Think about the celestial circle we call Earth, as well as all the other planets of our solar system. Imagine the way these planets move around the sun in an orbital fashion. The circle is the most prevalent pattern on land and in the sea. Consider the variety of flowers, fruits and vegetables with sacred circles. Think about a pinecone, the rings of a tree, ladybugs, shells, snowflakes, octopi, jellyfish, starfish, sand dollars, spiders and their webs. Consider weather patterns such as hurricanes and tornados. Mandala-like images have also been found in every culture, every content and in every spiritual tradition. Circular symbols have been found on the walls of caves documenting the very earliest records of modern man. The list of mandalas in nature and our physical world reality goes on and on.

My Mandala Experience

I first consciously stumbled on the mandala by accident while attending the University of Santa Monica in 2002. The process opened a door of creativity and intuition within myself and was accompanied by a profound experience of peace. The first mandala I drew evoked a sense of serenity I had been seeking for years. I had tried many anti-anxiety medications, anti-depressants, acupuncture, herbs, massage and more in an attempt to alleviate a sense of dread, fear and panic. While meditating helped me calm down and relax, creating mandalas took this sense of peace, safety and contentedness to the next level. Making mandalas soothed me, and continues to soothe me in a way that I cannot explain, describe or logically comprehend. To this day whenever I draw or paint a mandala my mind relaxes, my heart expands and I feel as if my soul begins to hum. I love creating mandalas and I love teaching others about this powerful healing practice.

After my introduction to the mandala I was so intrigued I decided to do some research. I found a mandala retreat in Northern California and knew I had to go. It was a fabulous experience and I created many healing images for myself. At one point during the retreat, we were asked to create a symbol for someone else. There were about 40 people at this retreat and each of us drew the name of someone else, then created a small mandala for them. When it was my turn, I picked a name of out a bowl that was being passed around. The name I drew was "Ann." I did not know her, and, in fact, we had not even met. During a brief guided meditation, we were asked to turn inward and ask our heart or Higher Self for the perfect healing symbol for this person. I was surprised that not much came forward for me—just a little white bird flying quickly through my mind's eye. I was perplexed as to why I did not get anything more. Usually when I turn inward and ask for a healing image, I receive colorful geometric designs, or a clear and powerful image. So I tried again, and again I received the same simple image. With some concern and trepidation, I created the mandala with a little white bird in the center of it and hoped she would not be disappointed.

After all the mandalas had been given and received, Ann came over and asked if she could speak with me. Nervously, I said yes. She proceeded to tell me that the simple little mandala I had gifted her with was an answer to a prayer. I asked her how so. She shared the following story with me. "Tammi, before I came to this retreat, I chose a name for my new business, but was not certain it was the 'right' name. I lit a candle and said a prayer. I asked God to give me a sign if this was the right name." Then she shared the name of her business with me. "I named it 'White Bird Flying.'"

I was astonished! In that moment I realized I could relinquish my judgment and doubt around my intuition, and deeply trust my inner knowing. I now understand and accept there is a deeper part of me that knows things I consciously do not, and I am so grateful for that partnership. I have seen miracles like this happen repeatedly in my classes and I now know everyone has the ability to access gifts, creativity, intuition and the wisdom within.

Everyone's experience with the mandala is different. The common denominator is that each person gets exactly what they need. Although skeptical, at my prompting, my husband Steve begrudgingly participated in one of my mandala classes. Although he is not a painter, he had to admit it was an incredible experience and that he was blown away by what he created. In fact, everyone who comes to one of my mandala classes is astonished by what they manifest. They often say: "I can't believe I did that." I remind them that this is sacred art, a co-creative process. They didn't do it alone; Spirit did it *through* them. When we learn how to trust the process and create in this way, the experience of collaborative co-creation can translate into every other area of our lives.

My Prosperity Mandala

Several years ago I set an intention to create more prosperity, so I decided to do a "Prosperity Mandala." A green and gold swirling image showed up in my mind's eye. I created the image on card stock with colored pencils. I showed a friend my mandala and she loved it. She asked me to paint one for her. It took me a moment to realize I had just commissioned my first mandala painting! I immediately went to the art store and bought supplies.

Later that evening, through laughter and tears, I began to create a 3' x 3' prosperity mandala painting. A month later, when it was finally complete, I packed it up, carefully tucked it into my car and brought it to my friend. I felt a bit afraid as I carried it up to her office. When she opened the door and saw the mandala, she smiled, then started jumping up and down. She excitedly shared with me how much she loved it.

It was surreal and thrilling to see how my personal brand of creativity made someone else so happy. Then she wrote a check out to me for $2000. I was stunned. My prosperity symbol was really working! I have since used that same image on candles, cards and in my prosperity support classes. In fact, it is the image I used on the cover of this book.

I love creating mandalas and introducing others to this powerful and sacred practice. In mandala workshops, the first thing I guide my students to do is "centering" and setting their intentions. Next I perform a guided meditation and invite them to ask their hearts or Higher Selves to reveal the perfect healing symbol for them. Then I have them create their symbol with colored pencils or paint and embellish them with crystals, gold leaf and glitter. When they are finished creating their mandala, I have them place their hands over it and ask inwardly if there is any message or wisdom the mandala has to share. The messages can come forward as one word, a sentence, a poem, or pages of channeled material. The final step is to thank the mandala, and Source, knowing everything that has been intended and asked for is being provided and that all needs are being met. The synchronicity after these classes results in transformation, healing and manifestations of prosperity that are nothing short of miraculous and an incredible joy to witness.

I have cultivated a wonderful friendship with my creativity, intuition, Higher Self and Inner Being, and am absolutely confident of the immense power that resides in my own heart and soul. I trust the information and images my inner realms reveal to me and am blessed to support others in doing the same. You too have the ability to cultivate your creativity, access answers to your questions and tap into the profound wisdom within you.

Grace, intuition, beauty and wisdom are always accessible, everywhere and to everyone. It is not just around you, but in you. All that is required is your sincere desire and heartfelt invitation. If you turn inward with an open and inquiring mind, you will discover a wealth of symbols, support, magic and miracles in the very center of your Self.

Exercise #1: Research Creative Classes in Your Area.

Creative classes can be found through continuing education programs, the Learning Annex, or with local teachers, artists and healers. Check out advertising in your local papers and/or magazines. Open your mind and let your heart and soul guide you to something that would be fun for you to do. Do not pick something you think you "should" do, or that you would even necessarily be good at. Adopt the beginners mind and be willing to not know, make mistakes, look silly and have fun. This is about opening to the mystery of creativity and the doorway to the Divine within. Take a deep breath and invite the child like qualities of excitement and joy to be your guide.

Some examples of creative courses may include (but not be limited to): paper making, card making, welding, crystal classes, sculpting, computer classes, pottery, photography, photoshop, singing, music, dancing, movement, playing an instrument, intuitive development, meditation, sewing, quilting, knitting, painting, jewelry making, faux finishing, poetry, drawing, woodshop, furniture making, training animals, gardening, feng shui, chakra classes, creative writing, storytelling, basket weaving, acting, costume or set designing, the healing arts and more. The sky is the limit! We are connected to a Source of Infinite expression, vitality, aliveness, vibrancy and creativity. If none of these suggestions spark your interest, just set the intention to naturally, gracefully and easily find the perfect course, class, adventure or endeavor to help you tap into your divinity, your creativity and your wealth of wisdom within.

Exercise #2: Create Your Mandala Prosperity Symbol.

Allow yourself to have fun with this process. If you find the prospect daunting or intimidating, just keep it really simple. My first mandalas were in crayon on newsprint. From there, they expanded and evolved. Next, I used colored pencils, then small water color painting, then small acrylic paintings and now I do very large paintings with crystals gold leafing and mixed medium. Even if you create a very small crayon mandala, it can still be very powerful, healing and extremely revelatory. Just set your healing intentions and most of all HAVE FUN with the process!

1. Assemble your supplies. This includes paper, which can be a piece of typing paper, newsprint, construction paper, poster board, drawing paper or canvas. Next, find what

you are going to draw or color with. This can be crayons, pastels, colored pencils, magic markers or paint. You will also want a compass, or you may use a cup, saucer and/or plates for different sized circles. You may also want a ruler or straight edge to make straight lines.

2. Draw your circle on the paper by using your compass or tracing around your cup, saucer or plate.

3. Turn inward and take a few relaxing, healing, cleansing breaths and allow yourself to relax.

4. Once your thoughts have slowed down, ask your heart or Higher Self for the perfect Prosperity Healing Symbol for you right now. Patiently allow it to come into focus in your mind's eye. Let it happen in its own time and its own way.

5. You may see the image in its entirety or perhaps only get a sense of where to start. Trust the process and give yourself permission to create it. There is no "right way" to create a mandala. Do not put pressure on yourself. Allow the process to be fun and simple.

6. If you get stuck while creating your mandala and not sure what to do next, take an easy breath and turn inward, then ask your heart or Higher Self to reveal your next step.

7. Once you have completed your mandala, you may want to embellish it with glitter, crystals, items from nature or anything else that calls to you.

8. When your prosperity mandala is done, put your hands over it, close your eyes and ask inwardly if it has a message

or wisdom it wants to share with you. Listen quietly and patiently for what comes forward. It may be silence, it may be one word, a sentence, a paragraph, or pages of channeled material. Trust however this unfolds for you.

9. You may want to write this message on the back of your mandala or in your prosperity journal.

10. You may also go back now (or at any time) and ask your mandala any questions you have, including how you can manifest greater prosperity in the world. Listen quietly and patiently. What you receive may be expected or unexpected; logical or illogical; something known or unknown. Just open your heart and mind, and you may be quite surprised at what you receive.

11. Place your mandala where you will see it often. Invite and allow it to support you in continuing to consciously claim and attract your divine prosperity.

This process may not seem powerful to you. However, I have had many students come back to me after creating their prosperity mandala and tell me this was the *most important* piece of their prosperity puzzle. Open your mind and give it a try! Even if you do not become addicted to the mandala process, it is an incredible tool to support you in aligning with your Higher Self and opening the door to your inner wisdom and inspired creativity. If you do enjoy this exercise, allow your mandala adventure to evolve and just keep creating. If you want to know more about the mandala, or see some of my paintings, I invite you to go to www.journeytocenter.com to look at the images in my gallery and the written articles.

Unlocking your creativity is the true key to your prosperity. What it takes to become truly prosperous is a creative, open and flexible mind. There is virtually no limit to the knowledge you can acquire and the creativity you can express. What you have in your imagination and your heart is far more valuable than what you have in your bank account. And by virtue of tapping into your creativity you will be supported in eventually *expanding* and *increasing* what is in your bank account!

Your mind is connected to Universal mind, and as you open to your own brand of creativity, you will become a powerful vortex and more fully aligned with the Creator. This can help you tap into your genius, expand your brilliance, understand your uniqueness and attract your abundance. Invite your creativity to help you understand these Truths: You are PRICELESS! You are VALUABLE! You are SPECIAL! You are UNIQUE! You are WORTHY! And you are ADORED!

Chapter 13

Seeing is Believing

*You must understand that seeing is believing,
but also know that believing is seeing.*

~Denis Waitley

For many people the process of visioning, imagination and manifesting may not be all that effective if they do not see it exemplified in the world; there are times we need to see it to believe it. In order to "prove" to our subconscious mind that something is possible, we first need to see it manifested as an actual living, breathing human example.

I used to think men were untrustworthy because that had been my personal experience. And it was going to continue to be my experience because we always manifest what we think and believe. I finally came to understand I was going to continue to attract untrustworthy men until I changed my mind about this limiting belief. So I consciously made the decision to find examples of both men, and couples, to be my "new positive role models."

I found two couples where I could witness the husbands consistently treating their wives with respect and kindness. They were also honest and loyal. The women were also devoted, respectful and kind to their husbands. A friend said to me "I think there are things going on behind the scenes that aren't so great." But I did not care, I did not want to focus on "behind the scenes." Like going to the theater, I wanted to focus on what I wanted to see. I did not want to spend time sneaking around looking behind the curtains and under the stage. Those details were none of my business.

I was clear about what I wanted, and was consciously choosing to take responsibility for creating a new reality for myself. I finally figured out it was important for me to focus on what was good and right with men and relationships, and give up focusing on what was bad and wrong. I was going to "cherry pick" and direct my attention to the qualities and living examples I wanted to manifest in my own life. As I consciously observed these lovely couples, I witnessed their healthy communication, solid boundaries, heart-connection, laughter and joy. As I observed them, my mind and heart opened the possibility that one day it could happen for me—and so it did! I documented that healing journey in my book *Manifesting Love From the Inside Out.* This exercise was a positive and powerful way of healing the limiting content that had been taking up residence in my subconscious mind since early childhood. I eventually came to realize I needed to implement this powerful healing technique with prosperity and wealth as well.

For a period of time I harbored an unconscious notion that someone could not be spiritual AND prosperous. I had painful experiences with financially affluent people that I deemed as negative, so I unconsciously "threw the baby out with the bathwater" so to speak. I finally understood in order to open my mind to the possibility of "spiritual prosperity," and create it for myself, I needed to consciously pay attention to it being exemplified in the world.

From my perspective, one of the greatest role models of this positive prosperity paradigm is Oprah Winfrey. I decided to pay more attention to her: what she believed, what she taught, what she has learned and how she did it.

Oprah as a Living Example of Prosperity

Media mogul Oprah Winfrey has a net worth of $2.7 billion. She rose from poverty, abuse and prejudice to become one of the most influential people alive today. Choosing to consciously observe her as a living example of divine prosperity has supported me in healing the limiting belief and ridiculous notion that wealth and spirituality are mutually exclusive.

Oprah's diverse format includes world and humanitarian issues, health and spirituality. She has interviewed the non-famous and famous alike and is credited for revolutionizing the television talk show platform with her program airing in 140 countries. Oprah has published five books and two magazines, one of which was named the most successful start-up ever by *Fortune* magazine. In 2006 she added a radio network to her media empire with "Oprah & Friends" on XM Satellite Radio. In 2007, Oprah opened the Oprah Winfrey Leadership Academy for Girls in South Africa, a boarding school for poverty-stricken girls. Oprah is currently at the helm of her biggest vision yet, her television network, OWN, which is filled with uplifting spiritual content and conscious programming.

In 2009 Oprah was asked to give a graduation speech to the students of Duke University. In her speech she shared that while she is happy and proud of her financial success, true happiness lies in helping others. Oprah stated: "It's great to have nice homes and it's great to have a private jet. Anyone who tells you that having your own private jet isn't great is lying to you. You may achieve great things, but you haven't completed the circle of success until you help someone else move to a higher ground and get to a better place."

Oprah revealed her number one secret to success: "Believe in yourself. I am who I am because I trust my gut more than anyone else's opinion," she said. "That is my best advice to you —trust your gut. You know what is right and what is wrong. Trust your gut and stand in your own shoes and you will be a huge success."

Oprah shared other pearls of wisdom about manifesting success: "Give back and you will be a success, summon courage in the face of adversity and you will be a success, see the possibilities of what you can become, and not just what you are, and you will be a success, live with humility and you will be a success, stand in your own shoes and be generous enough to say kind, affirming words to those that long to hear them—and you will be a huge success."

Oprah has given millions of people, including myself, the courage to dream big by living her best life. She is a living example of authentic power, creativity, big thinking, service, philanthropy, spirituality, wealth and generosity. Oprah is clearly aligned with her divine purpose and has manifested immense prosperity. With regard to prosperity, her conscious and subconscious minds are congruent. She is consistent in her actions, words and deeds. She knows she is worthy and deserving of her staggering wealth and harbors no guilt. She makes no apologies for her success and supports others in doing the same. When she was asked about how it feels to be so successful, she said: "It feels like peace." Peace is a very high vibrational state, which I personally aspire to live in more and more consistently.

It may be important to mention, when looking for role models, we are not comparing ourselves to another (which *never* works out well) or competing with any one in any way. I love something I heard Oprah once say: "People say they want to be like me. Look, I got that down! Go out and be the best YOU you can be!" Oprah also shared a funny story about when she was an anchor at a news station and attempted to be like Barbara Walters. While reading the teleprompter, she mispronounced the word "Canada" and said something like "Cun-Auda." While still on the air, she busted up laughing. In that moment, she decided that, rather than emulating another or aspiring to be like someone else, she was going to be her authentic self and the very best Oprah she could be. Another great life lesson from a very wise woman!

Everything under the sun exists, so you have the powerful choice and opportunity to look for what is right in any situation and every circumstance, or to look at what is wrong; for what is good, or what is bad; for what is positive and wanted, or what is negative and unwanted. Only you can do this for yourself.

You can argue for limitations

or focus on unlimited possibilities.

Your choice and your focus will predict and create your future

I invite you to figure out what you want and look for living examples that model the qualities and characteristics of what you would like to claim for yourself, because I assure you *it all exists.* And then CHOOSE YOUR WORDS WISELY!

Speak the words and utter the messages that are congruent with the direction you want to go in your life. If you are going to talk about what is wrong with the world, how bad the economy is and how limited the resources are and then expect to hit the lottery, it is not going to happen. Focusing on and speaking about the negative is not going to attract the positive. Not only is it illogical, it is impossible.

Your words have the power to create poverty or prosperity.

In order to manifest what we want it is vital to be consistent and congruent with our vision and our words. In the Bible, John 1:1 it is stated, "In the beginning was the Word, and the Word was with God, and the Word was God." Words are extraordinarily powerful and literally create our lives. Words can place us in poverty or they can support us in manifesting a life of prosperity, fulfillment and joy. "For by your words you will be justified, and by your words you will be condemned." Matthew 12:37.

The spoken word holds tremendous power, continually assisting us in creating our lives. Most of us talk a lot, and it is easy to take the power of our words for granted. But just like these two quotes from the Bible, words not only have power, words ARE power. The words you speak are not only heard by other people, but heard by the Universe, your unconscious mind and your Self. You are constantly programming your world, your subconscious mind, your navigation system and your future with the words you speak and the thoughts you think.

With the correct and skillful use of the spoken word, we can more easily overcome obstacles and financial struggles and manifest greater success and prosperity. The spoken word can bring to life our deepest intentions and soul's longing. In order for our words to be as effective as possible, they must be full of integrity, positive, consistent and congruent with what we want to create.

Exercise #1: Look For Role Models

1. What is it you want to create? Look around for role models that exemplify your highest ideals. Remind yourself if they can do it, that means it can be done! We are all linked up to the same source of power and we all have the opportunity to create empowered, prosperous and fulfilling lives. It is not that the power to prosper is in some people and not in others, it simply means that some people have tapped into it and others have not.

2. Write down the qualities you perceive as admirable in your role models.

3. Observe this list and these qualities you have identified. Now consider and acknowledge each of these qualities existing in you as well. We often admire in others disowned aspects of ourselves. What we see in them may be what we need to look for, acknowledge and further cultivate within ourselves. So take a moment and acknowledge yourself!

4. Know the information that comes forward in this exercise can also be a guiding light for you as you move more in the direction of your life purpose, your passion and your prosperity.

Exercise #2: Claim Your Wisdom Word

1. Turn your attention inward and ask your heart or Higher Self what quality or characteristic you would benefit from more fully inviting into your life right now. Listen patiently for the still small voice to reveal its wisdom.

2. After your "wisdom word" shows up, create an affirmation around it. You want your affirmation to feel good when you say it or think about it. You want it to make your heart sing, make you happy and energize you.

3. Start your day with your affirmation, repeat it to yourself when you are waiting in line at the grocery store or at a stop light. Repeat it before you go to bed. You have more power than you think and using the power of your words can energize you, encourage your prosperity and support you in manifesting your heartfelt dreams.

Here are some examples I have personally used:

"I am a magnet for magic, miracles and money"

"I am living a joy-filled, fun-filled prosperous life!"

"I am confident and courageous and I speak from my heart!"

"I am of service, I am glamorous and I am prosperous!"

"I am an affluent artist!"

"I am the child in whom God is well pleased."

"I am relaxing into my faith, living in my loving and attracting my prosperity."

"I believe in myself and am worthy of money, love, fulfillment and FUN!"

What are some messages you can share with yourself right now about your immense value and innate worthiness? What are some words that make your heart sing and feel expansive as you consider them? Write these messages down and refer to them often. It is great to have cheerleaders in your life, but real change occurs when you become the authentic, inspired, consistent, kind and loving cheerleader for yourself!

Chapter 14

The Purpose of your Life

I am here for a purpose and that purpose is to grow into a mountain, not to shrink to a grain of sand.
Henceforth will I apply ALL my efforts to become the highest mountain of all and I will strain my potential until it cries for mercy.

~Og Mandino

I break down work into three categories: job, career and life purpose. I have experienced all three. I have worked as a waitress, in retail, as a secretary and a massage therapist. These were my "jobs." I participated in these activities, not because I loved them, but to make money and pay my bills. I have also worked as a hairdresser, model, spokesperson and actress, these were my "careers," employment that I received education for, enjoyed and was proud of. I currently work as an artist, sacred art facilitator, author, radio host and counselor, and believe I have discovered my "life's purpose." I love what I do and I get paid to play. I am of service, I am prosperous, I feel vibrantly alive and am deeply fulfilled. I am by no means fully realized, or think I am in "full bloom," but I do have the strong sense I am on the right track, heading the right direction and in aligned partnership with the Creative Force of the Universe.

I agree with this quote from Rick Warren, minister and the best-selling author of *A Purpose Driven Life*: "If you're alive, there's a purpose for your life." I don't think we can be truly happy or fulfilled unless we discover our purpose and start living it. We all have amazing gifts and a seed of brilliance within. Our brilliance waits patiently to be activated and wants to be expressed.

What Is Your Entelechy?

A word that can be used to describe that seed of brilliance is "entelechy." Entelechy comes from the Greek word *entelecheia*. The root *ekhein* can be translated to mean "to have" and *tele* means "perfection." It is the essence of divine potential in all things. For example the entelechy of an acorn is to be an oak tree, the entelechy of a caterpillar is to be a beautiful butterfly and the entelechy of sunflower seed is to be a glorious, golden sunflower.

Every human being has a seed of potentiality lying deep within.

It is up to each individual if this vital force remains

dormant, or if they choose to say yes,

fan the flame and activate the seed of divine expression.

Maybe you are one of the fortunate few who are abundantly clear about your life's purpose. Or maybe you are like most people, hoping your purpose will show up and make itself known to you. It may help to know that no matter where you are on your life's path, your purpose is already in progress. James Hillman has a wonderful quote: "You are born with a character, it is given, a gift, as the old stories say, from the guardians upon your birth . . . Each person enters the world called."

Perhaps your calling made appearances early in childhood. What was fun for you? What did it mean to play and what did it feel like? Children do not have to think about these things, for them, it just IS! When we are fresh from God, we have an innate sense of who we are, what we enjoy, what makes us happy and why we are here.

Your soul's purpose may have revealed itself in adolescence through your interests. It can also be glimpsed at by virtue of what you admire and respect in others. Your purpose may be seen in the things that come easily to you, in certain natural abilities and "gifts" you don't think are all that important or any big deal. Another very strong clue about what you came here to do, is hinted at when you lose track of time while immersed in an activity.

If you are not clear about your purpose, ask your soul or Spirit to show you - then pay attention! Open your mind to celebrate, enjoy and express who you are at the deepest level. Set the intention to open your heart wide, live in your loving and take a stand for what matter most to you. Opening your mind and heart to finding purpose, as well as the value in all things, can create an internal shift and raise your vibration in such a way that allows doors to open and invites synchronicity in.

As you open your mind to exploring your life's purpose, be like a spiritual scientist. Know when you ask the questions, the answers *can* and *will* reveal themselves. Be like a curious seeker, out to locate your buried treasure, knowing with certainty it exists. And because you are searching for it, you are guaranteed to find it.

When you start looking at your life with the intention to know your purpose, you can look at everything that happened, or did not happen, as important and necessary information. You can use your intuition and observe patterns to find deep meaning. What were some of the things you heard repeatedly from teachers, friends, parents or even strangers? A powerful exercise is to gather information about yourself; ask your friends and those who know you well what they perceive to be your greatest gifts. Then listen carefully to their feedback and maybe even write it down.

We live in a Universe that conspires to inform us.

It wants to dance and play WITH us and THROUGH us.

We just need to extend the invitation

and stay open to receive it!

We only need to ask the questions we want to know the answers to, then open our minds, hearts, inner ears and spiritual eyes so we can see, hear and receive the feedback. The more open we are to finding meaning, guidance and information both inside and outside of ourselves, the more likely we will find it. Once we extend the invitation, we can start to perceive the information and recognize the patterns. As we do this, we have the opportunity to start connecting the dots and begin to line up with our purpose, passion and prosperity.

I love this wise and wonderful quote from P.T Barnum: "We are all, no doubt, born for a wise purpose. There is as much diversity in our brains as in our countenances. Some are born natural mechanics, while some have great aversion to machinery . . . Unless a man enters upon the vocation intended for him by nature, and best suited to his peculiar genius he cannot succeed." In other words one person's dream job is another person's nightmare!

Diane's Divine Purpose

A friend of mine, Diane, was a waiting tables and not loving her job. I asked her what she would do if she hit the lottery and did not have to work anymore. She pondered the question for a moment and then a sparkle showed up in her eyes. She told me she would love to teach children, teenagers and adults about nutrition, how to cook healthy meals and create beautiful desserts. I am certain my face contorted as she shared her ideal dream life with me. I thought to myself: *EGADS!* What a nightmare! That sounds *AWFUL!*

After Diane considered what would be really fun for her, it put the wheels of her imagination into motion. She decided to take some action steps and follow her joy. Diane volunteered for a continuing education program and offered a class about simple, healthy cooking. Then she created a cookbook she made available online and later went to print with. Next Diane created a website and made her services available locally. Her vision continued to expand as she made her teachings and philosophies available through teleseminars. Diane's "dream-job idea" has gracefully evolved into her life's purpose. She is no longer waiting tables, but is instead offering the wonderful gift of nutrition, food, her heart and her love to an audience that wants to receive her gifts.

Diane is now getting paid well to do the very thing she was willing to do for free. It didn't happen overnight, but it could never have happened at all if she had not opened her mind to consider what would really bring her joy, and then take the small consistent action steps in the direction of her dreams.

Intuition, gut instinct and following one's joy seems imperative in manifesting great prosperity. Something P.T. Barnum, Oprah Winfrey, Richard Branson, Bill Gates and my friend Diane all have in common is they are doing what they love, and their prosperity has followed. They are all aligned with their Higher Selves, in partnership with the Universe and living their life's purpose.

What is Fun For You? What Do You WANT?

My client, Barbara, called me with good news: "Yale wants to interview me!" "Fabulous," I responded. "For what?" Barbara proceeded to tell me she sent in her resume for a position as a "communications officer." "Oh, really?" I was confused. "What the heck is a communications officer? What does that mean? What would you do?" Barbara began to share her list of logical reasons about why this would be a great opportunity: she had the credentials;

there was a great salary; there would be benefits. Then I asked her: "But would it be fun for you? Is it really what you want to do?" Barbara was quiet for a minute and then mentioned the prestige of being associated with Yale, the lovely New England autumns and the brilliant academic minds she would be interacting with. I asked again, "Would it be fun?" She was quiet, so I continued, "Barb, what would be fun for you? What do you really, really want?" There was a long silence, she finally answered. "I want to do Shakespeare, I want to sing, I want to do films, I want to be a fabulous character actress." It seems Barbara's head wanted to go to Yale, but her heart wanted to sing, dance and perform.

A week later Barbara called me again: "Tammi, I have great news! I asked her if she got the job at Yale. Barbara responded: "No, thank *GOODNESS* that didn't happen! I just booked an audition to play this Russian woman in a film. I get to *act* and I get to *sing,* I am going to get paid to play!" She proceeded to tell me about another audition she had the following week for Beatrice in Shakespeare's "Much Ado About Nothing," and her audition for a big national commercial. Barbara thanked me for helping her get clear about what she really wanted. I reminded her all I did was ask her what she really wanted. She answered the questions for herself and then took some wonderful action steps on her behalf; she searched for acting opportunities and then submitted her head-shots and resume. Now the Universe could support her in living the life she really wanted, deserved and desired.

Our life's purpose is always fun. It is not what we *should* do, but rather what we *want* to do! If we do not take the time to consider, identify and claim it, it will not be able to show up. And even if it did, we may not recognize it or be ready for it! So take some time to ask yourself: What would be fun for me? What do I really, really want?

What Is Your Authentic Shape?

It is everyone's right to be prosperous, successful and fulfilled. God is here to experience the physical world through us and playing small does not serve Him. We are here to grow, evolve and expand, mentally, emotionally and spiritually. But each of us has to choose for ourselves if we are going to settle and simply *survive* or open our hearts and *thrive*. The truth is every one of us has our own magic and inalienable right to fully develop, celebrate and express our unique selves. The desire to prosper is not only our potential and our right, but a cosmic urge woven into the very fabric of our being. So where do you fit in the bigger scheme of things? There *is* a piece of the worldly puzzle that is meant *just for you*.

You have a piece of the puzzle

that no one else can fit into;

it is your authentic shape.

You possess a unique combination of experiences, propensities, proclivities, gifts, talents and interests that no one else in the world has. As you open your mind to this possibility and Truth, your life's purpose can start to come into focus and reveal itself to you.

The Purpose of MY Life!

Years ago, I opened my mind to the possibility of life purpose—I wondered glumly if had one. Meditating one morning about what my purpose might be, nothing remarkable revealed itself. But later, while getting a massage, a very intuitive massage therapist made a comment about my purple glittery toenail polish. "Tammi, I love your sparkly toes!" My response to this little compliment was something like: "Yeah, thanks, I just don't feel that planet Earth is my home. I don't fit in here . . . it just isn't sparkly enough." Then this wonderful and amazing woman uttered a sentence that changed my life forever: "Well maybe that *is* your purpose, to bring the bling to planet Earth." A light went on inside of me—I felt I was just given my job description!

Years later, I am confident that bringing the bling *is* my purpose. I bring sparkle and beauty to planet Earth in many different ways: through my art that features lots of crystals, glitter and gold and through my art classes and teaching others "bling techniques." I bring my own unique brand of sparkle when I sit in my loving, witnessing acknowledging and reflecting the Divine beauty, light and power of others. I assist others in cultivating their physical beauty with makeup and makeovers. I love to offer support about hair, fitness, nutrition and wardrobe. I have also recently started the non-profit foundation "Art and Soul". I work with women and support them in cultivating confidence, claiming their creativity, owning their beauty and knowing their power. My life's purpose and path has been guided by love, service and joy.

Once I opened my mind to the possibility that I had a purpose, and started asking the questions, the answers began to reveal themselves. Once I started accepting myself just as I was, without apologies or excuses, life began to shift and transform around me. Yes, there were lean years, and it took courage to keep showing up on my own behalf, but the rewards and positive feedback from the Universe was always there. I started relaxing into faith and acknowledged if God was on my side, how could I fail? I began to understand as long as I kept loving myself, believing in my gifts and trusting God, success was inevitable.

There is a Divine plan for everyone, and turning inward with the intention to find it is available to us all. You must be prepared for changes, they may come quickly or they may take time, this is where the qualities of patience and faith are necessary. Flowers bloom in God's time; we cannot force the rosebud into its fullness and we cannot demand the immediate full Divine expression of ourselves.

Healing, growth and evolving in consciousness is a

PROCESS, not an EVENT—

a JOURNEY, not a DESTINATION!

Often when I counsel people they say: "Yeah Tammi, I would like to find my purpose, but in the meantime I have to pay my bills." I certainly understand this and I have personally made the gradual transition from working to pay my bills and *striving*, to living my purpose and *thriving*. The process can be like having both feet in one area of the garden, then we realize we long for something more, to be somewhere else. We may decide to put a toe on another area, then set our foot down, then gradually shift our weight, until we are finally ready to put both feet on the other side of the garden.

Most people don't go from sitting still to soaring, and most people don't just quit their jobs and immediately step fully into their life's purpose (although it *can* happen that way.) Too much change all at once can feel scary and unstable. A gradual transition can allow you to feel more supported, safe and solid.

"Sometimes you have to crawl,

before you walk,

before you run,

before you fly."

The "life purpose journey" can be like going into the mystery, an adventure into the unknown and it takes trust, perseverance and immense courage. The core qualities that will support you *the most*, is the unshakable confidence that on the deepest level you *KNOW* you have great value, that you are loved, you possess important gifts and are worthy of your heart's desires. As Oprah has wisely suggested: *"Believe in yourself!"*

But What Do I DO?

I know from experience how scary it can be to step more fully into ones life's purpose. I have walked through my own fear, anxiety and dread as I opened my mind to discovering my entelechy and life's purpose. In the past, really believing I was supposed to do television, I was excited to be involved with a pilot. However, after a significant investment of my time and energy, the project seemed to stall. I was frustrated, and grew tired of waiting...I was not enjoying the disempowered experience of waiting on someone else to do their part. I finally decided to turn inward with the intention of hearing the wisdom within and to figure out what my next action steps should be.

After meditating and quieting my mind, I asked my Soul or Higher Self: "What would you have me do?" The answer I received in response surprised me greatly: "Write." I was not a writer and had no conscious desire to write. I was an actress and spokesmodel for goodness sake! I was certain I had heard this message incorrectly. So I got quiet and posed the question again: "What would you have me do?" Again I received the same information. "Write." My response: "Write? Write *what*?" My Higher Self responded: "Write about what you know." I was not loving what I was hearing and retorted: "But I don't *know* anything!" Then I was reminded: "You know how you got from a pattern of unhealthy relationships to one that works." Well, yes... I had to admit, I did know that.

Throughout my twenties and thirties, I had experienced dozens of unhealthy, unhappy, dysfunctional relationships before I embarked on my healing path and eventually manifested a wonderful man and a healthy, happy marriage. Then I heard: "Well, not everyone knows that." Inwardly I was beginning to understand that perhaps one day, I could be a way-shower for others wanting to heal their hurt and manifest a healthy, happy, spiritual partnership. Shortly thereafter, I could clearly see the vibrant purple book cover with a heart in the center and a crystal inside the heart. The title came in loud as clear as well: *Manifesting Love From the Inside Out*. And so I knew it was time to write.

Here is a concept one my teachers and friends, Gavin Frye, shared with me: "I lean into things to see if God endorses them." I decided to lean into writing; to "try it on" and see if it was a fit. If not, I could always stop. Shortly after I received my inner prompt to write, I decided to go back to school. Part of the required curriculum was a writing class. It seemed I was being supported not only in writing, but also in becoming a good writer. I also received positive feedback immediately. During one of my very first classes I was asked to read my assignment out loud as an example of a well-written paper. I was stunned! I will admit, I still had resistance about writing the book, it seemed like such an overwhelming and daunting project, but every time I sat down to meditate and listen to the still small voice of my Higher Self, the message came through loud, clear and consistent.

As I leaned into writing my book, I was met with green lights, support, acknowledgement, encouragement and open doors. Eventually I went everywhere with my manifesting love notebook. I was always prepared to write down thoughts and ideas whenever they occurred. In fact, I slept with my notebook next to my bed and took notes when nocturnal inspiration would strike. I continually chipped away at my short term and long term goals and *Manifesting Love* finally came into being.

My book was self-published and a grassroots endeavor. When it first came out I sold a copy to everyone I knew. Then I thought, "Now what?" That was when I was asked to make my book part of the curriculum at a work release program. The girls involved in the program and I went through the book one chapter at a time. I witnessed the transformation of many women who had previously identified themselves as bad, as prisoners, as being wrong and unlovable. They began to identify themselves as spiritual beings, lightworkers and love bugs! I felt I was a witness to miracles in the making.

One day, after class, one of the girls came to me and said: "Tammi, I used to judge women like you, but now I realize we are just alike." Hearing this statement, along with witnessing the extraordinary transformation of these girls, blew my heart wide open. In that moment I realized my Higher Self knew what she was talking about when she told me to write—and I was so glad I listened, mustered up the courage, created the goals and continued taking baby steps until the project was complete.

I have sold thousands of copies of *Manifesting Love* to date and it feels as if it is just now starting to gain momentum. A few months ago I received a phone call from a woman wanting to order 15 copies for all of her friends. She told me it was the best self-help book she had ever read and that it had completely transformed her life. I told her I was honored. When she identified herself as Vanna White, to say I was surprised would be a massive understatement!

Recently I received this email from a reader:

Greetings Dr. Tammi,

I have to say that an angel must have told my pediatrician to recommend your book to me. Trust me, I have read LOTS of books but "Manifesting Love From the Inside Out" goes beyond being your typical self-help book. Your book is so intelligently and spiritually written.

As I read more of your book, I feel like I am truly on that path of healing and becoming WHOLE . . . or better seeing that I am already WHOLE, I just need to embrace it. Thank you for writing "Manifesting Love." I truly believe this is a book that every woman (and man) should read.

Yes, I am ready for healing, wholeness and great love!

Thank you beloved sister!

Tamu Ngina

Tamu touched my heart and was my Earth Angel. I felt she was a wink from the Universe to let me know I was right on track and heading the right direction.

Here is a portion of a review I received on Amazon that absolutely blew me away:

How do you comment about such a profound work? I cannot easily express how amazing this book is. I know many men do not read self-help books but as a man,

I am telling you guys out there to let down your guard and read "Manifesting Love From the Inside Out!" Tammi is the most amazing teacher and her exercises are POWERFUL!

Tammi absolutely nails the idea that loving yourself IS the path to loving others. While transformation of this kind takes some time, you will slowly but surely (or even quickly) begin to notice how your inner love for self radiates out to others.

Tammi has lovingly taught me to face my fears, inner monsters, shame, and regrets, and turn them into a loving beacon for the love and wholeness. Why wait any longer? If you're reading this, especially you guys out there, you are looking for REAL answers to your life. You will only find those answers within. If you do not know HOW to look within, Tammi will teach you. I PROMISE you, I GUARANTEE you this book will transform your life.

Love is not confined to eros - Love is THE pure energy that you can utilize for every area of your life. I am a heterosexual normal guy. I'm telling you, this book is a life changer.

Trevor

As I read Trevor's review, I was stunned, I felt I was shaken to the very core of my soul self. Tears pricked at the back of my eyes and I was awash in goose bumps. While in the throes of my suffering, pain and poverty, I had no idea I that I had any value, and that one day I would able to help others. But here I am today living a fulfilling life of creativity, prosperity and service. I continue to receive incredible feedback from readers all over the world and I am honored, humbled and astonished. I am awestruck by the grace, miracles, support and love that is now a part of my life every day. Yes, it took work, practice, diligence, courage and time, but now writing comes naturally and easily. I enjoy the process, and get positive feedback that my musings and messages support, uplift and inspire others. Was it the journey easy? No. Was it always fun? Definitely not. Was it all worth it in the end? Absolutely!

You too have unique, profound and amazing gifts to offer the world that are immensely valuable. It is not always easy to figure out what they are, but I guarantee you they are woven into your DNA. Finding your hidden treasure takes courage. Locating your riches takes commitment. Your remarkable gifts are waiting for you to claim them and then share them. I am on the side lines cheering you on, so are your angels, so is your soul, so is the Universe and so are the future recipients of your special brand of magic!

You have profound and unique gifts to offer!

You are priceless, important and valuable!

You have something extraordinary to share with others

and the world!

If You Want Something Different, Do Something Different

As I have mentioned before in this book: "If you do what you have always done, you will get what you always got." So if you are ready for greater prosperity and a more fulfilling life, listen to your inner promptings and take the little steps.

The longest journey begins with that first small step.

And consistent small steps in the direction of your

heart and soul's promptings ensure

you will eventually be living the life of your dreams.

What I have found is that for each small step I have taken, I am met with miracles, grace and positive feedback. I believe for every step we take towards God, God takes 10 steps joyously towards us.

My purpose and co-creative journey continues to unfold and evolve in interesting and unexpected ways, and has been far from a direct, straight and clear path. Sometimes it seems it has been more winding and circuitous than necessary, but that is life! Often on this human adventure we have the opportunity to try different things. This can support us in refining our desires, getting clear about what we do want—and what we do not want. Life can be like a buffet, we get to go back repeatedly and refine our choices and desires.

Being of Service and Following Joy

For a period of time I owned a studio/gallery where I featured my artwork and taught classes. I found it deeply fulfilling and had a lot of fun. However, after two years it was starting to feel like a burden and it was not bringing me the joy it once had. The neighbors were getting really nasty as well. My husband asked me if I was happy, if this was really what I wanted to be doing. From his perspective I was getting "hints" that maybe it was time to surrender the gallery and move in another direction. I told him I felt a like a gerbil on a wheel, running fast, but not really getting anywhere. However, I had concerns about letting my studio go. I was of service in the community and I did not want to disappoint anyone. Steve reminded me being a martyr and sacrificing myself for others was an outdated paradigm. I knew he was right, but I still was not quite convinced.

With the intention to gain clarity, I called my good friend Penny about my dilemma. After patiently listening to my list of pros and cons about keeping the gallery, Penny shared the following true story with me: A reporter was following Mother Teresa around. As he witnessed her lovingly cleanse the helpless and the homeless, he held a handkerchief over his nose, repelled by the stench. Later he spoke with her and said: "How do you do what you do? I would not do it for a million dollars." Mother Teresa replied, "Neither would I." It took me a moment to figure out the moral of the story, but the light bulb finally went on. Mother Teresa was doing what she was doing out of her loving and her joy. Then Penny said: "Tammi, you are of the greatest service when you are in your joy. From my perspective it seems you are happiest when you are connecting with others from your heart and having conversations about healing and consciousness." She was right. And finally I was clear—it was time to put my gallery on the market.

You are of the greatest service to the world

when you are in your joy!

I talked to my husband and told him I agreed with him, maybe it was time for me to step onto a bigger platform where I could reach more people (although I had no idea what that might look like!). He thought so as well, so we decided to put my gallery on the market "just to see what would happen."

Steve and I have continued the habit of "leaning into things to see if God endorses them." So I leaned into letting go of the gallery. I thought perhaps we might get a nibble or two and possibly sell it the following spring. What happened instead was we got an offer the first day, then a second offer, then a bidding war. My gallery was in escrow within the first week! From my perspective, this was astonishing. At this time real estate was *not* moving. My husband reminded me we had invited Spirit in, leaned into it and apparently God was giving us the thumbs up and endorsing everything that was happening. Certain doors were shutting and other doors were opening.

Shortly after the closing, I was asked to do a radio interview about my book. I was a little nervous, but said yes. It ended up being a lot of fun and I loved the experience. A week later I heard from the president of the network. He loved my interview and asked if I would be interested in hosting my own show. I got dizzy and my mouth got dry. I think I squeaked out the words "No, thank you" through what felt like a mouthful of cotton balls. Later that evening I told my husband about the "funny invitation" and his response was: "This is the opportunity you have been waiting for!" No, this was *NOT* the opportunity I was waiting for. I had no conscious intention of doing radio. Steve reminded me that just a couple weeks prior I had said I was ready for a bigger platform where I could reach more people. (Be careful what you wish for—and what you say out loud—because you might get busted on it!).

After some prayer and meditation, and a big glass of water, I called the president of Empower Radio back and said yes, I wanted to do the show. I was afraid, really afraid, but I chose to walk through the fear. My supportive husband reminded me courage is not the absence of fear, but the willingness to do something in spite of the fear.

My first radio show, "Journey to Center," was really scary, but each week I felt a little more confident, a little more comfortable and started having a lot more fun. Hey, if manifesting divine prosperity and tapping into one's life's purpose were easy, everyone would be doing it! Sometimes I think it might be easier to just go get a job, but then I quickly remember I asked God to use me for His purpose, and to live up to my greatest potential. Then I take a deep breath and utter a heartfelt prayer of gratitude.

Your Purpose is Within You

You are an intelligent, creative and powerful being. Your outer reality is a reflection of your attitude, beliefs, thoughts, words, choices, your "yeses" and your "no's." You are a spiritual being living a temporary human existence and are always connected to the Source of life. You have guardian angels, friends in other dimensions and otherworldly support here to assist and guide you. But you need to be able to ask for help, be willing to listen and receive it when it shows up!

Your purpose is within you.

You were born with an inherent driving force

that desires and deserves success.

Joseph Campbell once said the basic theme of all myth (the archetypal stories by which we live our human lives) is that there is an invisible plane supporting the visible one. The truth is the invisible plane is supporting you and prompting you towards your purpose. Open your mind and ask the questions you want the answers to, then pay attention to your dreams, revelations, meditations, synchronicity, flashes of insight and messages from others. Everything is possible. Just opening your mind to this notion and living from this knowing invites information, miracles, grace and support.

I believe finding your purpose is more than a title, a degree, a label or a job description. I believe it is an agreement to go into the mystery, partnered with Spirit and your intuition. It is about learning to use your heart as your compass, your feelings as your map and joy as your guide. It is about learning to love and honor yourself more consistently, and sometimes it means moving forward in spite of your fear.

Finding your purpose is also about discernment; do you want to say no to something because it is really not a fit? Or are you scared because you are being presented with an opportunity to up-level and stretch out of your comfort zone? If you are not clear, you can always request information from your dreams and during your meditations. You can also ask God for help, hints and clues to support you in going in the direction He would have you go. The door to Spirit is always open and you can always ask for assistance and clarity so that you might achieve your purpose and potential; experience your greatest happiness; and manifest your most significant contribution to the planet.

Know that even if you think you have found your life's purpose,

it can continue to morph, evolve, expand, shift and grow

as a living breathing energy and unending lifetime adventure.

What I have come to realize is that living on purpose means you are a channel for Spirit: a conduit for healing; a paintbrush in His hand; or a flute He plays beautiful music through. In shamanic traditions it is referred to as becoming like a "hollow bone." When you become a hollow bone, you are no longer living primarily from the small ego self, motivated by fear. You reside in humility, openness, a sense of worthiness, peace and deep faith in the goodness of the Universe. Spirit can now come straight to you and work through you.

To quote author, teacher and wise woman, Carol Adrienne: "Living on purpose means you are an opening through which God flows. Your purpose, is not a thing, place, title or even a talent. Your purpose is to BE. Beyond any narrow category of occupation, the purpose of your life is to develop in your capacity to love."

When you know this and live from this posture and perspective, life becomes about being of service in a way that brings wonderful things to others and simultaneously gives you great joy. Living on purpose is about cooperation with the Universe and connection with other beings. It is about giving generously and receiving graciously. It is the ability to tap into imagination and inner wisdom and then taking the action steps. It is about intention and attention, integrity and responsibility. It is making choices and decisions based on inner guidance and external hints and clues.

Stepping into your purpose and authentic power means relinquishing the victim stance for good. It is surrendering to Divine will, and becoming flexible, compassionate, patient and kind. It is celebrating, honoring, respecting and loving yourself, so you naturally and easily celebrate, honor, respect and love others. Living on purpose is about continually stretching, evolving, morphing and expanding. It is moving beyond current boundaries and finding the balance that includes both stability and growth; curiosity and creativity; knowing and not knowing. When you stop creating, expanding and learning, is when you start to get old—and each of us gets to decide for ourselves when that happens.

To live on purpose is to live with an open heart and mind,

always on the lookout for the things that keep you

vital, vibrant, enthusiastic and alive.

Within each one of us is a wellspring of creativity and beauty. I believe if more people turned inward with the intention of hearing "the still small voice" and followed through with the wisdom they receive, everyone could have a miracle-filled and prosperous life. It is not always easy, and it does take courage and commitment, but the rewards for saying YES to this adventure are beyond what the ego and the conscious mind could ever create by itself or logically comprehend.

Each of us has an energy within that seeks expression and perfection; something innate that continues to prompt us forward, onward and upward. Our souls urge us to venture into the unknown, into the mystery, to expand into greater fulfillment, continued expression, and an evolving sense of "beingness." The very foundation of the human experience is to reach for and relax into a sense of aliveness, beauty, meaning, connection and creativity.

I believe we all have the ability to be continually blooming lotuses of creativity with infinite petals; kaleidoscopes with unending images, to perceive, explore and share. Anything is possible, as we are part of an unlimited Universe. In truth, God is here to experience and express Himself in us, with us, around us and through us.

This is your purpose:

*To feel happiness, joy and celebration in what you do
and who you are!*

The reason for your life, is to dance in your own light!

When you start to enjoy life as a journey rather than a destination you can start to live your life from an expanded and joyful state. Celebrating yourself and dancing in your light is what will sustain and nurture you at the deepest level, it will also bring joy to those around you. Exploring, experiencing and celebrating your Soul Self is what will help heal the world AND give God the greatest of glory!

Chapter 15

Let Your Light Shine!

There is a fire inside. Sit down beside it.
Watch the flames, the ancient, flickering dance of yourself.

~John MacEnulty

In A Return to Love Marianne Williamson shared with us this timeless, powerful and magnificent quote: "Our deepest fear is not that we are inadequate. Our deepest fear is that we are powerful beyond measure. It is our light, not our darkness that most frightens us. We ask ourselves, who am I to be brilliant, gorgeous, talented, fabulous? Actually, who are you not to be? You are a child of God. Your playing small does not serve the world. There is nothing enlightened about shrinking so that other people won't feel insecure around you. We are all meant to shine, as children do. We were born to make manifest the glory of God that is within us. It's not just in some of us; it's in everyone. And as we let our own light shine, we unconsciously give other people permission to do the same. As we are liberated from our own fear, our presence automatically liberates others."

Claiming our light can be scary, saying yes to shining can be daunting—in fact, for many, it may be preferable to live in poverty. God has so much in store for you, you just have to know your value and your worth and be willing to claim it. In Matthew 5: 14-15 Jesus said: "You are the light of the world. A city set on a hill cannot be hid . . . Let your light so shine before men, that they may see your good works and give glory to your Father who is in heaven."

You do not have to work hard to turn on your light . . .

if you are breathing it is lit.

It is a matter of relaxing,

allowing the wattage to increase and letting it shine.

The following summary includes 30 suggestions, exercises and action steps you can take to activate your entelechy, claim your brilliance, align with Source and live a life of purpose. They are also the most important qualities for you to cultivate as you continue to expand, grow and spiral upward on your manifesting prosperity adventure.

1. *Commit to Yourself.* Every relationship and business endeavor that succeeds first starts with commitment. Commit to yourself, commit to your human experience, commit

to Spirit and to your prosperity journey. The roots must go deep in order for the branches to go high. Commit to YOU and ground yourself in the world! This will help you create the solid and stable foundation you will need to manifest success.

2. *Set Your Intentions and Write Them Down.* Everything that comes into being begins with intention: from the home you are living in, to the clothes you are wearing; from the car you drive, to the book you are reading. What are *your* intentions? Claim them and put the Universal wheels into motion on your behalf. Next, write them down. It has been said by many manifestation experts, the number one predictor for successful manifesting is taking the time to write things down. Write down your intentions and journal your progress to ensure that they are anchored and activated in physical world reality.

3. *Invite Spirit to Partner With You.* The same energy that moves the planets around the sun can support you on your journey and in manifesting your prosperity—but not without your consent and not without your invitation. Extend the invitation to Spirit and align with the most powerful partner of all. Co-creation is the most fun, fulfilling and satisfying kind of creation there is!

4. *Pay Attention to Your Thoughts and Words.* The musings of your mind, and the words you speak today, are what create your tomorrows. Your thoughts and conversations are akin to the steering wheel in your car. Pay attention! Relinquish

any oppressive, disempowering and negative material and replace it with positive, optimistic and empowering material. Take responsibility! Think and speak in a way that steers you towards the future you want, deserve and desire.

5. *Claim Your Value.* We all manifest what we believe we deserve, so consciously claim your value and your worthiness. We are all precious and important from God's perspective, but until you know it and claim it for yourself, it will be impossible for you to manifest it. Look in the mirror, into your own eyes, and say aloud "I am wonderful, and am magnificent and I am WORTHY! I deserve to manifest all of my heart's desires!"

6. *Choose Faith!* Everybody experiences fear. The difference between those who are successful and those who are not, is that successful people do not let fear prevent them from moving forward. Remember, courage is not the absence of fear, but moving forward in spite of fear. Faith is a choice and is always available to us. The next time you feel fearful, ask yourself: What would faith say? What would faith do? Go the direction of faith and know you will be supported by legions of angels, seen and unseen.

7. *Tithe 10% of What You Receive.* Pay attention to all the money you manifest and tithe ten percent to the people, places or organizations that feed you spiritually. Remember this is the only time in the Bible where God says: "Prove me wrong!" Give God the chance to partner with you in your prosperity process. Trust Him and acknowledge Him in all things—

including your finances—and be prepared for miracles.

8. *Give Generously.* Give of yourself, share your time and your heart. Be of service and be kind. Do unto others as you would have them do unto you. Think about what you want and pray for others to manifest those same things. Life is like a boomerang, what you put out, *you will* get back. This is the law of attraction, karma, cause and effect. If you want more love, give more love, if you want more appreciation give more appreciation. As you generously give, you invite and naturally attract more kindness, more opportunities and greater prosperity.

9. *Receive Graciously.* Receiving graciously is the other half of giving generously. After you give, open your heart to receive with grace and gratitude. Whether kindness shows up as a compliment about your eyes, about the work you do, or a friend buying you lunch, open your heart and receive with loving appreciation. This will support you in ascending upward into realms of synchronicity, support and sweetness. Gracious receiving guarantees that support and unexpected gifts from the Universe will continue to show up in unpredictable and remarkable ways!

10. *Connect With Your Inner Child.* The foundation of your beliefs about money, your value and the nature of life were formulated when you were a child. You can connect with the young one inside of you here and now and share the information you would like them know, believe, understand and claim. Not only will it support you in deep healing, it

can also alter your Money Blueprint and help you accept your value in a very powerful and life-altering way.

11. *Make Friends With Your Subconscious Mind.* If you are ready to manifest prosperity, you will need the consent, approval and partnership of your subconscious mind. Set the intention to cultivate a friendship with your subconscious mind, clear out any limiting beliefs and then upload new, positive and prosperous content. This will open the pinch in the middle of the hourglass so prosperity can naturally flow to you with grace and ease.

12. *Align with your Higher Self.* Open your heart to making friends with your Higher Self. Invite, align, embrace and merge with your Higher Nature and your Soul Self. Meditate and listen to the still small voice within. Pay attention to your dreams and open the door to the wisest and most brilliant aspect of yourself. Tap into, invite and allow the Divine Within to express through you. By aligning with your Higher Self you will remember your true purpose, find fulfillment and begin to prosper at the deepest levels.

13. *Make Friends With Your Saboteur.* We all have an inner aspect that wants to keep us safe . . . even at the expense of keeping us small. You can go inward with the intention to connect with this powerful part of yourself. Ask it to become your ally, partner and friend in the prosperity process. Not only will you feel more congruent, empowered and confident, you will have a solid, honest and consistent source of support in the world.

14. *Do Things That Make You Feel Prosperous.* Getting into the *feeling* state of prosperity will help you attract prosperity. What makes you feel valuable, rich, wonderful and worthy? Flowers? A walk in the beauty and generous bounty of nature? A spa day? A soothing candlelit bubble bath? Prosperity is a mindset, a state of being and a *feeling.* What would give you the experience and feeling of prosperity? Do it, revel in it, and know this will attract abundance to you.

15. *Make Space.* Get rid of what you don't want to make space for what you do want. Clean your closets, organize your garage, do a cleanse to release toxins from your body. Weed your garden and get rid of old debris. Then lovingly prepare the space in your home, heart, body, mind and life for what you would really like to fill the newly opened spaces with.

16. *Forgive.* Make a conscious choice to forgive and release the people and experiences that keep you energetically bogged down. Release the heavy garbage bags of guilt. It is hard to fly while holding onto the heavy, toxic energy of hate, anger, resentment and shame. Loosen the load and lighten up by opening your mind, heart and soul to forgiveness. Forgive everyone and everything—including (and perhaps especially) yourself!

17. *Gratitude.* Gratitude is one of the highest emotional vibrations we as humans can experience. By focusing on what we are grateful for we raise our vibration and naturally attract even more to be grateful for. Be grateful for all the

lessons and blessings in your life and all the blessings that are on the way to you now. This energetically rolls out the red carpet in your life and optimistically, enthusiastically and joyfully invites more blessings, miracles, love, support and prosperity!

18. *Self- Compassion.* Choosing compassion is extending kindness, love and empathy to yourself, as well as acknowledging the fact that sometimes this human experience hurts. The energy of self compassion comes from claiming your connection to Source and feeling that sweetness. Consciously choosing compassion energetically keeps the door open to attract and receive the kindness and support from others. Self-compassion also invites and attracts miracles, synchronicity, divine guidance and divine prosperity.

19. *Set Goals.* What is the big picture of your life? Set long term goals and then consider the short terms goals that can start to move you in that direction. Remember the longest journey is filled with many small steps. Acknowledge, celebrate and reward your big goals and your small ones. Connect with a friend over your goals and enjoy the journey together.

20. *Visualize.* See your success and prosperity in your mind's eye; imagine it, visualize it, feel it and enjoy it, then, write it down. Remember, where you go in your mind, you eventually go in your life. Use your imagination as a tool and a friend, and have fun with your inner adventures and inner world. Then prepare for shifts, changes and adventures in your outer life and outer world.

21. *Make Good Friends With Money.* Take responsibility for your relationship with money. Respect it, appreciate it and love it! Create a budget, prioritize, consider needs vs. wants and pay your bills on time. Also, cultivate an inner relationship with money. Ask for the archetype of money to show up, ask questions about how to become better friends with him or her: listen, accept, appreciate and acknowledge this persona. This inner relationship can help your outer manifestation of money to flourish.

22. *Surrender.* Surrender your fear, surrender your stress, surrender anything and everything that is no longer serving you. Then, claim what you want and surrender it to Spirit for the highest good of all concerned. What the Universe has in store for you may be even better than your wildest fantasies! Claim your preferences but release your attachments. Hold your hopes and dreams lightly in your hand, or place them in your God Box knowing there is no better place for them to be. Then keep your eyes, ears, mind and heart open for the guidance, open doors, signals and winks from God.

23. *Pray.* Allow your relationship with God to deepen and expand. Explore the friendship by having authentic, intimate conversations. Share what is on your mind and in your heart, what you fear and what you love. All healthy relationships include communication, and prayer is the most powerful form of communication of all. Prayer works and God is *always* listening.

24. *Meditate.* After you have prayed and shared what you have to say with God, silence your mind so you can hear what God has to say to you. When you quiet your monkey mind and relax the active beta brain waves, the still small voice from within can be heard. Meditation provides you with the opportunity to access profound inner wisdom as well as receive personal messages from your Higher Self and from Source. Try it, trust it, explore it and you will not only experience peace, but also reap amazing rewards.

25. *What Do You Want? What is Fun? What Brings You Joy?* Ask yourself: "What do I really, really want? What is truly fun for me?" No one can answer these questions for you. And if you do not take the time to answer them for yourself, you certainly won't manifest the answers. You are here on Earth to learn, play and to have a great time. What does that look like and feel like for you? Follow your heart and let it be your compass; do what brings you joy and allow it to be your guide. If you do this, you will certainly end up someplace extraordinary, magnificent and amazing.

26. *Cultivate Creativity.* If you are breathing, you are an aspect of the Creator, therefore innately and naturally creative. Open your heart and mind to create and play. Extend an invitation to your imagination to explore and express yourself in the deepest of ways. Remember the most incredible inventions, solutions and successful endeavors did not come from logic, but from imagination. Write, paint, sing, play or dance! Whatever your soul wants to birth and/or do, invite it, listen to it, activate it, allow it and EXPRESS IT!

27. *Look for Role Models.* Look for living, breathing examples of what you hope to manifest one day. Look for great relationships and people who are prospering in joy, integrity, passion and compassion. Everything in the world exists; focus on what you want, look for who else is doing it and know that *ANYTHING* is possible.

28. *Positive Affirmations.* What are some words and phrases you can use as a mantra to help you maintain your vision, value, passion and purpose? Words are powerful and a wonderful way to claim your intentions and desires. Plug your affirmation in while waiting in lines or sitting in traffic and make great use of that "downtime." Put notes in your car and on your mirrors, on your dresser and your refrigerator. The more you remember to use your affirmations, they more they can *and will* work for you!

29. *Honor Yourself.* Treat others the way you want to be treated, AND treat yourself the way you want others to treat you. If you want the world to honor you, honor yourself. If you want to be acknowledged and appreciated, acknowledge and appreciate yourself. If you want love and respect, love and respect yourself. If you want the world to be gentle and kind to you, be gentle and kind with yourself. Outer reality is a reflection of inner reality. If you want outer reality to change, you must change your inner world and how you treat yourself. Check inside of yourself often and ask yourself: "What honors me now?" and follow through with the information and wisdom that comes from within.

30. Let Your Light Shine! You are a unique aspect of the Divine, here to express, create, experience and explore in your own special way. Relax into your authentic shape and know there is a spark of Divine Light in the very center of your Self. Do not hide this light, allow it to shine. Celebrate yourself in all you do and know you are glorifying God in the process. You did not come here to play small or be invisible, you came here to be the light of the world—trust in this Truth! Have faith in this process. PROCLAIM and ACCEPT that you are remarkable, glorious, fabulous and amazing! If someone does not see the value in your light, do not take it personally, it has nothing to do with you. Keep shining and then move to the next room and share your light there! Keep dancing in your light and you will find you are not dancing alone.

Deepak Chopra has said, "Within each of us is the embryo of God, and all the embryo of God wants is to be born." We are each a unique, beautiful, extraordinary expression of the Divine and seen equally through the eyes of our Creator. It is how we feel about ourselves that determines what we manifest in our lives.

Here are some questions for your consideration: Are you going to say YES to the spark of God within? Are you worthless or priceless? Do you want to expand or contract? Are you ready to claim your brilliance? Are you ready to create, prosper and play? Are you going to allow your light to shine? Only you can answer these questions for yourself, and your answers will dictate the quality of your life, the direction you go and what happens next. You are singularly responsible for your prosperity and your experiences.

Each of us is consciously or unconsciously creating our lives and would do well to take full responsibility for ourselves. Life is a creative medium and we each get one; we each have the capacity to shape our lives exactly as we choose. When we remember this truth, and deliberately choose our desires and beliefs, we have the opportunity to master our reality. We all have access to the exciting possibility of living a life of full expression, profound fulfillment, immense prosperity and otherworldly joy.

If you have come to the end of this material, you have undoubtedly learned some things about manifesting prosperity from the inside out. If you have started a tithing and forgiveness practice, I am willing to bet you have had some significant changes occur in your financial life. If you have participated in the exercises, listened to the guided meditations, started a meditation practice and connected with your Higher Self, I know you have experienced some powerful shifts in your inner reality and outer world.

If you are paying attention to your dreams and inwardly asking questions about your life's purpose and what brings you joy, I suspect you have had some sparks of inspiration and noticed some interesting signs from the Universe. If you have connected with your saboteur, I am confident you have an important friend and ally which has helped you in multiple ways. If you have cultivated an inner and outer friendship with money, I am sure you are manifesting more money. If you are setting goals and taking action steps, I would imagine you and your life is in the process of profound transformation.

If you are cultivating your creativity, I am confident you are feeling more joyful, alive and fulfilled. If you are treating yourself with kindness, generosity and respect, I know the world is responding in kind. As with anything, what you put into it is what you get out of it. Prosperity consciousness is a habit, a way of being and an adventure that can be explored and expressed for a lifetime. I encourage you to continue your journey with intentions of grace, ease, creativity, expansion and great love.

As time unfurls and life unfolds, know your purpose will continue to morph, evolve and expand. Your desires and priorities may shift and so will the search for what is yours—and for what is yours to do. People who are truly successful and fulfilled are those who have found the safe space of home inside of themselves. My prayer for you is that you have found the sweet, peaceful place of home and are deeply in touch with the rich, sacred sanctuary within.

I am honored to have you as a part of this prosperity adventure and I hope I have supported you on yours. My intention and deepest heart's desire is to have assisted you in more fully understanding your value, knowing the Truth of who you are, and in claiming your Divine inheritance. I also pray you continue to expand in your creativity, prosperity and joy.

You are the light of the world and the child in whom God is well pleased; what better reason could there be to celebrate? Keep your eyes focused on the star of your own inner guidance and allow your light to shine everywhere you go, and in everything you do.

If you have prosperity stories you would like to share, questions you would like to ask or if I can support you in any way, please be in touch with me at www.tammibphd.com or email me at tammibphd@gmail.com.

Abundant blessings of reverence, respect, divine prosperity and great love from my heart to yours.

Namaste

Tammi Baliszewski, Ph.D.

Are you ready to take prosperity to the next level?
Go to www.tammibphd.com and
check out her radio program, products, services and classes.

Bibliography

Adams, J.Q.; Pearlie Strother-Adams 2001
 Dealing with Diversity. Chicago, IL: Kendall/Hunt Publishing Company

Adrienne, Carol 1998
 The Purpose of Your Life, New York: William Morrow and Company

Beattie, Melodie 2007
 Gratitude, City Center, MN: Hazelden Publishing

Benson, Herbert. (Dec 1997).
 "The relaxation response: therapeutic effect". *Science* 278 (5344): 1694–5. PMID 9411784.

Branson, Richard 2005
 Losing my Virginity: The Autobiography, London: Virgin Books

Brehrend, Genevieve 1921
 Your Invisible Power: Working Principles and Concrete Examples in Applied Mental Science, Stilwell, KS: Digireads.com Publishing,

Carnegie, Andrew 2006
 The "Gospel of Wealth" Essays and Other Writings, New York: Penguin

Dement, William (1960)
 The effect of dream deprivation. *Science* 131: 1705-1707

Eker, T. Harv 2005

Secrets of the Millionaire Mind: Mastering the Inner Game of Wealth, London: Piatkus

Fillmore, Charles 1936

Prosperity, Unity on the Web, http://websyte.com/unity/pro. htm

Fisher, Charles (1965)

Psychoanalytic implications of recent research on sleep and dreaming: Empirical findings: *Journal of the American Psycho-analytic Association*

Fromm, Eric. (1965)

The Forgotten Language; An Introduction to the Understand-ing of Dreams, Fairy Tales, and Myths. New York: Hold Rine-hart and Winston LLC

Gaines, Edewene 2005

The Four Spiritual Laws of Prosperity, New York: Holtzbrinck Publishers

Holmes, Ernest 1984

Science of Mind, Camarillo, CA: Devorss and Company

James, William 1985

Psychology a Briefer Course, University of Notre Dame Press.

Jung, Carl 1964

A Man and His Symbols, New York: Dell Publishing

Nelson, Martia
   Coming Home: The Return to True Self, www.martianelson.com

New International Version Bible, The Old and New Testament

Myss, Caroline 2003
   Sacred Contracts, New York: Three Rivers Press

Wallace, J. & Erickson, J. 1992
   Hard Drive: Bill Gates and the Making of the Microsoft Empire, New York: HarperBusiness.

Williamson, Marianne 1992
   A Return To Love: Reflections on the Principles of A Course in Miracles, New York: Harper Collins

Zweig, Michael 2004
   What's Class Got to do With It, American Society in the Twenty-first Century. ILR Press

http://www.gatesfoundation.org/about/Pages/bill-melinda-gates-letter.aspx

http://www.okmagazine.com/2009/05/oprahs-words-of-wisdom-for-college-grads-14213/

http://www.sciencedaily.com/releases/2008/07/080724215644.htm

http://www.sciencedaily.com/releases/2010/03/100319210631.htm

http://viewonbuddhism.org/Meditations/dalai_lama_meditation.html